Glencoe
The Infamous Massacre 1692

About the Author

John Sadler has had a lifelong interest in Scottish military history. He now combines writing with lecturing in History at Newcastle University and working as a battlefield tour guide, living history interpreter and heritage consultant. His other books include *Culloden: The Last Charge of the Highland Clans 1746* ('Drawing extensively on first-hand accounts, paints a vivid picture of the campaign and battle' *Scotland in Trust*) and *Scottish Battles* ('Sadler is as good a storyteller as he is an historian' *The Scotsman*). He is a keen re-enactor and a long time member of the Sealed Knot Society. He lives in Northumberland.

Glencoe
The Infamous Massacre 1692

JOHN SADLER

AMBERLEY PUBLISHING

This one is for Rosie

This edition first published 2009

Amberley Publishing Plc
Cirencester Road, Chalford,
Stroud, Gloucestershire, GL6 8PE

www.amberley-books.com

Copyright © John Sadler 2008, 2009

The right of John Sadler to be identified as the Author
of this work has been asserted in accordance with the
Copyrights, Designs and Patents Act 1988.

British Library Cataloguing in Publication Data.
A catalogue record for this book is available from the British Library.

ISBN 978-1-84868-515-4

Typesetting and Origination by Diagraf (www.diagraf.net)
Printed in Great Britain.

'All the way, the road had been among moors and mountains with huge masses or rock, which fell down God knows where, sprinkling the ground in every direction, and giving it the aspect of the burial place of a race of giants. Now and then we passed a hut or two, with neither window nor chimney, and the smoke of the peat fire rolling out at the door. But there were not six of these dwellings in a dozen miles; and anything so bleak and wild, and might in its loneliness, as the whole country, it is impossible to conceive.'

Charles Dickens

Contents

Acknowledgements

I must firstly acknowledge my own particular limitations in this field of Scottish history, most notably my lack of Gaelic, which some may judge a fatal flaw. For any inadequacies which result from this lamentable defect I can only apologise. Another difficulty that confronts all writers on the subject is the correct spelling of place and personal/family names. Dr Stevenson refers to this in his preface to *Highland Warrior*. Like him I have adopted the anglicized form in most cases, unless the original is well established, thus Coire Gabhail rather than 'Corrie of the Capture'. For the most part however, I have used that form which is likely to be easiest for non-specialist readers, such as Ranald, rather than Raonull or the Norse Ragnald, though I use Alasdair for Alexander. For clan surnames I have retained the convention of using 'Mac' and prefer MacDonald to MacDonnell (MacDhomhuilll), unless speaking of the MacDonnells of Antrim. I entreat the purists to excuse any offence, as none is intended.

The author is grateful for the assistance of the following, without whom this book could not have been written: Adam Barr for the photography, Chloe Rodham for the map, Richard Groocock at the National Archives, Tristan Langlois at the National Army Museum, Lee Deane of National Trust for Scotland, Ailsa Mactaggart of Historic Scotland, Charlotte Chipchase of Royal Armouries Leeds,

Helen Nicoll of the National Museum of Scotland, Shona Corner of the National Gallery of Scotland. Winnie Tyrell of Kelvingrove Museum Glasgow, Tobias Capwell of the Wallace Collection, Alan Cameron of the Clan Cameron Trust, Mairi Mooney of the West Highland Museum in Fort William, Denis Rixson and Cron Mackay in relation to maritime aspects, and to Graham Trueman, Rosie Serdiville, Lauren Thow, Catherine Turner, David, Michelle, Jonathan and Daniel Hern and Martin Keegan.

All errors and omissions remain the sole responsibility of the author.

Belsay, Mid-Northumberland, Spring 2008

Introduction

They were kneeling in a small box-shaped pit sunk into the stone floor huddled together in fear, their arms and hands entwined in support. Normally the hole would have been used to store grain and covered with the wooden trapdoor that now lay upright on its hinges behind their backs. It would have been the ideal place to hide. Close the lid and the pit would be nearly invisible. There would have been just enough room for three people to lie beneath it. What gave them away? I wondered. A cough? A sob?

Two of the women were in their twenties, the third was an old lady. Someone had shot her in the mouth and her shattered dentures cascaded with her own teeth down her front like mashed melon pips. One girl had been shot repeatedly in the chest. It was difficult to tell if the other had had her throat cut or been shot; a great gash of blood crescented her neck. The expression on their faces had survived the damage. It was so clear. A time valve that opened directly onto those last moments. So you saw what they saw. I hope beyond hope that I never see it again.

Anthony Loyd[1]

Thus the author describes killings that occurred in Bosnia in the nineteen-nineties scarcely more that a decade ago and in a European country. Such horrors are collectively covered by the modern expression 'ethnic-cleansing' and this present work is concerned with a similar atrocity committed on British soil over three centuries ago. The Massacre of Glencoe had a loud and dreadful resonance, set against the splendidly primeval backdrop of the Glen itself and yet it has, to a degree, been subsumed in the mass-tourism culture of the Scottish Highlands. This has successfully marketed the region's violent history as a colourful and exotic tapestry with distinct Hollywood overtones. Feature films, such as the highly successful if wildly inaccurate pastiche *Braveheart*, have added an Arthurian gloss. Nothing in the events of that night in February 1692 is in the least romantic. It was mass-murder, pure and simple, bloody, squalid, cruel and, for the most part, merciless. The grim and arresting tableau above is precisely the type of circumstance enacted in Glencoe during that dreadful darkness.

'Ethnic cleansing' may be defined as little more than a re-packaging of genocide; it has been described as:

> ... At one end it is virtually indistinguishable from forced emigration and population exchange while at the other end it merges with deportation and genocide. At the most general level, however, ethnic cleansing can be understood as the expulsion of an 'undesirable' population from a given territory due to religious or ethnic discrimination, political, strategic or ideological considerations, or a combination of these.[2]

Genocide is not a new feature of inhumanity – the twentieth century includes some frightful examples: the forcible movement of the Armenian population by the Ottoman Empire in the First World War and the slaughter of Jewish communities by the Germans in the Second, which transformed the business of mass-killing into an industry. Jews were subjected to murderous pogroms in England and Europe during the Medieval period, and other, equally repugnant examples abound. What makes Glencoe unique is that the killings represented murder under trust, and were apparently ordered or at least sanctioned by central Government, and that the action represented a clear demonstration of a policy aimed at emasculating if not removing elements of the Norse-Gael population of the Western-Scottish Highlands. Simple killing was by no means uncommon, the clans were fractious and frequently savage. Had the same number of MacDonalds fallen in intercnine strife, in battle against Government forces or by the hangman's rope, the business would have been no more than a footnote in history.

One singularly murderous incident was the quaintly named Battle of the Spoiling of the Dyke, which occurred on Skye in 1578. This arose as part of a bitter and sanguinary feud between Clan Donald and MacLeod. The latter descended upon and took up Eigg, herding the MacDonald islanders into a cave where they were summarily butchered. In reprisal, the men of Uist attacked Skye, targeting Trumpan Church in Waternish where the congregation gathered in worship were immolated. Only one young woman, dreadfully burnt, staggered free and lived long enough to raise the alarm. MacLeod from Dunvegan, his tacksmen big with vengeance, caught up with the raiders by Ardmore Bay, and none of the MacDonalds was spared. The corpses were roughly interred in a crude trench and a turf dyke toppled over, hence the name given to the encounter.[3]

This, then, is an account of an atrocity, an act of pure murder, which reflected badly on all who were involved. The victims admittedly were no innocents: the MacDonalds of Glencoe had blood of most of their neighbours on their hands, and the majority of their contemporaries viewed them as a contagion. Had the death of the twelfth MacIain and many of his name occurred at the conclusion of judicial proceedings, it would have distressed few beyond an immediate affinity and cheered many. What did appall was the manner of their extinction and what it implied. Mass-murder, sanctioned and carried out by the state, was not an acceptable remedy for lawlessness, however rife and incorrigible. Whilst the parallels with contemporary horrors are clearly present, they should perhaps not be unduly laboured the Massacre of Glencoe must firstly be viewed in the context of the period in which it occurred and in the circumstances, which led up to the act itself. Nonetheless, if we consider the wording of the infamous order itself, the intentions appear abundantly clear and such an order could easily have been issued in relation to a twentieth-century atrocity:

> You are hereby ordered to fall upon the Rebels, the McDonalds of Glenco, and putt all to the sword under seventy, you are to have a special care that the old Fox and his sons doe upon no account escape your hands, you are to secure all the avenues that no man escape. This you are to putt in execution at five of the clock precisely; and by that time, or very shortly after it, I'll strive to be att you with a stronger party: If I doe not come to you att five, you are not to tarry for me, but to fall on. This is by the Kings speciall command, for the good and safty of the Country, that these miscreants be cutt off root and branch. See that this be put in execution without feud or favour, else you may expect to be dealt with as one not true to King nor Government, nor a man fitt to carry Commissione in the Kings service. Expecting you will not fail in the fulfilling hereof, as you love your selfe, I subscribe these with my hand att Balichollis [Ballachulish] Feb: 12, 1692
>
> [signed] R. Duncanson
>
> For their Majesties service,
>
> To Capt. Robert Campbell of Glenlyon

Over the distance of three centuries this remains a chilling command. It is utterly unequivocal and backed by a clear threat: Glenlyon is to kill every person under three score years and ten, in effect the entire population. The order does not appear to discriminate between adult males and non-combatants. In July 2007 the International Court of Justice's decision in the matter of *Jorgic v Germany*, the specific facts of which need not concern us, was reviewed by The European Court of Human Rights, which debated if the establishment of a viable case against a defendant in respect of ethnic cleansing amounted to genocide. The court felt this was not necessarily the case, but in certain circumstances one might very well be the equal of the other:

> That is not to say that acts described as 'ethnic cleansing' may never constitute genocide, if they are such as to be characterized as, for example, 'deliberately inflicting on the group conditions of life calculated to bring about its physical destruction in whole or in part' contrary to ... provided such action is carried out with the necessary specific intent ... that is to say with a view to the destruction of the group, as distinct from its removal from the region ... [4]

On this basis, the order to Glenlyon looks very much like an invitation to genocide, if we accept the MacDonalds of Glencoe as a distinct ethic group, even if the order was intended to apply to males only. Driving their dependents out into the teeth of a Highland winter would still suffice, as would burning their steadings, looting or destroying their food stocks. It is not the purpose of this narrative to embark on a lengthy debate as to the legal definition of what occurred, other than to establish that it represents a heinous act and to accept the bitter truth that such instances continue to occur. The subject of the Massacre remains highly sensitive today. At the time it reflected the alienation of the Jacobite Tory clans from the mainstream political establishment of both kingdoms, following the 'Glorious' Revolution of 1688 and the Whig supremacy.

To trace the roots of the story we must delve into Scottish history of the fifteenth century, the *Lin nam Creach* – 'The Age of Forays' – a period of near anarchy which followed the final abolition of the Lordship of the Isles by James IV of Scotland in 1493. Prior to that time Clan Donald had been supreme, descendants of Somerled and the Norse Gael tradition. Increasingly, in the course of the sixteenth century, this traditional dominance was challenged by the emerging power of Clan Campbell who would, in due course, and in the personages of the Campbell Dukes of Argyll, come to dominate the Whig faction. As the sixteenth century wore on. religious tensions, following the Scottish Reformation, added to the alienation of the Norse-Gael clans and helped to foster an increasing divide in Scottish society, between those in the English-speaking Lowlands and the Gaelic-speaking glens.

The Lowlanders' disaffection with their Highland contemporaries the *Mi Run Mor Nan Gall*, deepened in the seventeenth century at the point the Tory Clans stepped fully onto the national stage, when they followed Montrose and MacColla during the long and bloody tribulation of the civil wars. Further religious division occurred during the post-Restoration decades in the reign of Charles II, when strenuous and violent efforts were made by the Government to impose an episcopacy on the Scottish Church. At the same time the Duke of York (the future James II of England, VII of Scotland), emerged as a champion of the Tory clans against the encroachment of Clan Campbell, and presided over the humiliation of Argyll, thus creating a bond between clansmen and the House of Stuart – the genesis of the Jacobite Movement.

Following the Revolution of 1688, the Tory clans rallied to Graham of Claverhouse, 'Bonny Dundee', and inflicted a major reverse on Williamite forces at the Battle of Killiecrankie. This and the continuing struggle against James' adherents in Ireland caused deep unease in the administration, which determined to bring the clans to heel by forcing an oath of loyalty upon the recalcitrant chiefs. MacDonald of Glencoe was a small sept, living within the dark majesty of the glen that bears their name. As a thorn in the sensitive flesh of the Williamites and the Whig clans, they 'punched well above their weight'. MacIain, their chief was late in submitting so that his oath was technically invalid. This prompted Sir John Dalrymple, Master of Stair and Scottish Secretary, to possibly resolve upon a 'final solution' for this troublesome tribe: an object lesson to the rest.

From this was conceived and executed the infamous Massacre, in the bitter cold of a February night in the remote Highlands. Murder under trust: the atrocity perpetrated by soldiers billeted upon their victims. Men, women and children shot down, clubbed and bayoneted, the dazed survivors fleeing, barely clothed, into the teeth of the icy wind. It was an act of savagery condoned by the Government and instigated by one of its principal servants, an attempt at genocide in Britain. Indeed the Massacre could be said to have led directly to the final carnage on Drummossie Moor, which finally ended a very long chapter in Scottish history. A chain reaction which paved the way for the subsequent harrying of the glens and ultimately the Highland Clearances in the late eighteenth and nineteenth centuries.

In modern terms this was 'ethnic cleansing' at its worst and most thorough. Increasingly marginalised by their remote and anachronistic way of life, their religion, language, dress and dogged adherence to a failing system of clan and chief, the Highland Clans who did not espouse the Whig cause, were perceived as entirely pernicious by a rapidly developing Lowland culture, increasingly alienated from and ashamed of the Gael.

A modern paradigm for a successful exercise in ethnic cleansing comes from the civil wars in Bosnia during the 1990s, where a five-stage process was perfected:

1. Concentration – surround the area to be purged, like beaters and huntsmen
2. Decapitation – identify and murder key political and social leaders, priests and professionals, deprive the mass of victims of leadership
3. Separation – segregate those capable of bearing arms from the rest
4. Evacuation – expel all non-combatants from the target zone
5. Liquidation – murder all those capable of bearing arms.[5]

Since the late seventeenth century the Massacre of Glencoe has remained as a stain upon the British polity. Rather than a successful object lesson to the Tory clans, it became a symbol of intolerance, a demonstration of the administration's view of Highlanders as 'untermenschen'. And so it has remained, for many the Massacre of Glencoe symbolizes, to this day, the determination of the Lowland majority to crush the Highland way of life by any and all means, and that natural justice, humanity and decency need not feature: 'Only just now, my Lord Argyle tells me that MacDonald of Glencoe has not taken the oath, at which I rejoice. It is a great work of charity to be exact in rooting out that damnable sept, the worst of the Highlands.'

Queen Boudicca, in AD 61, probably represents the first known instance where the native British Celts rose up against not only the Roman invader, but against those Celts who had 'collaborated' by adopting the ways of the oppressor. Her campaign consisted of destroying the towns and the centers of Roman influence, together with their entire populations, many of whom were done to death with singular, prolonged cruelty. Colchester, London and St Albans were given to the flames, and the death toll is said to have reached 100,000, (although this is probably an exaggeration).

On St Brice's day 1002 King Aethelred "The Unready" (actually Un-raed or 'ill-advised'), Saxon King of England, ordered the massacre of all ethic Scandinavians living in the north and east of England – the 'Danelaw'. His orders were carried out with enthusiasm. Following the Norman Conquest, in 1069 – 1070, the northern English rose against the Normans and purged their towns of the invaders with blood and fire (Gateshead, York). William I responded with the Harrying ("Harrowing") of the north, a planned campaign of slaughter and devastation – 'he created a desert and called it peace'. Later, in 1190, there were serious anti-Semitic disturbances in York, which led to the slaughter and/or mass suicide of the entire Jewish community within the walls of Clifford's Tower. Later Edward I ("Longshanks") expelled all Jews; many were put to death or callously abandoned on shifting sands waiting to drown.

Edward I (latterly also "Malleus Scottorum") set the tone for three-centuries of border conflict, when he ordered the massacre of the entire population of Berwick in 1296, and only called a halt when he saw one of his knights dismembering a heavily pregnant Scottish woman. By which time, it is said, some 7,000 had perished. Later, both William Wallace and Robert Bruce responded in kind in

Northern England, particularly Northumberland. As late as 1542, English Middle March Warden, Sir Robert Bowes requested that Henry VIII authorise the wholesale slaughter of the English inhabitants of North Tynedale, on account of their contribution to lawless behavior. To his credit, Henry sternly reminded his subordinate that the rule of law must prevail. Two years later when giving his deputy and brother-in-law Edward Seymour orders concerning a punitive expedition against the Scots, the King showed no such restraint. His orders are clear and concise – the Scots are viewed as *untermenschen* and are to be treated accordingly. The murderous brutality of the Border Wars reached their nadir.

The era of the civil wars in England and Scotland saw several such atrocities, (I have, for the moment, not included Ireland, where ethnic cleansing featured very heavily). In 1645, female camp followers from the Royalist side were slaughtered or mutilated by victorious Parliamentarians at Naseby. They were accused of being Irish Papists (In fact most were Welsh, but spoke Gaelic, with little English, and this was sufficient to condemn them). At Philiphaugh in the same year, Scottish Covenanters surprised the Marquis of Montrose, and his Irish troops, after surrendering, were handed by the military to the 'mercy' of the Kirk. The men were summarily shot in batches against the wall of Newark castle (traces of which remain), whilst the women, to conserve valauble ammunition, were simply drowned in the river, and their bodies piled on the bank. The final chapter in the reduction of the Jacobite clans, after Glencoe, was the harrying of the glens in the summer of 1746, following their defeat at Culloden. The Highland way of life, dress, religion and culture were to be extinguished, and the mainly Scottish agents of 'Butcher' Cumberland set to their work with a will. Previously, on the field, Highland wounded and captives had been shot or bayoneted without quarter, and without too much enquiry as to who might be a rebel and who an innocent bystander.

My own association with Glencoe spans half a century, for most of my childhood holidays and many since have been spent in the shadow of the Big Herdsman – *Buachaille Etive Mor*. Frequently huddled under sopping canvas, pitched along the broken line of the old road, whilst the modern A 82 thunders down the Pass. This bears the million or so visitors, many of whom rush heedless in their urgency to reach Fort William. As one approaches from the south past Bridge of Orchy over the barren span of Rannoch Moor, the placid waters of Loch Tulla to the left, there comes a point lifting toward the higher ground of the Black Mount, when the long saddle of the mountain comes into view. In this writer's admittedly biased submission, it is one of the finest sights these islands have to offer. There is a clear sense of transition, of moving into another, altogether more dramatic landscape, within which anything may be possible, a tangible sense of reaching out towards the distant past. It is awe-inspiring and, when dark thunderclouds roll across the tops, daunting. It is no wonder that some writers, including Dickens, found the place dreadfully oppressive.

For several decades then, I have assailed the numerous peaks in the Glen, *Buachaille Etive Mor*, the alpine crest of *Stob Coire nan Lochan*, the long ridge of *Aonach Eogach* and, of course, the twisting path of the Devil's Staircase, which has its own story to tell. Some four decades past, as a boy, I had a chance encounter and conversation with the late W.A. Poucher, then an elderly, elegantly clad gentleman whose genius with a lens captured so much of the spirit if the mountains. It was thus at a relatively early age I first read John Prebble's magisterial account of the Massacre, originally published in 1966 followed, some years later, by the previous 1933 history written by John Buchan. Having digested these, visited the surviving locations, tramped the lonely path to Kinlochleven and searched for the remains of Cromwell's fort at Inverlochy, a lifelong obsession developed, one which has since embraced a number of volumes on Scottish military history and frequently tested my family's patience to the utmost!

CHAPTER 1

The Glen of Dogs

'Glencoe has no melancholy except that which men bring to it, remembering its history'.

John Prebble

'His visage boisterous, horribly was graced
With still mustachios like two bending horns,
And turbid fiery eyes, as meteors red,
Which fury and revenge did threaten round.'

James Philip of Almericlose (Standard-bearer to Dundee describing MacIain of Glencoe. Translated from the Latin by Rev. Alexander D. Murdoch. Scottish History Society, 1888)

' 'Gael' – A Scottish Celt'

Oxford English Dictionary

A popular myth interprets Glencoe as the 'Glen of Weeping' – a handy notion for tourism development but not one founded on any reality, the epithet more properly applies to Glenfruin and arises from the sanguinary combat between Clan Gregor and the Colquhouns which occurred there in 1603, (see Chapter three). For most of its very long history the Glen was an isolated backwater, due to its remoteness and the excellent job done by primeval nature; for one violent night on 13th February 1692, events there filled the national consciousness, and the shadow has never completely gone away, as long as Scotland possesses a vibrant tourist industry it never will.

GEOGRAPHY OF GLENCOE

Long before the cultural divide between Highlands and Lowlands, vast volcanic upheavals drove the Highland Boundary Fault, like a swinging sword-blade, cutting from the Firth of Clyde in the south-west up to Stonehaven on the north-east coast; this is, in effect, the frontier of the north-western tip of Europe.[1]

Most spectacularly the line manifests itself in Gleann morn a-h Albin – the Great Glen which stretches for the best part of 100 km from Fort William to Inverness; during the Jacobite era three key forts would guard its length; Inverlochy, Fort Augustus and Fort George at Inverness.[2]

A vast upsurge in geological evolution which took place some 460 –470 million years ago produced the Caledonian Mountains, the shock and upheaval occasioned by a collision of several continental blocs. A mere 40-odd million years later, what would be Glencoe was dominated and forged by a handspan of major volcanic eruptions. As each vomiting of magma spewed out, tens of thousands of tonnes of molten rock in the remaining shell weakened and eventually crumbled. As the cooling stones began to fracture along the existing fault lines, a vast crater or 'caldera' was formed. Initially this basin was some eight kilometres in breadth and, as the molten surfaces cooled and solidified, magma was injected into the fault lines, creating ring intrusions that now gird the extinct volcanic peaks. Ice, wind and rain, and the great excesses of hot and cold, molded the landscape, developing over planes of geological time that we can only begin to comprehend. What remains is the jagged stumps of these distant eruptions that collapsed in the furnace of caldera.

What was left is now Glencoe: a U shaped valley some sixteen kilometres (ten miles) in length; narrow, some 700m (0.4 ml) across, and funnelling into the confines of the pass. Through the narrows, the glen angles to the right and northwards, entering the fertile plain toward Loch Leven at its western end. From the east the traveller approaches across the barren swathe of Rannoch Moor, 130 km2 (fifty sq. miles.) of waterlogged waste west of the loch. The moor is a bare and ancient landscape; the dank mosses studded with a mosaic of tiny lochans, stumps of vanished trees, largely devoid of sustenance for man and beast, an almost mythical emptiness where dragons, outlaws and elves might easily be imagined![3] Now the moor is traversed by the A82, but before the tarmac, the high pass over the Black Mount was frequently sealed by the winter snows and the glen shut in on the east. North of Loch Tulla the ground rises into the swell of the Black Mount, high enough to accommodate two Munros[4] – *Stob a'Choire Odhair* and *Stob Ghabar*.

As the ribbon of black tarmac runs dead straight and north-west above *Loch Tulla*, with a scattering of lochans, the Black Corries and the pimple of *Meall nan Ruadhag* to the right, the Kingshouse Hotel comes into view, its white walls profiled by the bulk of *Beinn a Chrulaiste* rising behind. To the left of the hotel the long shoulder of *Buachaille Etive Mor* lowers like a great sentinel over the southern flank. Beneath and on the eastern side a narrow road runs down the long, picturesque length of Glen Etive to the sheltered, fertile plain at the head of the loch. This landscape is a revelation. the shoulder of the mountain studded with scree and rock, bare and uncompromising. Glencoe is unique, epic and mysterious, and if history had not provided dark deeds, then legend must surely have created them. It is a place of romance, tinged with awe and an edge of danger. These peaks are now much frequented by climbers and ramblers, yet must never be trifled with, for even today the glen takes a toll of the unlucky or unprepared.

A narrow valley, the Lairig Gartain runs between the Big Herdsman and its lesser relative *Buachaille Etive Beag*. Next a trio of ragged fingers (*The Three Sisters*) pokes north-eastwards from the higher, lateral ridge of Bidean nam Bian that runs behind and forms the highest peak. Between the ridges of *Beinn Fhada* and *Gearr Aonach,* a precipitous scramble leads to the magical *Coire Gabhail*. Here, it is said, MacDonalds of Glencoe hid their lifted beasts when retribution threatened. The corrie itself is a flat-bottomed dish nestling between scree clad slopes: only one great, chunky, alluvial boulder dropped on the level plain but the ascent is truly alpine and would have required a most skilled herdsman to have driven cattle up its narrow and trickily uneven ascent. It resembles nothing more than a suitable ground for such fictional heroes as Holmes and Moriarty to resume their Homeric trial of strength. Westwards, the horseshoe of *Gearr Aonach* swings around through the peak of *Stob Coire nan Lochan*[5] toward Aonach Dubh, last and least of The Three Sisters, the high pointed ridge soaring majestically with yet higher ground across a narrow saddle behind.

Below the peaks and jutting ridges of The Three Sisters the River Coe tumbles down narrows, a rushing boulder-strewn cascade, cutting through the defile toward the small loch at Achtriachtan. Here the pass opens out as the road falls toward the valley floor and the western end. The landscape changes abruptly from the high and rugged to the rich and verdant, opening toward Glencoe Village and the shores of Loch Leven. Opposite the *Lairig Gartain* and climbing the northern rampart snakes the Devil's Staircase, a narrow pathway that cuts across to Kinlochleven at the head of the loch. This route would feature in the events of 13th February 1692. West of the Devil's Staircase crowds the long ridge of *Aonach Eagach*, ("The Aggy Ridge") mounting sheer from the valley floor, a long precipitous knife-edge, falling steeply to the northern side in a series of bared defiles. At its western extreme the ridge declines sharply toward the loch-side but then terminates with a flourish in the distinctive eminence of Sgur na Ciche – the rounded bell-like knoll of the Pap of Glencoe, a mammary allusion entirely appropriate.

The river, said to be the 'Dark Cona' of Ossian, rises at the north-eastern foot of the Little Herdsman and sweeps westwards, over the waterfalls, frothing and surging down the throat, through the quieter waters of the small loch, past Glencoe village and spilling into Loch Leven by Invercoe. The loch itself is a salt-water branch of the mightier Loch Linnhe. Ossian, legendary son of Fingal, spawned a romantic upsurge of Pan-Celticism of the most turgid variety in the ninetee century when James MacPherson allegedly discovered a corpus of lost verse. Most likely, this was complete tosh, but fitted the romantic mood of the time, when Tory clans were being refurbished as literary heroes.

Most settlement was and is located on the fertile tract by Loch Leven. From a tactical viewpoint the loch offered the best approach,: an attacker crossing Rannoch Moor would have been visible for miles, and the narrows easily defended: both flanks are effectively secured by nature, high and inaccessible ground everywhere – even the Devil's Staircase does not outflank the mouth of the pass. Glencoe forms part of the country of Lochaber.[6] In Gaelic the place is named Gleann Comhann, and is likely named so for the river running through. An exact translation is not possible, but the words may relate to some ancient tribe of inhabitants or even an individual Chomain or Comhan.[7] It was Macaulay who gave us Glen of Weeping but, as John Prebble suggests, the name may derive from the Glen of Dogs – an allusion to the fierce hunting dogs of the Feinn[8] or forms a reference to their natural warehouse for lifted kine and gear.[9]

Quite when man arrived in the Glen is unclear, whether our Paleolithic ancestors, hanging on the margins of retreating ice-sheets, penetrated this far is not known. It was only as the last of the ice commenced its final withdrawal that the climatic changes permitted the spread of vegetation: grasses and scrub, followed by forestation, anchored in peat. By 5000 BC the natural environment was largely formed and teeming with life, game and predators, deer, bears and wild boar, sharp-toothed hunters such as the wolf and wildcat. The latter, perhaps viewed fleetingly, briefly frozen against a high backdrop of moss and tumbled scree, survives. Mesolithic settlers came, most probably from Ireland, and cultivation began in the fourth millennium BC. The first evidence of human settlement in Lochaber dates from around 7500 BC at Kinloch on Rhum`; Cup marks from *c*3000 BC have been uncovered at Blarmafoldach. Within 1000 years there is evidence of cremation burials from Onich and North Ballachulish with a standing stone by the former. We might, then, surmise that the flat lands by Loch Leven were under the plough, some 4000 years ago or perhaps even earlier.

In the closing decades of the first century AD, Roman armies under Julius Agricola penetrated the Highland Line, advancing through Tayside and into the north-east. What effects, if any, were felt by the Iron Age farmers in Glencoe is uncertain. The period following the occupation remains equally obscure, *Tales of Fingal* or Fionn mac Cumhaill place the hero and his warband, the Fianna, in Lochaber. It was Fingal who constructed the Giant's Causeway to pave his path to the Scottish mainland. Legend relates that Fingal fought a great fight against a Viking host led by their King Earragan who brought two-score ship companies against the Irish band. After a hard-fought and satisfyingly bloody encounter the Norsemen were decimated. Only enough to crew two vessels survive to flee down Loch Leven. One of the Fianna, Goll MacMorna, accounts for the Viking chief.[10] Cumhall, the hero's father and former general of the Fianna, had also fallen to MacMorna's blade after he offended the High King, Conn of the Hundred Battles, from whom the chiefs of Clan Donald were to claim their descent:

'You Clan of Conn, remember this:
Strength from the eye of the storm.'[11]

The Lordship of the Isles

The Irish were established on the coast of Argyll during the time of
the Roman occupation, their great strength being the mighty stone
fortress of Dunadd.[12] Centuries of intermittent warfare with their
indigenous Pictish and Strathclyde British neighbours followed
,before in the ninth century, Kenneth MacAlpin united the tribes.
Next came those predatory Norsemen, their sleek, long-hulled galleys darting down the western seaboard ravaging and settling here
and there to mingle their blood with that of locals, and thus producing the Norse-Gael. Magnus Bareleg, King of Norway,[13] stamped
his iron will upon his scattered Hebridean holdings, until his death
paved the way for an ambitious Norse-Gael named Somerled to
carve out for himself a sea-kingdom in Argyll and the west.

Somerled won dazzling victories, creating hegemony over the
sea-lanes. For several decades he consolidated his power, defeating
his enemy Godred, King of Man, until the extent of his conquests
sparked friction with the King of Scotland. Malcolm IV had permitted land-hungry Norman freebooters to encroach on territories
claimed by the Norse-Gaels. One routier, Walter Fitzalan, provoked
a confrontation, and in 1164 Somerled mustered a sizeable force to
deal with these incomers once and for all. Not a good plan as it transpired, the mailed horsemen proved vastly superior to the foot-loons
of the Isles, Someled himself fell beneath their contemptuous blades
at Renfrew.

As the great man's blood congealed upon the field, his sons were
already squabbling over his vast patrimony. These were Dugall,
Ranald and Angus, and it was the middle one of these who first styled
himself 'King of the Isles'. From the loins of these successors, collectively named the MacSorleys, were sprung sons and grandsons whose
people became banded as clans – Dugall's heirs the Macdougalls;
Ranald's as Macdonalds and Macruaris. Donald of Islay, who died
around 1250, was succeeded by his mettlesome son Angus Mor,
active during King Hakon's doomed attempt to re-assert Norwegian

control. After the rebuff of the Norsemen at Largs and the collapse of their King's posturings, the Islemen found themselves as subjects of the Scottish crown: great men to be sure, akin to any feudal magnate, but not free princes as they would have preferred. During the late thirteenth century the Macdougalls grew in power and influence; it was their fatal misfortune to back the Balliol faction during the wars of Bruce. They were beaten and dispossessed after the battle of the Pass of Brander in 1308. Their cousins, the Macdonalds, who had succored the importunate King of Scots during the desperate days, and followed him to glory at Bannockburn, secured great advantage.

To the victors went the spoils, and Glencoe passed from Macdougall hands into those of Angus Og MacDonald. He, in turn, granted the land to his bastard, Iain Fraoch (anglicised as John of the Heather). From Iain's loins sprang Clan McIain Abrach – MacDonald of Glencoe. Though they might be the smallest sept of mighty Clan Donald, now reaching the very apogee of its influence, they shared common blood with kinsmen who inhabited and mainly controlled virtually all the Western Isles from Lewis, southwards across Skye, down to Jura and Islay. Lochaber, Ardnamurchan and Kintyre were theirs as was Antrim in Ireland. Lesser names living in Glencoe, Macruaris, Hendersons and others became John of the Heather's tenants, and the MacIain who fell in the slaughter of 1692 was the twelfth to bear his lineage and titles.

'Good' John of Islay, greatest and most influential of the chiefs of Clan Donald, whose proud title of 'Lord of the Isles' was no mere boasting, lived at a dangerous juncture, when nationhood was again threatened by Toom Tabard's son Edward, backed by Edward III of England whose pressure all but extinguished the precious flame of statehood. Almost, but not quite, in the dangerous politics of the mid-fourteenth century, the King of Scots could not afford to alienate sp great a magnate as John of the Isles, who, by careful management and the odd selective murder,[14] consolidated and expanded the full achievement of his dynasty. His son Donald inherited a stable and, by local standards, peaceable estate. It was unfortunate that Donald became embroiled in a quarrel over the disputed earldom of Ross, which he was able to claim by right of his wife. Disappointed by the high-handedness of the Albany Stewarts, he sought redress by force of arms and brought an army to the bloody field of Harlaw, by Inverurie, in July 1411. The battle was hard-fought but the Lowland levies under Alexander, Earl of Mar, bastard son of royalty, claimed the field. This was not the end of the Lordship, but it was the start of a slow decline, which terminated in the abolition of the title by James IV in 1493 and the eclipse of Clan Donald.

One of the consequences of the final collapse of Clan Donald's hegemony was the re-distribution by royal writ, of many of their holdings. MacIain was not dispossessed but found himself the feudal inferior of Duncan Stewart of Appin; some decades later the feudatory rights passed to Campbell, the Earl of Argyll. Such a transition was not unusual but a struggle for power in the west, unresolved by the official fall of the Lordship in 1493, was to lead to a bitter divide between these two great names, Campbell and MacDonald (see Chapter Three), which could be perceived as reaching its deadly denouement on that raw winter's night in 1692.

The Age of Forays

It was the intention of the Scottish crown, having disposed of the Lordship as a perceived over-mighty subject, to rule the fissiparous Islemen by proxy, relying on a network of local magnates. This experiment failed and ushered in a period of internecine violence known as the *Linn nan Creach*, The Age of Forays. This period also witnessed a hardening of the divide between Highlander and Lowlander, the former being regarded as ethnically 'different'. James IV was probably the last King of Scots to have a facility for Gaelic.[15] John Major, the chronicler of Harlaw, writing in the 1520s, described his upland contemporaries in pejorative terms: 'In dress, in the manner of their outward life, and in good morals, for example, these [Highlanders] come far behind the householding Scots – yet they are not less, but rather more prompt to fight ...'.[16]

With the violent near-anarchy of the Age of Forays, it was logical that the clan system would develop. Men would naturally join together and enter into understandings for mutual protection, and the shield of a great magnate is a powerful comfort in uncertain times. In the Lowlands, family connection remained strong, but was increasingly tempered by business and commerce, by the development of the Scottish polity and, ultimately, by the Reformation, which sharpened the divide with the recusant clans. Resentment went both ways. The Highlanders, as Dr Stephenson points out, saw their own notion of culture excluded and marginalized by an effete and decadent race who, whilst sharing a common bloodline, now affected to despise their cousins, the Gael.[17] Whilst the Highlanders remained, in the wider sense, an element within the Scottish polity, they were significantly removed from its more pressing influence, and saw no reason to desist from continuing much as before.

For its own part, the crown, without the resources or means to establish any meaningful manner of centralized authority north of the Highland Line, had to rely upon local magnates. If certain of the clans (MacDonald in particular) had cause to lament the collapse of the Lordship, there were others who sensed opportunity (most notably Campbell, MacKenzie and Gordon). Of these we are most particularly concerned with Clan Diarmid.[18] Their lineage, like that of the chiefs of Clan Donald, was impressive, possibly descending from a hero of the Fianna, or perhaps of British blood tracing back to King Arthur. The latter may in fact be, in general terms at least, correct, in that current researches would appear to locate the family's origin to Lennox in Strathclyde. By the thirteenth century an aggressive scion, 'Great' Colin, *Cailean Mor,* had lands in Argyll, which he held from the Scottish crown, and his successors claimed to be sons of this Colin, thus *MacCailean Mor.*

Like Clan Donald, Sir Neil Campbell wisely chose to back Bruce after the coronation in 1306 and his loyalty was equally rewarded.

With care, subsequent Campbell chiefs built upon this foundation and gradually but steadily increased their power. By the early fifteenth century they had added the lordship of Glenorchy to their titles. Sir Duncan Campbell, fourth Baronet, was elevated to the Lordship of Lochow by Robert III. His second wife was Margaret Stewart, a granddaughter of the King, albeit from the wrong side of the blanket, and his younger sons by her acquired Auchinbreek, Kilberry, Kildalloig, Ellangreg and Otter. Duncan's grandson, by his first marriage to one of the Albany Stewarts, was elevated to the earldom of Argyll in 1457 and established his seat at Inveraray, where his descendants reside to this day. Clan Diarmid had now fully arrived, but their ascent was only beginning. In 1500 the third earl was appointed as James IV's Lieutenant in the Isles, an appointment he held not just for the remainder of James' reign (brought to an abrupt and bloody conclusion by English bills at Flodden in 1513), but into the long minority of James V. As an adult ruler the new king proved both fierce and contentious, and relationships with his magnates were never satisfactory.

In 1529 the third earl died and Clan Donald protested to the crown that the Campbells were prone to exacerbating disorders, in order to garner laurels by seeming to uphold the rule of law. The fourth earl found himself temporarily incarcerated, and his commission offered to the chief complainant Alexander MacDonald of Islay. Unrest, however continued, and the King mounted a naval expedition into the west during 1540, partly to overawe fractious clansmen and extract oaths and hostages for future good conduct. Such raids did little good in the longer term, and James, already ailing from an unknown malady, declined rapidly after the humiliating defeat at Solway Moss in 1542, where his army was broken by 500 English marchers.

During the reign of Mary and her son James VI, the Reformation galvanized the face of Scottish politics and nationhood, and after the Union of the Crowns the long vicissitudes of the border were finally, if harshly, resolved. In the Highlands however, matters continued in the best traditions of violent anarchy. After the Battle of the Spoiling of the Dyke, the Glengarry MacDonalds kept the custom of church-burnings alive when, in 1603, they immolated the congregation of Kilchrist in East Ross. Five years beforehand the MacLeans and MacDonalds had met to settle their differences in a sanguinary trial of arms at Gruinart on Islay, where nearly 300 MacLeans fell.

Faced with such rampant lawlessness, the crown had a number of legal remedies at its disposal. Those accused could be summoned to appear before the Privy Council in Edinburgh, there to answer the charges laid against them and accept the penalty on conviction. If the accused, as they frequently did, chose to ignore the legal sum-mons, then they could be 'put to the horn' – outlawed. Where an entire group or clan was involved, then Letters of Fire and Sword could be issued – a draconian remedy that meant the guilty or those considered to be guilty could be harried by agents empowered to do so. This was a blunt instrument of policy apt to fuel further distur-bances, engender new feuds and be employed as a means of settling old scores. As a final and dreaded sanction, the state could proscribe the entire clan, as occurred with the MacGregors. This was the ulti-mate reprisal, the entire name ceased to have legal protection, they became non-persons. As John Prebble asserts: this was a licence for mass oppression and virtual extermination.[19]

Clan Gregor had found itself increasingly marginalized by the encroaching aspirations of Clan Campbell during the sixteenth cen-tury. The MacDonalds of Glencoe had been employed as hired muscle by the laird of Glenorchy as early as 1563. The seventh earl of Argyll also found employment for the Glencoe men as caterans. This same seventh earl, Archibald the Grim as he was known, having feuded with the Ogilvies, found himself at odds with Colquhoun of Luss. Despite the relentless harrying of MacGregors by Clan Campbell, Archibald had no difficulty in recruiting MacGregor of Glenstrae as cateran, the denouement of the latter's depredations was the savage little battle of Glenfuin (the true 'Glen of Weeping') where Glenstrae hammered the Colquhouns, 180 of whom, including a group of unarmed captives, were stretched lifeless. MacGregor was aided in this enterprise by a company of the Glencoe MacDonalds. It was the battered Colquhouns whose protests led to the severest of penalties being imposed on the entire clan, who thereafter could only survive by seeking shelter under the banner of different chiefs.[20]

Some years earlier in 1587, James VI had attempted to extend the concept of bonds by enacting statutory provision for the 'General Bond', which imposed a blanket obligation upon chiefs for the good behavior of those owing them allegiance. A decade after, the King required all men of property in the Highlands to show title to their lands, emphasizing that their tenure was dependent upon the operation of law rather than local custom. One of the king's ideas for controlling his wilder Gaelic subjects was to thin the blood of the Highlands by planting Lowland colonists in their midst, an expedient which was tried most notably, if without enduring success, on Lewis. The prime beneficiary of James' policies was Archibald the Grim, whose own settlement of Kintyre proved more lasting. He oppressed the indigenous MacDonalds and MacLeans. Happily for the Campbell chief, the Union of the Crown and the establishment of plantations in Ulster came at the most propitious moment. Not everyone viewed the inexorable rise of Archibald Campbell with equanimity: several influential voices, most vocally that of the Bishop of the Isles, expressed considerable reservations.

In 1608 the Bishop accompanied an expedition to the Isles under the generalship of Lord Ochiltree. Policy involved both stick and carrot. After attending a summit on Mull a number of the chiefs were placed in custody to better concentrate their thoughts, and subsequently agreed to enter into a series of measures, collectively referred to as the Statutes of Iona. These were far-ranging in scope and in no small part aspirational, but the Union had greatly added to the pool of resources available to the crown, and James was determined that these proud and arrogant peacocks should lay down their swords, behave as good citizens and act as officers of the crown. One intention was to facilitate the spread of

Presbyterianism and promote the use of the English tongue. These Statutes of Iona were by design or implication anti-Gaelic: their implementation would be likely to exacerbate rather than heal any rift between Highlands and Lowlands. It was not a solution to the Highland 'problem'.

The Statutes and the General Band did have an effect, insofar as the chiefs came to understand that they could not treat the authority of the monarch with cavalier disdain. This arose as much from the fact that repeated military intervention (James' generally putting some stick about), convinced the chiefs it was wiser to conform. Attempts at settling Lowlanders, which mirrored the process occurring in Ulster did not take, and the proscriptive elements contained in the Statutes, such as the discrimination against bards. Being considered by their heroic verses to incite recourse to arms, they in fact provoked little more than understandable resentment. James was, of course, administering similar lessons in the Lowlands. The notorious Border reivers, as fractious as their Highland contemporaries, had found themselves much curtailed after 1603 – a programme of ruthless suppression, largely complete by 1610. This ending of the Steel Bonnets was achieved by draconian and indiscriminate means, but it was effective: the truculent borders became the pacified middle shires. For the Highland chiefs the lesson was plain.

DOMESTIC LIFE OF GLENCOE

'I will doun in the lawland, Lord, and thair steill a kow.'[21]

A celebrated Irish epic the *Tain Bo Cualnage* tells the dramatic tale of a legendary Iron Age cattle raid, where Queen Maeve of Connaught is relieved of a prize bull, an affront that sparks all manner of reprisal. Some fifteen centuries after, the Gaels of the North-West Highlands of Scotland were enthusiastically perpetuating this tradition. Growing crops played a small part in the agricultural economy of the clans, their shaggy black cattle were the mainstay. Though they were termed black, the beasts came in a variety of shades. Longhaired with impressive horns, they were stocky, solid and hardy. They were the measure of a man's wealth.[22] The heroic association of cattle raiding with the dim, weird battles of long ago gave a veneer of romance to the squalid and violent business of rustling, which was both ceaseless and endemic. Though Clan Iain Abrach might be few in number, they performed prodigies when it came to the business of reiving. That they had few friends was not a consequence that caused them any disquiet. The beasts, besides being tough. were nimble, which was most useful in a breed that had to subsist in a harsh upland environment, and most convenient for the rustler who might have to move the stolen stock a considerable distance over rough ground before gaining the safety of his own country.

As a measure of their importance, a considerable corpus of legend and superstition was invested in the herd – no small wonder, for in a basic economy, the preservation of stock was quite literally a matter of life and death. The ancient flint arrowheads, littered by their distant ancestors of whom the clansmen were ignorant, were regarded as supernatural, shot by faerie folk, 'elf-bolts: the mystical qualities of a variety of stones were invoked as charms to ward off sickness'.[23] Despite the centuries of Christianity, old beliefs still lingered and great fires, through which the herds were driven for good fortune and the favour of ancient gods, were lit on 1 May (Beltainn) and 1 November (Samhain). Theft of cattle sparked many a feud and foray; the bloodshed which these unleashed only served to fuel the chivalric traditions.

Though great events might unfold in the wider world beyond the steep slopes sealing the Glen, MacIain's people lived through an essentially unchanging cycle, dominated by the seasons and the demands of herding. War, foray and the lure of plunder were relatively rare distractions, most welcome of course and providing the stuff of tales the bard would embroider through the dark, silent winter nights, when snow and wind and cold shut out the world for weeks or even months, and men had little employment other than to sit around the darkly smoking peat fires, sipping their whisky whilst remembering with advantage their own martial feats and those of their ancestors. East of the pass the land was barely habitable, the pattern of settlements clung, as they had likely done since Neolithic times, to the pleasant basin at the western end. Here a necklace of hamlets, Achtriachtan, Brecklet, Inverrigan, Achnacone, Leacantuim and, by the shore, Carnoch, sufficed to house a community of perhaps, at any one time 500 souls, of whom at best, a third could be counted as fighters.

Within these settlements dwellings were clustered and thrust together. There was nothing approximating to the life of towns. Close-packed, seemingly anarchic, the hamlets, termed 'baile'in Gaelic, most often translated as township with the tenure divided into strips or rigs, each worked by a family unit. This system of run-rig was common throughout the tribal lands. Travellers noted the dwellings of these Highlanders, which were of universal pattern throughout the glens, as being spectacularly squalid. In the censorious glare of their Lowland and English contemporaries, living standards of clansmen were a barbaric intrusion. Their bothies were low, of crude dry-stones, roofed with sods or thatch (a form of rope made from heather), devoid of comfort or sanitation and home to both man and beast, blackened by the aromatic and cloying fumes of burning peat. Addicted, in the pejorative view, to indolence, idle boasting, general lawlessness and endemic violence, the mountain men were without charm or quality. Celtic balladry would have to wait for the Romantic revival. These were a people driven apart, by geography, culture, attitudes, language, dress, politics and religion. They were a nuisance and an embarrassment, particularly to their Lowland neighbours who both feared and despised them. A Scotland which was on the brink of its own profound ascent into the Enlightenment, did not need beggars at the gate.

Around the gaggle of grey stone bothies people farmed the available land, and in Glencoe this was sweet and fertile – strips sown with oats, barley and kale, a few sheep and less goats. For transport they might keep short, sturdy garrons: and the chief went nowhere on foot. Gaudy as an Eastern potentate astride his pony, a slew of his people trotting after. During the long, dreary months of winter, the cattle were kept close by, for the cold months were a testing time, a spectre of famine hovering like Banquo's ghost. In the spring when a quickening sun revived men and beasts, the latter, having passed through Beltainn blaze, were driven out to summer shielings at the exposed eastern gateway and the hills of the Black Mount beyond. Here they would remain until summer sun dipped into autumn and the cycle was reversed.

When chiefs died, they were traditionally interred on the islet of *Eilean Munde,* which lies in Loch Leven, by the Ballachulish, famous for its productive slate quarries which flourished after 'The Great Sheep' had completed the work begun on 13th February 1692. The original chapel on the island is said to have been constructed by St Finian Mundus who came from Iona in the seventh century. His church was destroyed by fire after the fall of the Lordship and then rebuilt during the 1500s; falling into disuse by the middle of the next century. The burial ground was common to Clan Ian Abrach of Glencoe and also their neighbours, Stewarts of Appin, and Camerons. Remarkably, they managed to share the usage without drawing swords.

People lived as their fathers, grandfathers and the wealth of their ancestors stretching back time out of mind had lived: a bare and basic life, enlivened by song and the comfort of family and routine. Highland life was far from idyllic, the element of romance had yet to accrue. Life was hard, likely to be short and often brutal; infant mortality was high. But it was the only life they knew, any other was unthinkable. In endless winters, when life closed down and darkness was complete, famine and disease might take them off; in the light months, foray or feud might account for others. They lived with death as a constant companion and like all companions became accustomed to it. It is commonplace to determine the divide between what would become Whig clans (those who supported the Government) and Tories (who clung to semi-independence and latterly supported the exiled Stuarts) as, in no small part, a matter of religion. This divide, whilst it certainly did exist, may, nonetheless, be less clearcut than might it may appear. It is probably correct to assert that Catholicism could be identified with the Tories and Protestantism with the Whigs. In matters of observance however, many of the clans, most particularly those in remoter areas, practised a form of expedient faith which might involve elements of both, and which in fact indicates no clear affiliation. Though southerners might, and frequently did, find them uncouth, the Gael had an inbred respect for learning and culture. His chiefs would be educated in Paris, despite strictures to the contrary, with teaching of the commoners reliant upon local priests.

For the Glencoe men, Loch Leven provided a welcome and frequently abundant supply of herrings to Highlanders the long sea-lochs and the coastal waters were a natural highway. Their religion, up to a point, was constant and the political upheavals of the Scottish Reformation largely passed them by. MacIain, as befitted his status, had a spacious, unfortified dwelling in Carnoch, with a summerhouse nestling in the shelter of the rising hills of *Gleann Lac*. If MacDonald of Glencoe were not a great chieftain, such as Keppoch or Lochiel, he would still possess a small library, pine or oak chests to hold valuables, some glassware and a respectable cellar. He would have his bard to sing tales of ancestors, back to Conn of the Hundred Battles and the splendid deeds of his name. If, to the world south of the Great Glen, he and men like him were an embarrassing and unwelcome anachronism, on his own ground he was a free prince, father and protector of his people, and his word amongst them was law.

The Development of the Clan System in the Seventeenth Century

> What is properly called the Highlands of Scotland is that large tract of mountainous Ground to the Northwest of the Forth and the Tay, where the natives speak the Irish language. The inhabitants stick close to their ancient and idle way of life; retain their barbarous customs and maxims; depend generally on their Chiefs as their Sovereign Lords and masters; and being accustomed to the use of Arms, and inured to hard living, are dangerous to the public peace; and must continue to be so until, being deprived of arms for some years, they forget the use of them.[24]

> The usual habit of both sexes is the plaid ... the men wear theirs after another manner ...it is loose and flowing like the mantles our painters give their heroes. Their thighs are bare with brawny muscles. Nature has drawn all her strokes bold and masterly. What is covered is only adapted to necessity, a thin brogue on the foot, a short buskin of various colours on the legs, tied above the calf with a large shot pouch on each side of which hangs a pistol and a dagger ... a round target on their backs ...in one hand a broadsword and a musket in the other.[25]

These two quotations sum up a not untypical southerner's view of the Highlands, a barbarous tract of scruffy wasteland, somewhere north of Edinburgh. The late seventeenth century was not an age that necessarily admired wilderness – that would have to wait for the Romantics. The Highlands of Scotland constituted the most remote and inaccessible part of mainland Britain, their inhabitants separated from their fellow Scots and English not just by the inconveniences of topography but by perceived race, culture, language, custom, dress and religion. In the extreme north-west of Sutherland, where the waves batter distant Cape Wrath and the long sweep of Sandwood Bay, the Mackays held sway, staunchly pro-Hanoverian. South and across to Skye and Lewis, the MacLeods, a sept of Clan Donald lived around Loch Broom and what is now the pleasant fishing town of

Ullapool. MacDonalds (Clanranald) held Uist and Moidart, the MacLeans Mull, Clan Cameron claimed Lochaber, whilst Argyll to the south was the fief of mighty Clan Campbell. It was a wild land, untamed by major roads or highways, largely devoid of Government outposts; those there were decayed and undermanned.

Western sea and inland lochs provided the most natural arteries of communication. The soil was too poor to encourage husbandry. The mainstay of what was, at best, a subsistence economy, were the shaggy black cattle, acquired as often through foray as trade. In the years following the Jacobite Rising of 1715, as Marshal Wade was building his famous network of roads, he was assisted by his chief surveyor, Edmund Burt, who left a record of his time amongst the clans. As a rather dour Englishman, he was by no means enamored of his Highland hosts, nor for that matter their Lowland contemporaries. His were, however, perhaps the first general observations that many in England would have encountered and, though his account postdates our period by a full generation, it is nonetheless relevant: 'The Highlands are but little known, even to the inhabitants of the low country of Scotland ... to the people of England ... the Highlands are hardly known at all; for there has been less than I know of written upon the subject than of either of the Indies ...'.[26] In this observation he was likely to be correct. He noted with, perhaps a Whig bias, that the chiefs still enjoyed too much power for his liking: 'The heritable power of pit and gallows, as they call it, which is still exercised by some within their proper district, is, I think, too much for any particular subject to be entrusted with.'[27] He went on to expound, speaking of one of the chiefs:

> I have heard say of him, by a very credible person, that a Highlander of a neighbouring clan, with whom he had long been at variance, being brought before him, he declared upon the accusation, before he had seen the party accused, that his very name should hang him.[28]

As a good Whig, he deplored hereditary powers of the magnates, theirs from 'the mere accident of birth', whose power over their subjects exceeded that of any peer in England over his tenants. He was, however, no more impressed by those fervent sons of the Kirk, members of the 'Society for the Propagation of Christian Knowledge', who were, by that time, striving to bring the fuller appreciation of their joyless brand of Calvinism to the glens. Burt noted their task, which was in part to separate the Highlanders from their ancient, heathen tongue, though of course the radical ministers had to learn it themselves so they could communicate with their proposed congregations. The majority of these missions failed miserably, though some stalwart preachers like the Herculean Aeneas Sage enjoyed success and won through sheer indomitable persistence.[29] In addition to their feudal adherence, the clansmen's pride in their name confounded Burt – a southerner's view, with no attempt made to penetrate his subject's different understanding:

> This kind of vanity ... in people of no fortune, makes them ridiculous ... thus you see a gentleman may be a mercenary piper, or keep a little ale-house where he brews his drink in a kettle; but to be of any working trade would be a disgrace to him, his present relations and his ancestry.[30]

He was equally dismissive of the bagpipes, the butt of many a Lowlander's joke since, though this disdain was entirely founded in ignorance.[31] There is a view expressed by certain writers, that clan society was molded from the mists of time and therefore not subject to change. This was by no means true: the Highland way of life was constantly evolving. We have already seen how the chiefs, in the years between the end of the Civil Wars and the Glorious Revolution of 1688, adapted away from reliance on their swords to settle disputes. They found the hire of lawyers more cost-effective than the maintenance of caterans. In the seventeenth century, although the existence of Gaeldom as a cultural entity appeared imperiled by external factors, the Gaels proved resilient, and their literature and verse enjoyed a significant renaissance.[32] The 'Clan' still formed the basis of the social framework. These clans of the seventeenth century were not Celtic survivals from an age of heroes. Indeed, their origin can more properly be traced back to the fourteenth century. Chiefs might originally have held their lands without the benefit of feudal charter, but feudal tenure gradually became more commonplace.[33] Scotland as a nation was, during the late Medieval and Renaissance periods, plagued by a succession of minority kingships, and the inevitable factional feuding this entailed.[34] If the King, as tenant in chief, could not provide for his subjects or vassals, then they would find they had to make a shift for themselves.

This they did – the more aggressive increased their share at the expense of the weaker, and increasing power necessitated additional followers. This process could be cloaked or ratified in law by the lesser tenant agreeing to hold his land now from the greater and the Crown's acquiescence, sealed by deed or charter. As an alternative or as part of this process, the head of a family group or affinity could establish superiority over the lesser septs or branches. Lastly, men could enter into bonds or contracts whereby they pledged friendship and loyalty to each other. Where such an agreement was contracted between those of unequal standing, then the lesser party bound himself and his affinity to obey, the greater consideration being shelter under the great man's banner.

Feudalism, kinship and bonding ('manrent'),[35] became the cement that bound the fabric of society. It is from this backdrop that the clan system emerges, a response to the lack of effective royal authority. 'Clan' means 'children' – so there is a presumption all members spring from a common stock, a concept that the chiefs encouraged with their lengthy and often fantastical pedigrees, stretching their line back to Gaelic heroes of a distant past. In the glens of the west, the idea of loyalty to a chief gained favour as royal power waned. This was a reversal of previous precedents that had, themselves, declined when the Crown waxed strong. Throughout the period to 1700, clans could not be distinguished by tartans or even by surnames.

The former remain a later creation and, until the eighteenth century, many Highlanders did not possess a surname.[36] By the time of the first Jacobite rebellions this had begun to change, and those who followed a certain chief would adopt his name. By this means they would claim affinity with the chief, though they were not necessarily blood relations in any degree.

Below the hierarchy of chieftain and his kin, tacksmen and officers ranked men of other name, who owed allegiance through feudal or other ties and lastly, a smattering of caterans or outlaws whose loyalty was dictated largely by expediency. Grafted on to the body of the clan proper was the corpus of retained individuals who served the chief as officials, bodyguards, doctors, lawyers, harpers or pipers. Caterans had been present as an element in the fabric of Highland society certainly since the late fourteenth century. Both sides who fought at Harlaw in 1411, Donald of the Isles and Alexander, Earl of Mar, employed caterans as mercenaries. The name probably derives from the Irish 'cearnach' or soldier. If a chief claimed this paternal relationship to those who were in effect his subjects, he offered them a status higher than mere vassalage and implied a level of mutual obligation that might ordinarily apply only to those related by blood. In a violent and uncertain world, such as obtained during the Age of Forays, a man needed to belong somewhere and be able to call upon the shield of one far mightier than he.

Expediency, properly nurtured, could breed pride in the name and a willingness to identify closely with the chief, and this could, in turn lead to a very considerable degree of personal loyalty. Obviously, as generations passed and those of the blood married into those of lesser proximity, the net of kinship was cast wider. Those of the senior branch and senior members of cadet branches formed the clan gentry. In the earlier stages these held their lands as of right and through heredity, but latterly, it became the custom of many chiefs to grant formal leases or 'tacks'. In times of strife these tenants or tacksmen formed the officer cadre of the clan regiment. Their leases were usually heritable, and military service a condition of tenure.

Though the chief enjoyed great power, this was not, initially at least, without limitation or constraint. His position was not inexpugnable: he was expected to consult with a council of advisors and tacksmen. His successor was chosen from amongst a class of his immediate family, harking back to the old Celtic practice of tanistry.

By the late seventeenth century, however, the chief's position had developed into something more authoritarian and sometimes aloof. with the concept of primogeniture firmly established. This may sound retrograde, but the uncertainty of tanistry had sparked many a feud. Differences between various clan groupings were frequently exacerbated by a weak or inefficient royal authority. Lands were sometimes separately granted to different claimants who could then cite not only traditional tenure of long usage but also a viable feudal charter. A pernicious situation could arise where men living on a certain portion of land could find themselves obliged by charter to one feudal superior, whilst owing traditional allegiance to another. The Campbells proved particularly skilful in what could be termed 'aggressive feudalism'.[37]

In many ways this pattern did not differ overly from that established in the Lowlands. Change, and the widening gulf, came gradually spurred on after the mid-sixteenth century by the impetus of the reformed church, which drew the line between Calvinist Lowlands and the Recusant or Episcopalian Highlands. The pace of cultural change began to gather noticeably south of the Great Glen, as church lands were parceled out and the burgeoning middle classes created a more market-based economy with land and property being dealt in as commodities. As the cultural gap widened this was exacerbated to a significant degree by the lack of a common language. The ancient, guttural tongue of the Gael, melodic as it can sound to those suitably attuned, grated as harsh, barbaric and backward to those who looked more often to the south than north and west.

Gaelic culture was heartily despised by the Lowlanders who had no feel for its subtlety or tradition, and who saw learning as the province of formal schooling and university cloisters. Differences of language were compounded by marked variations in dress and by the Highlander's equally hubristic way of clinging to his own practice. Unsurprisingly the spectacle of everyday life in the Highlands failed to impress Edward Burt, who was solidly wedded to the virtues of regular industry. He found the cramped, earthy conditions in their bothies primitive in the extreme. This revulsion at the squalid conditions endured by the clansmen informs the writings of most of those (few) southerners who visited.

Their world seemed utterly at variance with the burgeoning cultural, commercial and artistic life of the Lowlands. The great age of the Scottish enlightenment, the time of Adam Smith, David Hume and a generation of Scots whose achievement was to turn Edinburgh and the Lowlands into the intellectual powerhouse of Europe, was just around the corner. This soaring upsurge was expected to co-exist with backward Highlanders, who appeared to have no more in common with their Lowland contemporaries than the native tribes of North America. What labour there was seemed to be undertaken by the females, whilst the men idled their time around in the smoky glow of peat fires, apparently with nothing resembling gainful employment to occupy them: 'Many are supported by the bounty of their acquaintances or friends and relations; others get their living by levying blackmail[38] and the rest by stealing.'[39] This may just be a southerner's pejorative view of a society he was unable and unwilling to understand. Such reports would only fuel the Government's alarm at the likely menace posed by these hardy mountaineers who, if they were nothing else, were natural fighters, hardened by their climate, their martial tradition, the practices of cattle raiding and the feud.[40] Someone who knew them better than Burt was Duncan Forbes of Culloden, Lord President of the Court of Session. He was a staunch Hanoverian, but had spent his life amongst the chiefs and was able to offer the Government the benefit of his accumulated wisdom:[41]

A Highland Clan is a set of men all bearing the same sirname, and believing themselves to be related, the one to the other, and to be descended from the same common stock. In each clan there are several subaltern tribes, who owe their dependence on their own immediate chiefs but all agree in owing allegiance to the Supreme Chief of the Clan or Kindred and look upon it to be their duty to support him in all adventures.[42]

Forbes explained why the Crown had, to a large degree, perpetuated the power of the chiefs, largely through an exercise of expediency:

It has been for a great many years impracticable (and hardly thought safe to try it) to give the Law its course among the mountains. It required no small degree of Courage, and a greater degree of power than men are generally possessed of, to arrest an offender or debtor in the midst of his Clan. And for this reason it was that the Crown in former times was obliged to put Sheriffships and other Jurisdictions in the hands of powerful families in the Highlands, who by their respective Clans and following could give execution to the Laws within their several territories, and frequently did so at the expense of considerable bloodshed.[43]

Whig clans such as the Campbells, who could muster 4,000 broadswords, accounted for a fair proportion of the 30,000 fighting men Forbes assessed as the total martial complement of all the clans. Of these, MacDonald of Glencoe was amongst the smallest, with 150 fighters at best. But the warning was clear. If a few thousand from Tory clans could shake loose Scotland, get the better of Crown forces in two major and several minor engagements, and then march, unchecked, as far as Derby (as they were to do in 1745); the threat from the whole was potent indeed. When they did muster the clothing, habit and arms of these Highlanders, it marked them utterly apart from their Lowland contemporaries. Edward Burt, as might be anticipated, found their manner of dress outlandish:

The common habit of the Highlander is far from being acceptable to the eye. With them a small part of the plaid, which is not so large as the former, is set in folds and girt round the waist to make of it a short petticoat that reaches halfway down the thigh, the rest is brought over the shoulders and fastened before, below the neck often with a fork, and sometimes with a bodkin or sharpened piece of stick, so that they make pretty nearly the appearance of the poor women in London when they bring their gowns over their heads to shelter themselves from the rain. This dress is called the quelt, and for the most part they wear the petticoat so very short that in a windy day, going up a hill, or stooping the indecency of it is plainly discovered.[44]

In battle, the plaid was customarily shrugged off before the charge bit home, and the warrior came into contact with only his long, saffron shirt (*'leine chrochach'*) to preserve modesty. Uniforms were unknown; everyday wear continued during hostilities. In some areas breeches were as common as the plaid.[45] Shoes, should the wearer possess them, were usually soft leather brogues, and everyone usually sported a woollen bonnet. The 'philabeg' or kilt probably came into use during the early eighteenth century and its creation is customarily attributed to an Englishman called Rawlinson.[46] The gentry wore fine hose or 'truibhs' (trews) which were essentially close fitting leggings akin to medieval hose, cut to favour the shapely thigh and calf of the wearer.

The plaid was a length of tartan cloth (Tuar = colour and Tan = district). Whilst different areas favoured certain patterns – the tartans, as we presently understand the term, did not exist. This garment was some two yards in length and twice that in width, gathered around the waist in a series of folds and held in place by a belt. The lower folds then fell down to the knee or just above in the manner of the modern kilt, whilst the top portion was gathered over the left shoulder to leave the right arm free (in the case of a left-handed swordsman this would naturally be reversed). This upper section could be adjusted to cover both shoulders in wet or inclement weather, and the plaid was very much all weather and all-purpose attire.

When the wearer needed both arms free, the bulk was secured over the chest by means of a brooch, the same as was employed to fasten the plaid when carried over the left shoulder. Putting on the plaid was no easy mater unless the wearer was accustomed. The preferred method (certainly that favoured by this writer) was for the wearer to spread the plaid upon the ground, arrange the pleats, then roll himself within, standing only once he had secured his plaid. Primitive as it might seem, the plaid was an eminently practical garb for mountain men. The saffron shirt worn underneath provided extra warmth and preserved modesty if the wearer stripped his plaid to cross deeper water. It doubled as a sleeping bag or bivouac, could be cast off with ease before the fight and recovered after.

An eighteenth-century English observer has left a vivid image of the various followers attendant upon a Highland chief. These included the Henchman, a kind of personal assistant and bodyguard, ('minder' in the modern idiom). He stood behind or at the haunch of his lord whilst the latter was at table. The Bard sang the praises of the chief and the deeds of his line, whilst the Bladier was the smooth tongued negotiator. Gilli-more was the sword-bearer and Gilli-casflue had the less edifying burden of carrying the chief over stream and bog, so as not to besmirch his finery. Gilli-comstrainie was to lead the lord's garron, Gilli-trusharnish's meaner function was to secure the baggage and finally the piper to play. This was an important post generally held by a man of rank, trained in one of the preferred schools to his art. Such was his status in fact, that he had a ghilly of his own to lug the instrument. Proud and haughty, the chief is a free prince amongst his people: his honour is their honour, his quarrel is their fight. From the highest to the meanest, these men see themselves as set above: saffron and plaid with the shine of burnished arms, the chief's bold feathers, his silver brooch and buckles on his shoes. A man who may have been educated in Paris, as versed in the classics as his English counterpart, and whose library and cellar would be the equal of any southerner.

WEAPONS AND WARFARE

The clansman's arms were as distinctive as his dress. During the earlier period the rank and file had relied on the bow, on spears and axes. The 'Lochaber' axe does not make its first recorded appearance until the sixteenth century. In its matured form this was a long handled polearm that featured a curved axe blade, elliptical in shape and finished with a hook set in the head of the shaft.[47] Swords were normally reserved for gentlemen; a decent quality blade was an expensive and prized item. Highland swords, in the sixteenth century, were characterized by the development of the double hander or *claidheamhmor*. This was a heavy double-edged blade, cross guard finished with distinctive drooping quillons terminating in pierced quatrefoils. Though such double-handers would have been rare by 1692 There is no reason to expect they were completely obsolete.[48]

During the late seventeenth century the design and construction of basket hilted broadswords was reaching its full and very fine flowering. Double-edged blades were mainly imported from Europe, many bearing the cipher 'Andrea Ferrara', but hilts were fashioned locally. By 1700 two major schools of design, at Glasgow and Stirling, were developing. The original simple framework of defensive bars, which had defined earlier 'Irish' hilts, was transformed into a rectangular framework decorated with circles, diamonds, clubs. The Allan family of Stirling were particularly noted. These weapons remain some of the finest produced by British craftsmen. Variants included a single edged version or 'backsword'[49] and some with curved blades.[50]

Descended from the medieval 'ballock' knife and later 'dudgeon' dagger, the Highland Dirk, fancifully named the 'Widowmaker', was a long bladed dagger, traditionally carried in the left hand, behind the shield or target, for parrying. Blades, habitually the length of the owner's forearm, were sometimes salvaged from cut down swords, but otherwise tended to be single edged and tapering, perhaps mounted with brass.[51] Bog-oak or myrtle were favoured for their stubby, pot bellied handles; the pommel disc shape and the whole hilt finished with a filigree of silver or brass. These are elegant, yet functional weapons, used like the medieval roundel dagger as an everyday tool as well as a means of dispatching foes.

The targe or target is a round timber shield or buckler, constructed from two layers of oak or perhaps fir, a couple of feet across, grain opposing and covered in supple hide. The basic product was decorated with brass studs and intricate tooling, and with a centrally mounted boss that could be drilled to accommodate a projecting spike, a useful device for parrying. Firearms were a relative rarity in the Highlands, but distinctive Scottish and Highland types, both pistols and long guns did exist, though perhaps never in significant numbers and were reserved for the gentry. They had an all-steel finish, no wooden stock or grips distinguished these pistols, or 'daggs'. Early examples were fired by the wheel-lock mechanism and latterly by the snaphaunce.[52] Its design was also characterized by the lack of the conventional trigger guard, which was a short stubby trigger with the distinctive 'fish tail' or 'lemon' butts. Latterly, flintlocks assumed dominance, and the weapons were carried in pairs and fitted with belt hooks rather than being slung in holsters.[53]

For the true Highlander war was an affair of honour, individual pride in feats of arms being the paramount aim. A man, standing in his clan regiment, would be judged by his kin and by his following. His was a martial society where the Homeric spectacle of the duel of champions was kept fresh by the bards, and the rant from the pipes called for individual feats of arms to rival the deeds of distant heroes:

> O Children of Conn of the Hundred Battles
> Now is the time for you to win recognition,
> O raging whelps,
> O sturdy bears,
> O most sprightly lions,
> O battle-loving warriors,
> O brave, heroic firebrands,
> The children of Conn of the Hundred Battles,
> O children of Conn remember
> Hardihood in time of battle. [54]

When the charge struck home it did so with fearful effect. A man, standing in the front rank, armed with broadsword and target, facing an opponent equipped with musket and bayonet, will use his target and the dirk, held behind in the left hand, to sweep aside the point of the infantryman's bayonet and deliver a sweeping cut to the neck or head – a killing blow. Razor-sharp edge of blade will slice through tissue and smash bones, biting into flesh and severing arteries; blood loss from the wound will be catastrophic, the fight ended in seconds.[55] Duncan Forbes, in his assessment of the fighting strength of the clans, did not grade the combatants in terms of worth. It would be false to suggest that every able-bodied clansman was a warrior, as most were not. Prowess in arms was generally reserved for gentlemen and professional fighters, caterans. They had the choice weapons, the training and motivation. The average commons would be ill armed and without much in the way of military kit. General Henry Hawley, who would fight at Sheriffmuir and would command the Government army at Falkirk in 1746, earned, perhaps unjustly, the reputation of being a martinet. He had little sympathy for the clans, and wrote somewhat dismissively of their tactics in battle:

> They commonly form the Front rank of what they call their best men or True Highlanders, the number of which being always but few, when they form in battalions they commonly form four deep, & these Highlanders form the front of the four, the rest being Lowlanders & arrant scum. When these battalions come within a large musket shott or three score yards this front rank gives their fire, and immediately throw down their firelocks and come down in a cluster with their swords and targets, making a noise and endeavoring to pierce the body or battalion before them – becoming twelve or fourteen deep by the time they come up to the people they attack.[56]

Hawley was to find these 'Highlanders' and indeed the 'arrant scum' sufficient opponents at Falkirk! Mustering for raid or foray, the numbers involved would be likely to be quite small. When, however, the clan was called to battle, then the organisational system employed was fairly conventional, with the commons being mustered in companies. The gentry would naturally form the officers, whilst the caterans might supply the sergeants. A traditional means of assembly was the fiery cross – two lengths of timber lashed together with a strip of, at least in theory, blood soaked linen attached. This device was passed, smouldering, from hand to hand through the chief's domain, the talisman of war.[57] The muster assumed ritual significance, and was ringed with superstition. If the company met an armed man, then this was a good omen. Any game that darted across the way had to be killed, else ill fortune would ensue. Should a barefoot female be encountered, then a drop of blood must be pricked from her forehead. The clan was distinguished not by tartan, but by its badge or emblem, a plant or herb, and by the slogan 'the wild summons to slaughter joy in the fight'.

In terms of tactics, clans were feared for their Highland Charge. This was not merely a wild rush upon the enemy, a desire to come to hand-strokes as quickly as possible. Obviously, any force that relies essentially upon the individual fighting prowess of its component members, and is generally deficient in firearms, would seek to come into contact as quickly as possible. A drawn-out advance, in the teeth of enemy fire, would winnow the ranks, and as the best-armed men were to the fore, the casualties would be inordinately damaging to the unit's cohesion and fighting capacity. Based on heroic tradition, the well armed gentleman or cateran was the cutting edge, and the followers or 'ghillies' were cast very much in a supporting role.

During earlier, smaller scale encounters, these may have stood back whilst the respective paladins slogged it out. For Montrose's, campaigns the ghillies provided, on a rather ad hoc basis, the missile arm, using their bows. Alasdair MacColla, during the civil wars (see following chapter), is credited with developing the wild rush of the Gael into a sound military tactic, deploying the men either in column or, sometimes, in a wedge shaped formation.[58] With the advent of firearms, the role of the missile arm changed. As relatively few clansmen, and those mainly gentry possessed long guns, a single volley was fired from extreme range before the charge crashed home. Ghillies would not, therefore, have had any kind of fire support role as before. The swiftness of the advance, essential to cover ground and maintain momentum, did not permit reloading.

Colonel O'Sullivan, Prince Charles's much-maligned Irish subordinate during the Jacobite rebellion of 1745–1746, was capable of some trenchant remarks, even though he has not enjoyed a good press amongst historians. He observed, prior to Culloden and as a criticism of the ground favoured for a stand by his fellow-officer and rival Lord George Murray, that:

> Any man yt ever served with the Highlanders, knows yt they fire but one shot & abandon their firelocks after. If there be any obstruction yt hinders them of going on the enemy all is lost; they don't like to be exposed to he enemy's fire, nor can they resist it, not being trained to charge [load] as fast as regular troops, especially the English wch are the troops in the world yt fires best.[59]

In this assertion, the Irish officer was undoubtedly correct. It would not be possible to expect from Highlanders the level of drill and the rate of fire that a regular battalion might deliver. Their tradition of war and lack of firepower both argued heavily against it. This is not to say, however, that they were without discipline, and those authors who regard a Highland army as a 'rabble' fall into the same trap as Edward Burt. Tactically, a commander of Highland troops had to choose his field with care. Level ground, with perhaps a slight downward angle, dry and not impeded by obstacles such as standing timber, walls or gullies was preferred. If the Highland formation could approach in dead ground (that is out of sight of the enemy), and then charge home over a short distance, prospects for victory were much improved.

At Killiecrankie, apart from Montrose' earlier victories, the Highland charge proved capable of shattering Government armies.

In this battle Government troops on Mackay's left were swept from the field with loss. This is not to say the deployment of the clan regiments was perfectly executed, it was not. The Camerons, instead of advancing directly upon Leven's regiment, echeloned to their left, and suffered fearfully from volleys poured into their exposed flank. A dry analysis of the fight fails to convey the impression that the charging clans clearly made upon raw troops. They came on, throwing off their plaids, as a body of men who knew their business, and at a rapid rate of advance, a far swifter pace than regular formations could attain.

With the rant of the pipes and the wild scream of the slogan, their onrush must have been fearful. Psychology in war is all-important, if underrated and difficult to fathom. These thundering clansmen, a steel tipped avalanche, with their great swords raised and the grinning blades of Lochaber axes swung by the commons, would be fierce enough to test the mettle of any young Lowlander recruited from an apprentice's bench. Cohesion in the clan regiment came from a long martial tradition, pride in the name and a consciousness of fighting under the gaze of one's peers. Those men the Highlander charged with were men he knew: some of his immediate family, others from the wider affinity. The clan regiment was bound together by its loyalty to the chief, by its long history, real and romanced, by the songs of the bards and the rant of the pipes. The men knew their weapons from long usage. They were physically fleet and hardy. Inured, as Forbes observed, to hardship, and therefore able to function with far less supply. For all of their shortcomings, these men, in their final burst of defiance, marched as far as Derby and shook the House of Hanover to its core.

CHAPTER 2

The Day of Clan Donald

'They bound their appetites by their necessities, and their happiness consisted not in having much but in coveting little.'

William Sacheverell (late seventeenth century)

'You remember the place called Tawny Field?
It got a fine dose of manure
Not the dung of sheep or goats,
But Campbell blood well congealed'.

Iain Lom

' 'Clan' – A group of people with a common ancestor, esp. in the Scottish Highlands'

Oxford English Dictionary

When, in 1603, the Union of the Crowns did finally occur and James VI of Scotland became James I of England, a long enmity was finally resolved – at least outwardly. Many English were unimpressed by their new king and his horde of Scots' carpet-baggers hastening south.

James had been an effective and largely successful ruler in Scotland, though he would be judged less favourably in England: physically unprepossessing, learned but not always wise, eternally fearful of the assassin's blade and with an unfortunate liking for young men. Early in his reign, the more extreme elements of the Catholic faction, disappointed in their hopes of greater tolerance, plotted to blow up King and Parliament: the Gunpowder Plot. This may have been a genuine conspiracy, or possibly a 'put up' job by Robert Cecil, Earl of Salisbury, intended to bring further opprobrium on the Catholic minority. If this was so, then it was successful.

THE CLANS IN THE CIVIL WARS 1640–1660

If he failed to win the hearts of his English subjects, James was at least always a wily politician, his son Charles I, on the other hand, was not. He was both tolerant and courageous, a tiny man who married a French Catholic and encouraged the Episcopalian Church championed by Archbishop Laud. Having stirred up resentment amongst his Scottish subjects by excluding the Lords of Session from his Privy Council, he then caused near panic by threatening to recover all lands sequestered since Mary's accession almost a century earlier! 'Laud's Liturgy' – the common perception attaching to the Book of Canons, considered by many Scots to smack of Popery, led to a spate of disorders, and spurred enthusiastic support for the Solemn League and Covenant of 1638. This was a clear statement of Scotland's religious affiliation and stimulated resistance to the Bishops. The Covenanters, as the signatories were labeled, with the bit now firmly between their teeth, sought, through the Scots Parliament, to abolish the Episcopacy altogether. This sparked the fiasco known as the First Bishop's War. Though Charles failed to raise a viable force, and a second attempt in 1640 resulted in a humiliating debacle in the Battle or more correctly, Rout of Newburn Ford, with the temporary loss of Newcastle to the Scots. The Covenanters, led by an experienced general Alexander

Leslie, who had served his apprenticeship in the Thirty Years War under Gustavus Adolphus, the Swedish paladin, fielded a well drilled and disciplined army of over 20,000 foot, horse and guns. Buying back Newcastle cost Charles some £200,000 in sterling. One of the King's early political opponents in Scotland, who was destined to become his most ardent champion, was James Graham, fifth Earl and later first Marquis of Montrose.[1] Like some of those who would follow him in the service of the Stuarts, Montrose remains a supremely romantic figure: being remembered for the successes he achieved in the field in spite of his political naïvety. He would fall foul of the problem of reliance on an army, modest in size, but composed either of Irish regiments or Highland clans. Such a popish following might serve to conquer Scotland, but the anathema attached to Rome would ensure no viable political consolidation. A string of victories, however brilliant could be and indeed was undone by a single reverse.

In 1639 the Committee of Estates became alarmed at the power of Huntly and the Gordons in the north-east, who were notorious recusants. Montrose was, at the start of the year, given a commission to raise sufficient men to ensure the back door was kept firmly bolted. Leslie took both the key bastions of Edinburgh and Dumbarton, which secured any easy access for Royalist reinforcements from Ireland. Huntly, however, scored an easy and largely bloodless victory at Turriff, but was by early April, sufficiently alarmed to submit to Montrose at Inverurie. Undeterred, the Royalists, led by an experienced officer, struck at the Covenanters before Turriff, and in the ensuing scrimmage drove them from the streets – the 'Trot of Turriff'. Montrose was able to restore the situation when he appeared with fresh levies, his overly optimistic assessment of the Royalists morale left Aberdeen exposed, and the city was soon occupied.

Lord Aboyne, Huntly's son, moved out to confront the earl Marischal and Montrose at Stonehaven. The fight was untidy and confused; the Covenanters guns did some execution, though they failed to follow up their initial success. When Montrose did move on, Aberdeen he was stopped at the Bridge of Dee by the Strathbogie men under Nat Gordon. After a stiff fight the Covenanting artillery found its mark, and flayed the defenders crowding the bridge. Montrose had won his first major victory, Royalist resistance was now all but broken. In England, the civil wars began with the raising of the King's standard at Nottingham in the summer of 1642; four years of civil strife followed with a great expenditure of blood and treasure on both sides. The King, who in several instances, proved himself no mean opponent, held off his enemies until losing the north after the battle of Marston Moor on 2nd July 1644.[2] Before then, the General Assembly in Scotland had accepted the terms of an alliance with the Parliamentarians, putting the Scots army, under Leslie, (now Earl of Leven) into the field.

Despite these setbacks, the King remained undefeated. The Covenanter army, which had performed indifferently at Marston Moor, became bogged down during the autumn at the siege of Newcastle, which obstinately held out for the King. A year earlier, Montrose in Scotland was finding himself increasingly at odds with the majority of the Covenanting faction, led by the Marquis of Argyll, *MacCailean Mor*, a wily politician and head of Clan Campbell. Though one of the first to sign the Covenant, Montrose remained a royalist at heart: opposing the policies of the King's unpopular ministers was a very different matter to taking up arms against the Sovereign. Montrose had latterly been a party to the Bond of Cumbernauld, the signatories of which were alarmed by Argyll's perceived personal motives and boundless ambition. The outbreak of war in Ulster and then in England continued the process of estrangement.

It was not until 1644 that Charles confirmed Montrose as his Lieutenant General in Scotland, and conferred his marquisate. The forces at his disposal, besides himself, included a total of two others. It was scarcely an encouraging beginning. An Irish brigade, under the paladin Alistair MacColla,[3] had been landed on the wild reaches of Kintyre and was harassing Clan Campbell on the Ardnamurchan Peninsula. These Irish comprised no more than three under-strength regiments and a tail of followers. MacColla, barely twenty-one (according to some accounts, Dr. Stevenson's chronology would make him somewhat older), was already a veteran, and is often credited with the development of the Highland charge as a tactical initiative. It is probably that he simply improved upon an existing arrangement. The partnership with Montrose was nonetheless viable and destined to achieve great things.

MacColla was not pursuing any identifiable strategy at this point, other than to raid Argyll's territories. He had escaped from the potential trap of Ardnamurchan[4] to descend on Lochaber. Alasdair MacColla, the son of Colkitto, was nominally a royalist, though he had already swapped allegiance several times. He was motivated in no small part by a personal crusade against King Campbell, as representative of Clan MacDonald South, whose previously considerable hegemony had been frittered away in intercinine squabbles then finally gobbled up by Argyll. From the outset, this phase of the civil wars in Scotland was very much a clan fight.

Montrose and MacColla met at Blair, and their combined forces, the Irish together with those the Marquis had raised, barely topped 2,000. His first objective was Perth, where Lord Elcho, with a crop of raw levies, prepared to make a stand. The clash occurred by the village of Tippermuir. The Covenanters enjoyed a distinct numerical supremacy: deploying on foot in the centre, whilst their horse, perhaps 800 strong, secured the flanks – a perfectly conventional formation. As well as numbers, the Lowlanders had the advantage of seven field pieces. Montrose drew up his meagre forces along a similar frontage – his men standing only three ranks deep as opposed to the Covenanters, six. The fight began with an exchange of musketry; Elcho's skirmishers recoiled and caused some confusion. Montrose chose the moment to order a general assault along the line. The veteran Irish showed their mettle, and the Highlanders, notoriously reluctant to withstand cavalry, managed to see off the horse who charged them. The encounter ended in a complete rout, and the Royalists entered Perth. The Year of Miracles had begun.

Alarmed by the debacle at Tippermuir, the burgesses of Aberdeen made haste to see to their defences. Battle was joined on 13th September, and after a stiff fight, the town was won, its defenders routed. Despite these fresh laurels, Montrose was far from secure. Argyll, alarmed at the unexpected threat developing at his rear, was on the march with substantial forces. The Marquis, whose scouting and intelligence gathering left much to be desired, was obliged to withdraw smartly from the city; MacColla had already been detached to reinforce the slender garrisons left in the west. The Campbells caught up with him at Fyvie, depleted in both numbers and supply. The fight that followed was a series of extended skirmishes, as the Covenanters sought to overcome the Royalists' hurried defences. It finally spluttered out in a muted war of outposts and sniping. Montrose got away, but Argyll would give him no rest. The Gordons cannily stood aside but when his remnant arrived at Blair Atholl, they were rejoined by MacColla, who brought in substantive reinforcements from the clans. The Royalists were now bolstered by MacDonalds of Keppoch, Glengarry, Clanranald and the Isles, MacLeans, Stewarts and Farquharsons.

It was time for sport. Montrose led his army in an extended chevauchee through the heart of the Campbell country. For Clan Donald, this was the stuff of dreams; emptying Argyll's fat byres, harrying his terrified tenantry and (the supreme joy) torching his capital at Inverary, all whilst *MacCailean Mor*[5] appeared impotent to intervene. It was a fine time indeed. Inevitably, once sated and laden with spoil, many Highlanders saw no need to continue, and quietly slipped of home. Very soon Montrose was reduced to 2,000 men at most. As he was preparing to storm down the length of the Great Glen and deal with Seaforth at Inverness, the Marquis was made aware that Argyll was mustering at Inverlochy, poised to bottle the Royalists in the confines of the Glen, with both ends firmly sealed. It was now that Montrose showed his genius as a commander of irregular forces. In the depths of a bitter winter, he led his remaining forces on a desperate march over the high ground to outflank Argyll and recover the initiative.

On the 2nd February 1645, Candlemas Day, the grey blades of Clan Donald swept down through the swirling mist to seek out the astonished Campbells by the shores of Loch Linnhe. Merciless and swift as wolves, the Highlanders closed the gap. The Covenanters, led by Campbell of Auchinbreck, still outnumbered their attackers by perhaps two to one. With the defiant Cameron rant 'Sons of Dogs, come and we will give you flesh' sounding in the still air, the fight was joined, the veteran Irish and Highlanders smashing through the levies. Auchinbreck and many of his name sold their lives as dearly as they could, but the day was soon decided. Argyll, safe aboard his galley, hoisted sail and cruised sedately away from the stricken field.

Having seen off Argyll, Montrose now stormed the length of the great Glen to take Inverness and Elgin. Lord Gordon, inspired by the Royalist triumphs, finally came off the fence. Aberdeen, Brechin and Dundee all fell. Once again, however, Montrose was nearly surprised by a fresh covenanting army under Hurry and Baillie, who obliged to withdraw hurriedly towards Brechin. Hurry was to prove more energetic than his predecessors, and a more worthy opponent. He was able to again surprise the Royalists by the village of Auldearn, near Nairn, on the evening of 8th May. Despite this good beginning, Montrose snatched a spectacular win, and from the wrack of their enemy's baggage the Royalists harvested much-needed muskets, powder and shot, pikes and provisions. The victory, though dramatic, was not yet conclusive. Both sides in the struggle were labouring under specific disadvantages. Apart from his redoubtable Irish regiments, Montrose was obliged to recruit primarily from the Highland clans and the Gordon affinity in the north-east. There was virtually no support from the Lowlands.

Though Hurry was chastened, General Baillie was mustering yet another army. Like his predecessors, Baillie was constantly frustrated by the intermeddling of the Estates, who appear to have learnt nothing from their catalogue of defeats. On 1st July, the Royalists splashed over the somnolent summer waters of the Don and instigated the battle of Alford – yet another victory for Montose who now appeared well nigh unstoppable. Once MacColla, with yet more Highland recruits, rejoined the army, the road south lay open. Montrose now commanded perhaps 4,500 foot and 500 horse, the largest force he was destined to lead. The next battle was fought on 15th August 1645 near Kilsyth, a crowning triumph for the Royalists.

Kilsyth was the only star in the slipping Royalist firmament. In England King Charles' veteran Oxford army had been utterly defeated by the Parliamentarians under Fairfax and Cromwell – the New Model or New Noddle Army, winning decisively at Naseby. The King now entertained great hopes that his invincible Scottish General would lead an army into England. In this he was to be sadly disappointed. The plain fact was that Montrose did not really have an army. The Highlanders were already stealing back toward their own glens, MacColla was again detached to secure the west whilst the Marquis sought to recruit in the borders. This was to be the second and extended harrying of Argyll – a bitter little war of skirmishes and atrocities, which would ultimately end in the ruin of the MacDonald faction. MacColla retreated to Ireland, since most of his followers and kin were either slain or dancing at rope's end.

Douglas brought in 1,000 riders, hardy borderers and descendents of the Steel Bonnets of Elizabeth's day, but that was largely it. Few others came forward, and faulty scouting once again precipitated a crisis. And this time there was to be no escape, no familiar warren of hills into which the army could retire. On 13th September Montrose was surprised at Philiphaugh by Selkirk, and his slender force overwhelmed. The Border horse promptly deserted, dooming the Irish foot that managed to surrender only with their womenfolk to be butchered en masse. The Kirk and its vituperative ministers browbeat David Leslie into breaking his word. The surviving male prisoners were shot in batches against the courtyard wall of nearby Newark Castle,[6] and the women, to save the cost of powder, were drowned. Leslie, even if he had besmirched his honour, had saved the Estates. The Year of Miracles was over.

Montrose had succeeded in escaping the field of Philiphaugh, though it might have been better had he fallen there. He spent the best part of the next twelve months skulking in the Highlands, seeking refuge wherever he could. In May 1646 Charles surrendered, not to Parliament but to the Scots, before the walls of Newark. One of his final commands was to his loyal Lieutenant in Scotland advising he should shift for himself. Montrose fled to the Continent. The relationship between the Committee of Estates in Scotland and Parliament, which was, for the moment, hostile and at best a marriage of convenience, began to founder. As the power of the New Model Army and the demands of the radical sectaries grew, Charles sought to exploit the differences. Since the Covenant was no longer as popular in Scotland and there were those who tired of the ministers ranting.

A resurgent Royalist faction, the 'Engagers' – partisans of a proposed compromise or 'Engagement' with the King, were gaining ground. Hamilton, their leader, was able to influence the Estates and, in 1648, led an army into England on behalf of Charles I. Hamilton's folly proved disastrous: his struggling and straggling regiments, blundering down the western side, were finally smashed at Preston. The Engagers, having at least temporarily got the better of the Kirk party led by Argyll, were still for political reasons, unwilling to admit the Royalists who had been out with Montrose and MacColla. Their army needed to be composed of the pure and Godly. There was no room for recusants.

With the Engagers defeated and Hamilton executed, Argyll soon recovered the reins of power. Any chance of a lasting settlement with the English Parliament was dashed when the Regicides there decided to cut off King Charles' head, which they did on 30th January 1649. This was too much, and the Scots rallied to the cause of the young Charles II. Even whilst he was in the midst of tortuous negotiations with Argyll and the Estates, Charles was prepared to authorize Montrose to raise an army in the Highlands. This last, quixotic campaign finally ended with the Marquis being betrayed by his hosts at Ardvreck Castle on the shores of Loch Assynt.[7] His ramshackle force had earlier been utterly routed at Carbisdale. Charles had no wish to be little more than a pawn of the Kirk party and, had Montrose been successful, then the spectre of another Year of Miracles might quickly have brought Argyll to heel.

For the Marquis of Montrose, all that now remained was for him to bear the ruthless humiliations heaped on him by his enemies and the sham of his trial with resolute and steadfast courage. Correspondence produced at the hearing, ostensibly from the King, stridently denied that Montrose had acted on instructions. This was inevitable given that the Marquis had failed to produce the expected trump. When King Charles II entered his Scottish capital, he would have passed the Tolbooth, where the severed head of his most loyal servant looked down.

Oliver Cromwell proved a good deal less easy to dispose of. On 3rd September 1650, despite being isolated in what appeared a most unfavourable position at Dunbar, he exploited Leslie's mistake and won a stunning victory. Regardless of the magnitude of this disaster, the Estates pressed on and Charles was crowned at Scone on 1st January 1651. As Cromwell's inexorable advance continued, and with Perth threatened, Charles boldly resolved to strike directly into England. His invasion finished in the streets of Worcester, where Cromwell won yet another dazzling success. In Scotland, General Monck continued the mopping up; Stirling fell, the Committee of Estates were mainly made prisoner. Dundee was stormed and ruthlessly sacked on 1st September, though it was not until 25th February 1652 that Dunnottar castle, the final bastion, capitulated.

RESTORATION 1660 – 1685

It might have seemed that the Stuart tenure, both in England and Scotland was at an end, but the great English experiment with republicanism did not long survive the death of its creator in 1658. It was General Monck who set about organizing the King's return. In April 1660 the wheel turned full circle, and Charles Stuart recovered his throne. He was to rule for a quarter of a century, but showed little or no interest in the northern kingdom. He never even set foot north of the border, preferring to leave matters in Scotland in the hands of a series of commissioners, to all intents provincial governors: Middleton, Rothes, Lauderdale and, latterly, his own brother, James Duke of York, a convinced Roman Catholic. The Committee of Estates, so rudely interrupted by Monck at Alyth, was re-convened and, in accordance with the strongly Episcopalian mood of the administration, now forbade ad hoc gatherings of worshippers or 'conventicles'. These were open-air meetings, where services were conducted by Presbyterian ministers, away from the Episcopalian pulpits favoured by the Government. Another casualty of the new face of Scottish politics was Argyll, whose supposed treachery justified his execution. The Act Recissory was then passed, and, at a stroke removed the statutory privilege the Kirk enjoyed – the legislative position was returned to that which had obtained in 1633, before the Covenant.

James Sharp, the ambitious Archbishop of St Andrews and Primate of Scotland, proved the perfect instrument to undertake the new policy. To those who had supported the Solemn League, Bishops smacked of Popery and were to be resisted. Those ministers who demurred were progressively purged, and in November 1666, popular outrage spilled into an insurrection. Harried by Sir Thomas Dalyell of the Binns,[8] the rebels headed for the Pentland Hills, where they were dispersed in a skirmish at Rullion Green, the dragoons killing perhaps fifty of them.

In the short term, the rattled administration reacted sharply: thirty-three men who had been 'out' with the Pentland Rising, as the affair was known, were hanged, and more shipped to the Colonies. Though Lauderdale's time saw something of a relaxation, the business of the Bishops had triggered deep resentment, particularly amongst the more radical Presbyterians in Galloway.

By 1679 matters in the south-west were sliding out of control, and a show of force involving billeting Highland companies forcibly in the area did not prove conducive. The Highland host, though apt to be light fingered, were not unduly savage; but to the radicals the mere idea of a force of savage clansmen, most likely Catholics on their very doorsteps, was an added injury. In that year Archbishop Sharp, the perceived instrument of repression, was ambushed and done to death by a group of extremists. This was the signal for a further and far more serious insurrection. The conventicle that assembled on Loudon Hill on 1st June comprised perhaps 15,00 protesters, armed with an array of miscellaneous weapons. Whilst the ministers exhorted, a young firebrand named William Cleland assumed some form of military control.

He was to be opposed by James Graham of Claverhouse, latterly Viscount Dundee, hero or villain depending on conscience. Kneller's portrait shows a handsome, even slightly effeminate young man, arrogant, perhaps petulant, but for many, the ideal *beau sabreur*. He was prone to contention, but considered loyal to his friends, amongst whom were numbered the slain Archbishop and James, Duke of York. Cleland made the best use of both ground and manpower – Clavehouse rashly chose to make a frontal attack, dismounting his dragoons in a skirmish line. As they advanced, secure in their superior musketry, the rebels surged forward on the flanks. Withdrawal became a rout as Claverhouse's wounded horse bolted: three-dozen troopers lay dead.

The rebels surged forward to assault Glasgow, but were seen off after a stiff fight. As the Government forces regrouped at Stirling and cast about for recruits, Charles sent his illegitimate son James, Duke of Monmouth as commander in chief. As the administration recovered its nerves, the rebels fell to wrangling. The Duke was able to assume the initiative, and a confrontation ensued at Bothwell Bridge. After some attempts at conciliation, firing broke out, and a firefight raged for the next couple of hours. Finally, the bridge was successfully stormed, and the royal guns were deployed to rake the rebels with a storm of round-shot. A rout ensued, amidst much slaughter in the pursuit. Lauderdale's career was a further casualty of the insurrection, and he was succeeded by Monmouth who, admirably, persisted with attempts at reconciliation, including an Act of Indemnity. He, in turn, wßas followed by the Duke of York, who was not only the King's brother but also his likely successor should Charles, as appeared likely, die childless.

James was possessed of both integrity and courage, but lacked either wisdom or tolerance. His appointment was a dangerous choice: a rabid Catholic was bound to stir yet further resentment in a divided realm and his authoritarian measures, including a 'test' for clerics, alienated even staunch Episcopalians. In the hills and glens of the south-west a guerrilla style war of murder and repression continued with Claverhouse, supported by 'Bluidy' Mackenzie[9] the duke's principal agent. This was the 'Killing Time' – a dark era of relentless harrying. Richard Cameron, something of an extremist even by radical standards, was one of the rebel leaders. He was killed in a scrimmage in July 1680 and bequeathed his name to Angus' regiment, who became the Cameronians. In time they would serve the Government well.

JAMES II 1685 – 1688: 'THE GLORIOUS REVOLUTION' AND THE HIGHLAND PROBLEM

When Charles II died in 1685, he was replaced, as expected, by James, who was the seventh Stuart King of Scots to bear that name and destined to be the last. James VII of Scotland and II of England had no talent for compromise. He failed to take that part of the Coronation Oath guaranteeing the Anglican supremacy; conventicles in Scotland were again proscribed, attendance now being made a capital offence. Monmouth launched his doomed rebellion in the south-west; his makeshift army was destroyed at Sedgemoor and his head lost with it. James' daughter Mary was married to the Stadtholder William of Orange, the staunchest of Protestants, indefatigable enemy of Frenchmen and Catholics. The Dutchman, sensing the mood, and aware of discontent in England, prepared his ground carefully, being quick to reassure Scots that the Presbyterian Church would be safe.

James Stuart found he had few allies remaining in Scotland and even fewer in England. The 'Glorious Revolution' of 1688 was largely bloodless, and William soon sent his father-in-law fleeing into exile. The Protestant champion was soon writing to the Estates, and the Convention, summoned in March the following year, voted on 9th April, to nobody's surprise, in favour of William. There was, however, at least one dissenting voice: Claverhouse, now Viscount Dundee, remained unshakeable in his loyalty to James. With characteristic élan he stormed out of the Convention and refused all pleas to return. These entreaties soon turned to threats and, when he maintained his obduracy, he was, on 30th March, proclaimed a traitor at the Mercat Cross. It is unlikely that many of his former colleagues believed they had heard the last of Bonny Dundee.

The Graham was to draw heavily on the loyalty of the Highland clans to the house of Stuart, though the Year of Miracles had ultimately achieved nothing for the Gaels. They had won victories, but in the final analysis had crushed neither Campbells nor Covenanters. Their participation had, however, brought the clans out of their dark and brooding glens and nearer to a national stage, charging with MacColla for a greater cause than individual enrichment. True, there was great satisfaction to be had from sparring with the Campbells, and even more from spreading fire and sword through Argyll's wide and gilded lands. Their stand in part championed Catholicism, and in some cases, the Episcopalian face of Protestantism; but above all, they fought for their King. It has been suggested most persuasively that Tippermuir in 1644 ushered in a major change in clan society that continued to hold, though falteringly, until the reckoning on Culloden Moor in 1746. '... In the long run the real significance of [Montrose'] wonderful campaign was its effect on the Highlanders. These astonishing victories put fresh heart in them.'[10]

This view could be challenged in that Montrose was, of course, a Lowlander, and Argyll had plentiful support from the Highlands besides his own clan, including the Mackenzies. The image of a Highland army, dressed outlandishly, muttering strange oaths in their heathen tongue and looting indiscriminately, became something of a bogeyman for Lowlanders, and may have deepened the cultural gap. Though the Highlanders opposed Argyll and could thus have shared a platform with the Royalist Engagers, the need, on Hamilton's part, to maintain political support in the Lowlands precluded any pact with 'malignants' who had fought with Montrose and MacColla. The defeat suffered by the Engagers at Preston and their subsequent collapse removed any possibility of co-operation, though an attempt by the Kirk party to establish some form of control over Inverness by the installation of a garrison there produced an armed response from the Mackenzies, who had previously proved loyal.

When the Regicides took the final step of executing Charles I, the Kirk party set its face permanently against England and thus presented the Highlanders with a dichotomy. Engaging with the Argyll faction would be the lesser of two evils, since despite the long history of antipathy, even Clan Campbell was preferable to English republicans! The Kirk would only bend its collective knee to Charles II if he would accept the Covenant, itself an anathema to the clans. It was this crisis that led to Montrose last, ill-fated attempt, and even though it failed utterly, it did motivate the Kirk to offer some scope for compromise. Terms had been reached even before the disastrous encounter at Carbisdale removed the Marquis from the board. The Regicide had stimulated the swell of popular discontent with the Kirk, who had, after all, only recovered with English aid. Their moral tirades were wearisome, and the popular mood shifted in Charles' favour.

Cromwell's invasion of 1650 proved a further stimulus: the Kirk might rant over religion, but to the majority of Scots, the matter was one of resisting the ancient enemy, having the person of their King at their head added further weight to his legitimacy. Despite the odds, the Kirk steadfastly, if foolishly, stood by its refusal to admit recusants and malignants into its hallowed ranks. With Cromwell triumphant at Dunbar and the Kirk's star visibly waning, Charles was moved to consider raising a Highland force to seize power – this near coup, 'The Start', did not proceed, but the possibility frightened the Kirk into opening its ranks to the untouchables. From December 1650 Highlanders began to be actively recruited and bled for their King in the battles of Inverkeithing in July 1651, where the MacLeans suffered grievous loss, and later in the streets of Worcester, where the MacLeods, amongst others, took many casualties.[11] Despite this support, many of the clansmen stayed at home – some were financially wasted by the earlier wars, more feared that to quit their own areas would be to invite their harrying by less scrupulous neighbours. Many chiefs still preferred a purely parochial interest to a national one.

For instance, Argyll in April 1651, did not raise his tenants from Lochaber, and this spread the suspicion, based on precedent, that once the Camerons and others had quit their glens, the Campbells would be emptying the byres. At the same time, Cameron of Lochiel[12] was robustly enforcing his feudal rights against MacDonald of Glengarry and Keppoch, collecting loan installments at swordpoint.[13] Despite these obsessions with largely domestic matters, the clans were moved to support the King. His rule was preferred to that of the Covenanters and certainly to the English yoke. Once Argyll had submitted, the traditional hatred of *MaCailean Mor* could once again be coupled to support for the House of Stuart. In spite of this, continued opposition to the English invader foundered, due in no small part, to poor leadership, but also to natural friction between clansman and Lowlander. Officers and men quarreled, duels were fought, the common purpose subverted.

By the time English troops began to penetrate into the west, resistance spluttered and failed in a welter of petty rivalries, and the conquest proved easy. Ironically, the occupation of the Highlands during the Commonwealth brought some benefits: an evenhanded administration, unfettered by local jealousies and archaic feuds. As the chiefs accepted the inevitable, they entered into terms with the

English, finding caution[14] and calming their followers. The invader's policy was one of stick and carrot: as a reward for acquiescence the chiefs retained all of their privileges and even the right for they and their 'tail' to continue to bear arms for self-defence.[15] Old disputes were dealt with through arbitration. If this was tyranny, then it was not without its merits. The stick came in the form of a string of outposts, the largest of which was at Inverlochy. Lochiel's Camerons refused to accept such an imposition tamely, and the garrison was not established without loss.

Cannily, Lochiel soon came to appreciate the beneficial aspects of English rule, since to secure his co-operation they were inclined to provide often generous incentives, and mitigate his own indebtedness by settling his outstanding arrears to the Mackintoshes. He also did not scruple to act against Glengarry when the latter rebelled. He afterwards claimed to have been holding the confiscated lands in trust for their rightful owner. It would be unlikely that Glengarry derived any comfort from this! There had been bad feeling between the two men, and MacDonald went on to accuse Lochiel of profiting from the rents due to him. This was not the only way the Cameron chief managed to profit. His was the only sept permitted to carry weapons: any found in arms could be sure of immunity if they took his name, becoming Cameron adherents, meaning he could maintain a monopoly on armed force. For Lochiel the Restoration did not bring the rewards he had anticipated – given his conduct as at worst a collaborator and certainly an opportunist – this is perhaps unsurprising. Even Glengarry, considerably more active, though he earned a peerage and a pension, was denied his prime objective – the earldom of Ross. Perhaps this was an echo of the old claim before Harlaw in 1411, but no administration would be likely to grant such a major boost to Clan Donald.

With Argyll shorn of life and lands, it would have appeared that the day of Clan Campbell was over, but Lord Lorne, the dead marquis's son, despite being in disfavour and under sentence of death himself, did manage to avoid the axe and to begin clawing back his lost lands. Ultimately it did not suit the Crown to completely emasculate the Campbells. As the generally preferred tool of Government in the Highlands, their extirpation would have left a dangerous vacuum. Lord Lorne, who had succeeded to his father's title, had a significant financial burden in that the Huntly lands, confiscated by the Covenanters, now reverted; but the transfer of the Gordon's indebtedness, which Argyll had assumed would in part legitimize the grant, remained and therefore imposed a crushing liability.

This crippling legacy necessitated some ruthless cash-flow management in the west, where he, in turn, oppressed his debtors to make up the losses. This rapacity did nothing to endear him to the clans. His position was not a happy one: the son of a traitor, and therefore continually suspect, yet at the same time, a principal agent of the Government. The earl's need for cash ignited a local feud with one of his principal debtors, MacLean of Duart. Argyll had tried to assign the benefit of MacLean's mortgages directly to his own creditors, but MacLean refused. This sparked what amounted to a local war as the two squabbled. Duart was massively in debt, and the cost of defying his principal creditor only swelled the burden. As the two sides allowed the conflict to escalate, inevitably other clans were drawn in; Argyll had few allies and MacLean found support amongst the other Royalist clans.

In law, Argyll was in the right and, as mortgagee, entitled to enforce possession of the MacLean lands in Morvern, title to which was encumbered by the debt. Though this was a vicious little war of raid and counter-raid, such as any of their ancestors would have recalled from the Age of Forays, there was a significant difference. Argyll, for his part, had only taken up arms to enforce his legal rights; he had the law and the authority of the Crown on his side. Nonetheless, the feud with MacLean alarmed the other chiefs, who were deeply suspicious of Argyll's motives and methods. Keppoch, Glengarry and Lochiel all dispatched broadswords to aid MacLean, generally for a price, of course, which exacerbated his already dire fiscal problems.

Highland chiefs of the late seventeenth century were markedly more reluctant than their heroic forbears to rely on their swords.

They now liked to have at least some legal pretext before taking up arms. Many had dispensed with force altogether and relied on their lawyers. Clan society was becoming less militaristic but considerably more litigious.[16] In part this was due to the widening role of the chiefs. The events of the 1640s had thrust them onto a national stage: the idea that they were serving their anointed King had taken root. They themselves, as they moved from being Gaelic chieftains to Scottish gentlemen, came to perceive the notion of clan warfare as backward – embarrassingly so – harking back to a savage past which earned nothing but scorn from their Lowland contemporaries. This increasing sophistication did not necessarily mean the glens were more peaceful: there remained a pernicious infestation of broken men and caterans. The troubles of the civil wars had left many homeless and destitute; economic developments, which might be thought beneficial, in fact served to aggravate the problem.[17]

The English garrisons had been withdrawn to assuage national pride, and this removal acted as a further inducement to lawlessness. Even MacDonald of Keppoch, seeking to impose some order within the sept, fell foul of the rougher element, and was, with his brother, murdered in 1663. His successor was one of the prime culprits.[18] A remedy proved impossible to find; garrisons could not be maintained; the raising of Highland companies foundered, as did efforts to compel the chiefs to act on their own initiative. Despite the rising tide of anarchy, the Highlands, at this time, were not considered a priority. The ruthless nature of the religious establishment meant that the Government's eyes were firmly fixed on the disturbances in the south-west. Conventicles were considered a far greater threat that the clans, and the dispatch of Highlanders as unwelcome guests billeted on their dissenting Lowland contemporaries was an example of the administration's trust in their loyalty. Lauderdale obviously had no fears the rot would spread, nor did it. Even the traditional links with Ireland, which had tended to promote fissiparous tendencies, had withered in the 1650s. The presence of the Highland Host, some

5–6,000 strong, did nothing to improve the Lowlander's perception. The clansmen plundered at will, but in many cases, returned as swiftly as they had come, for fear one of their neighbours might be doing likewise at home!

By 1678, opposition to Argyll's oppressions was growing, and not just in the Highlands. This might never have amounted to a viable threat, but the equanimity of the nation was upset by the 'Popish Plot' of that year. This was a fiction, but one that caused panic in the breasts of all true Protestants, who feared the King was to be murdered along with many of their persuasion and the Catholic James installed. This led the Privy Council in Edinburgh to review their relaxed approach to the Highland clans, so many of whom comprised recusants. Argyll was now viewed as the paladin who would suppress these rebellious tendencies; this was despite the entreaties of Glengarry and others that they were utterly loyal. In the prevailing climate of paranoia, these overtures were seen as nothing more than cunning posturing.[19] Argyll's mercantile assault on MacLean thus gained a new and wider legitimacy. The earl pursued his second attempt to gain Morvern with vigour, but a fresh panic arose when the Conventiclers rose and Argyll was ordered to desist and prepare to head south into Galloway. He did nothing of the sort, and doggedly pursued his goals in the Highlands.

Lauderdale's fall, in the wake of the rebellion, removed one of the principal props securing the Campbell's position, and when James replaced him, circumstances shifted unfavourably. The Duke of York had primarily been sent to Scotland to remove him from the centre of controversy in England. His aims were divergent from those pursued by his predecessor. His eyes were firmly fixed on the English throne, and to ensure his accession he would, as a Papist, need the support of the clans, making them the obvious resource. Permitting Argyll to oppress them at will was clearly contrary to his policy of courting the chiefs. By the early part of 1680, James had devised a proposal or 'Scheme' which, whilst it would not emasculate the earl, would certainly clip his wings, and provide for wider distribution of authority in the Highlands: 'The extraordinary favours and partialities formerly shewn to the Lord Argile, could neither be answer'd nor without much difficulty amended, since that family had been so much advanced and with so much power put imprudently into their hands.'[20] He proposed that the Crown should pick up MacLean's burden and free him from the crushing burden of his debts. This timely investment would doubtless secure the grateful MacLean's eternal loyalty and reduce Argyll's holdings. He further proposed that the policing of the Highlands should become the joint responsibility of the four leading magnatial families: Argyll, Atholl, Huntly and Seaforth, each of whom would become a paid officer of the Crown. Argyll's arrogance buoyed the cause of his opponents, and opposition was growing. James was not necessarily amongst these: having no personal antagonism and a resistance to proposals that the earl's conduct should be subject to a Parliamentary inquiry.[21]

What brought matters to a head was the Test Act, a draconian move that required, in effect, all men to swear to support the likely succession of James. Argyll opposed the measure, thus suddenly raising the spectre of his father's appeal to ultra-conservative Protestantism. This was a very dangerous situation and one that naturally alarmed James. Very soon the earl was on trial for his life, which was found to be forfeit. It remains highly doubtful that James, or for that matter his brother, intended to carry out the full sentence of the law. Rather, Argyll was being taught a lesson, which they sought to, 'make use of this occasion to get him more into their [Charles' and James'] power, and forfeit certain jurisdictions and superiorities which he and his predecessors had surreptitiously acquir'd and most tyrannically exercised.'[22]

The whole sorry business proved a serious blunder. Argyll's refusal struck a chord with all Scots who feared a Catholic succession, his previous excesses and unpopularity were forgotten, worse, he escaped from confinement and fled to the Low Countries which vitiated any hope of a compromise. The outlawed earl's son, another Lord Lorne, was permitted to come into part of his inheritance, though his father's sprawling legacy was vastly shrunk. He lost titles, most of the lands held through feudal superiority, a significant part of his income. These confiscations were used to pay off his father's outstanding indebtedness. This was undoubtedly music to the ears of *MacCailean Mor*'s legion of enemies.

James was still struggling to find an effective policing system for the Highlands. His scheme to employ the magnates came to nothing; he recruited two more independent companies, their complement drawn mainly from the Lowlands,[23] though these achieved little or nothing. Lastly, he planted a garrison briefly at Inverlochy, before Lochiel sent them packing. An attempt to set up a panel of commissioners to mete out justice in the turbulent glens began well, particularly in the east, but foundered when the justices came into contact with the wily Lochiel.[24] To strengthen their authority, Lieutenant General Drummond was detailed to provide the commissioners with some military muscle. He was presently sending back wildly optimistic reports of his and the commission's successes.

Charles II died in 1685. The work of Drummond and his colleagues became redundant when Monmouth's abortive rising in England was accompanied by a landing in the Highlands, led by the fugitive Argyll. The earl's adventure was a stillborn thing: he was as doomed as his principal. His track record as a rack-renting landlord was inauspicious: he had no natural charisma or military credentials, and the Government had already installed Atholl as Lieutenant in Argyllshire. His zeal, and the enthusiasm of the clans in receiving carte blanche to harry the Campbells, ensured the venture quickly collapsed. Argyll was taken, and the sentence of death, which had hung over his head for the previous four years, was now carried out. Determined to stamp out any embers of dissent the Government authorised sweeping measures against any Campbells remaining in arms. The disturbances spawned a new wave of lawlessness; private grudges were cloaked as loyal endeavours, swarms of landless men emerged to loot and burn. The painstaking work of the earlier commission was washed away in a fury of violence.

Drummond, now Lord Strathallan, was sent back with more troops to bring the situation under control. As before, he responded with enthusiasm, but achieved little success. By the time of the 'Glorious Revolution', three years later, matters had scarcely improved. James showed a partiality toward Lochiel, whose record as a loyal servant of the state was distinctly mixed. It appears the Duke was impressed by his swashbuckling manner and easy charm. Certainly his cunning and ready wit served to extricate him from a number of scrapes. Lochiel may have succeeded, at least in part, in convincing James that much of the trouble in which he'd been embroiled was caused by the mire of confused land holdings and the complexities of an outmoded feudal system. This would not explain why he harried the garrison of Inverlochy, or so readily obstructed the work of the commissioners.

One anecdote, which illustrates the Duke's perhaps reluctant fascination with his Highland subject, concerns the conferring of a knighthood on Lochiel in 1681, the year of Argyll's fall. As a gesture, James offered to dub the Cameron with his own sword, which, embarrassingly, refused to budge from the scabbard. The chief was obliged to free the blade and offer it, hilt first, to the future King. James wittily observed that Lochiel's sword obeyed no hand but his own. There was a barb within the humour – the duke was well aware that Lochiel was motivated entirely by personal goals.[25] James may have viewed the Camerons as partial successors to the Campbells, once the latter had been stripped of much of their authority, which was a natural counterpoise.

Lochiel, generally, had the ear of the other chiefs, though his relations with Argyll were cordial. Perhaps too cordial, as there was suspicion the wily chief was playing a double game during the earl's abortive revolt. Sufficient mud stuck for Lochiel to mount a hasty dash to the Court to reinforce his loyalty to James – who jovially, if pointedly, referred to his guest as 'the King of Thieves.'[26] Throughout the Restoration period, as Professor Stevenson relates, the Government had been far more occupied by the threat posed by Lowland conventicles than any from the Highland chiefs. Some attempts to stamp out lawlessness had been undertaken, but these had, at best, been half-hearted and largely starved of resources.

It appears correct to assert that James, as King, gave little thought to any fundamental reform of the pernicious web of feudal complexities that obfuscated property matters. When in exile, however, he was quick to promise he would, 'free them from all manner of vassalage and dependence on the great men their neighbours.'[27] He was prepared to undertake that all would be free of feudalism and subject only to the rights of the Crown. Destroying the overweening power of Argyll and the Campbells, notwithstanding the fact it had largely come about as a result of miscalculation, put heart into the Royalist clans. Not only did they discern the practical benefits, they were able to conflate the twin ideals of support for the Stuarts with detestation of the Campbells. It proved a far-reaching set of circumstances. James VII, therefore, had both destroyed the beast of oppression, and at least in part, recognised the efforts of the loyal clans during the civil wars.

These events, which occurred during the 1680s, caused many of the clans to see their loyalty to the dynasty in terms of personal loyalty to James: the Jacobite faction[28] could therefore have been said to have been born at this time in the Highlands. The happy coincidence of disposing of the Campbells cemented the loyalty of the Royalist clans, who traditionally associated the Argyll faction with radical anti-monarchist tendencies. They saw the Campbells as a major and continuing menace, since any Government of which they were an active part must, inevitably, also constitute a threat. In reality, the Stuarts had, in historical terms, done little to stimulate loyalty amongst the Gaels. They had been the instrument of Clan Campbell's rise after the demise of the Lordship and, in general, had found little to interest them in the Highlands. Neither Charles I nor Charles II found any appeal in their native realm whatsoever, far less the Gaelic Fringe.

The early alliance between the ruling house and the Highland clans, through its generals Montrose and MacColla, had largely been directed with expediency. The echoes of that alliance with changing circumstances forty years on forged a much closer bond. Professor Stevenson points out that the problem posed by the fissiparous tendencies of the Gaels changed in the course of the seventeenth century. James VI was plagued by the endemic lawlessness of the clans and their extreme reluctance to bow to central authority. Merely defying or, more usually, ignoring the King did not imply the chiefs disputed his right to rule. That was never in question – it was more a matter of how much interference could be tolerated.

BONNY DUNDEE AND THE CAMPAIGN OF KILLIECRANKIE

After 1688, William III and his Hanoverian successors were to be disturbed by an altogether different problem – the archaic loyalty of the clans to a redundant royal family and a threatened way of life. This loyalty to the Stuarts was largely one-sided and dictated, as before, by a measure of expediency. The exiled dynasty was to prove cynical in their use of their Highland sympathizers. They wished to bring their cause onto the national stage and recover the thrones of both England and Scotland, since the latter, alone, would never suffice. The clans were a source of manpower, a reserve of natural fighters who could form the hardcore of a Stuart army. They saw the Highlands as a jumping off point, firstly for the Lowlands, then the whole of Scotland and on to the greater prize of England.

As time passed, these became increasingly unrealistic goals and, by adhering to them, the chiefs only succeeded in widening the gulf separating Gael and Lowlander. Even if the sting of the *Mi run mor nan Gall* has been overstated, the general contempt for the 'Mackes' or 'Maks' persisted; loyalty to the house of Stuart in an age of Whig supremacy could only serve to deepen this divide. Worse, when the cause finally expired, the reaction of a nervous administration would result in a brutal and bitter repression. It was this fountain of sentiment that Dundee now hoped to tap. He had few friends in the Lowlands: the Estates had effectively marginalised his faction completely. With a mere handful of diehards he raced first for his seat at Dudhope, before withdrawing into the Highlands to avoid the net that was fast closing. Pausing in Glen Ogilvy to preach the gospel of revolt amongst his wife's people, he went next to Keith, then on to Elgin and Forres. Whatever his limitations, Dark John of the Battles did not lack charisma. He had that essential pull which Argyll had so noticeably lacked.

The Government was far from blind to the growing threat, and had appointed Hugh Mackay of Scourie as local commander. He could immediately field three regiments of foot and one of horse. Having captured one of his gallopers at Cairn o' Mount and learnt of his imminent peril, Dundee made a dash for the relative sanctuary of Castle Gordon. Here he was joined by a body of north-eastern gentry under the earl of Dunfermline. Now the western clans began to respond, Keppoch chose the moment to descend upon Inverness and extort a ransom, which he preferred to call a debt, from the burgesses. Outraged, the wronged citizenry demanded redress from Dundee, as this piece of banditry had been carried out in the name of James VII. All he could do was offer a receipt in the King's name and promise future redress. It is unlikely this would suffice to win many friends in the town.

From near Dalwhinnie the rebel Viscount issued a summons for a general muster in Lochaber on 18th May. Again he slipped past Mackay's patrols and relieved Government tax collectors of their funds at Perth. Having re-distributed this sudden wealth, and warned off some of the local lairds who might have been leaning toward the Williamites, he approached Dundee to try and suborn his own former regiment. The men were more than willing, but the Government's watchful eye was too close to facilitate a mass defection. Mustering beneath the standard at Killiecrankie was a fine array from the Jacobite clans: Lochiel, MacLean of Duart, (who had ample cause for gratitude to James), Clan Donald, Stewart of Appin, MacNeil of Barra, MacLeods from Skye and Raasay, Frasers, MacNaughtons, MacAllisters, MacLachlans and Lamonts.

Mackay was now forced onto the defensive as the Jacobites took Ruthven Castle,[29] whilst Keppoch found time to settle another outstanding matter by harrying the Mackintoshes from their stronghold at Dunachton. The Williamites were chased into Strathbogie, where Mackay might hope to better employ his cavalry. He was also reinforced with further two-foot battalions, as Dundee fell back into Badenoch. On 9th June several hundred MacLeans took on the Government dragoons and saw them off in a sharp little skirmish; the panicked Williamites obligingly left most of their weapons and gear behind. Blighted by the inevitable defections, Dundee retired into the relative fastness of Lochaber. Despite the slenderness of his support, he resisted offers of mediation and found the price on his head raised to the very considerable sum of £20,000 – a measure of the Government's alarm. At this time, Blair Castle, seat of the marquis of Atholl, was held by his son Lord John Murray.

Blair was a key position, and best kept out of the hands of the Williamites with whom, it was feared, the Peer's true sympathies lay. Stewart of Ballochie, the Marquis' factor and a convinced Jacobite, was detailed to seize the place. On 26th July Dundee arrived with 2,500 broadswords at his back. Mackay, whose numbers were greater, had not been able to advance past Dunkeld. Should the clans risk a general engagement? Numbers of the chiefs preferred to retire, but Dundee was supported by Lochiel, who despite the weight of his sixty summers and his somewhat chequered history, still commanded widespread respect, and advocated making a stand. Their counsels carried the day; the Jacobites would test their resolve in battle. In the quickening glow of a summer's dawn Mackay marched his battalions from Dunkeld, a great slew of scarlet, toiling toward the narrow defile of the pass of Killiecrankie. By mid-morning the lead elements were at the foot of the narrow ascent, where the Garry foamed over brown speckled stones and the path wound uphill for nearly two miles, a wilderness of rock and scrub. Once the men had rested, they commenced the tortuous climb, for the horse and guns this was especially difficult and only the very lightest ordnance the 'leather' guns could be hauled up the defile. It is possible that Jacobite snipers harassed the troops. The terrain was certainly ideal but the Williamites emerged substantively unscathed, Mackay set up his HQ at Urrard House and planned his deployment.

His left was to be held by a commanded body of shot led by Lieutenant Colonel Landers, with the foot regiments of Balfour, Ramsay and Kenmure in line stretching eastwards. He placed his horse in the centre with Leven's, his own and Hasting's forming the right. Like a legendary host from a distant, heroic past, the clans came sweeping around the summit of *Craig Ealloch*. Seeing the Jacobites poised to occupy the higher ground, Mackay moved his line forward, in a quick scramble to gain advantage. As the Williamites reached the line of the Urrard Plateau, they found a dip to their front with another rise beyond. Mackay considered his position adequate for defence, though not a suitable platform for launching an attack of his own.

To conform to Dundee's perceived deployment, the Williamite general had to shunt or echelon his battalions to their right. The river, quite wide and swift flowing, lay at his men's backs, meaning that to retreat now would be difficult. Lander's chosen men were still posted on the extreme left of the line, with Hasting's exposed flank covered by a small tributary of the Garry. As his line was stretched over the rim of the plateau, he ordered the foot to deploy in three rather than their customary six ranks. In practical terms, such a move offered better opportunities for telling volleys against the rush of the Highland charge. However, the plan began to come unstuck when the Kenmure's, located in the centre, failed, for whatever reason, to conform, and remained bunched in the denser formation. A gap of perhaps 150 yards now yawned between them and Leven's men to their right.

Mackay's line comprised perhaps 3,500 feet, and Dundee's a full 1000 less. The MacLeods held the right, next an Irish composite battalion under a Colonel Cannon; then the MacDonald regiments – Clanranald, Glengarry and MacIain with the Glencoe men. To the right of Clan Donald stood Grant of Glenmoriston, a small mounted squadron in the centre. The left comprised Lochiel, MacLean, MacDonald of Kintyre, MacNeil then MacDonald of Sleat. Dundee himself took station on the extreme left his followers were most anxious he should curb the reckless rush of his own impetuous valour and stay out of the fight. The strong summer sun was shining directly into the eyes of the clansmen, and Dundee was not minded to attack whilst such a disadvantage obtained. The afternoon passed in a bickering of the light ordnance (which performed poorly) and sharpshooters. Lochiel dispatched a platoon of marksmen to occupy a bothy in the no-mans-land between the two armies, and these opened a harassing fire. A company of Williamites led by Mackay's brother was sent forward to dislodge them. At 8.00 p.m. the shadows begin to lengthen, the fierce sun is calmed, and Dundee chooses this moment to launch his attack. His men are fewer and, like Mackay, he has been obliged to extend his line; to do so he must increase the distance between each of the clan regiments. As it is he who is assuming the offensive, this was is dangerous than the gap that has opened between the Kenmure's, who were raw, and the steadier Leven's.

With their slogans ringing in the evening air, the clans swept forward. Almost immediately, the charge ran into difficulty, the nature of the ground caused the Camerons, who were targeted on Leven's, to move sharply to their left and bunch with the MacLeans and MacDonalds, who were seeking to engage Mackays. Lochiel's men were winnowed by volleys from Leven's, and Mackay sent his cavalry forward to exploit the hole in the Jacobite Line. They, in turn, were charged and held by Dundee's horse. As they routed, the Williamite troopers careened into the ranks of Kenmure's, precipitating the disintegration of both this and several companies from Leven's Regiment.

On Mackay's left, Balfour, commanding the battalions on that flank, saw only the collapse of the cavalry and Kenmure's. He assumed, the day was lost too soon, and tried to withdraw in an orderly manner. This proved a most dangerous manoeuvre: the difficult terrain and the wild charge of the MacLeans, supported by a formation of the Athollmen, swiftly turned retreat into rout, and the hacking blades of the Highlanders took a fearful toll as the panicked men stumbled toward the formidable barrier of the Garry.[30] In fact, the position on Mackay's right was not yet hopeless. The charge had scattered several companies from his regiment, but Hastings and the remnant of Leven's held firm; they were able to fall back and form a defensive hedge around Urrard House. Mackay, who had not lost his nerve even if he had lost his army, was able to withdraw the survivors under cover of darkness.

They probably had not realised that a volley from Leven's had claimed the life of James Graham. He had ridden forward with his troop of horse, and now paid the price of glory. He had won the field but lost his life, and with his death, any hopes of a Jacobite victory in Scotland that year faded with the summer light. Dundee was buried in the chapel at Blair, his body wrapped in a plaid, and joined to the pantheon of heroic failures. A romantic figure and clearly charismatic and competent, there was, however, no plan for succession. He was the fount and inspiration of the Jacobite army.

Killiecrankie must therefore rank as a phyrric victory. The Government side undoubtedly came off far worse in terms of casualties, though the clans, particularly Lochiel's Camerons, suffered heavily in the opening bout of musketry[31] Deprived of their revered General, the clans appointed Colonel Cannon to succeed, a neutral choice unclouded by partisan rivalries. If the Irishman was acceptable to the clans, he had none of the dead man's charisma. With the declared object of taking Perth, the Jacobite army advanced down the line of the Tay as far as Dunkeld. It was here, by a fine twist of irony, that Dundee's former nemesis William Cleland was stationed in command to 1,200 Cameronians, the cutting edge of Protestant fervour. On 21st August the Highlanders attempted to storm the town; however, this was not the kind of fighting they were used to: the Lowlanders having barricaded the streets, loop-holed and fortified houses.

The streets resounded to the crack of musketry and the cries of men wounded and dying. Cleland had built a final redoubt enclosing the cathedral and Dunkeld House, two of the most prominent and substantial buildings. As fires spread through the houses and bothies, the clansmen stripped lead from the roofs to make good their dwindling supplies of shot. Time and again they came shrieking from the smoke to storm the barricades, and every time they were thrown back. Shot in the liver and wounded in the head, Cleland dragged himself into Dunkeld House so his men would not lose heart as they saw him fall. It was a death Dundee would no doubt have applauded. Nor was his sacrifice in vain, for the grimed and exhausted defenders held on as the attack faltered and failed. Several hundred Jacobites had died in the fruitless assault.

Cannon withdrew to Lochaber so the clansmen could lick their wounds, and planned for the next year's campaign. In April 1690 Major General Thomas Buchan arrived to take command and drum up fresh recruits. It was an uphill struggle: barely 1,500 could be mustered. Lochiel and the other chiefs, deprived of Dundee's inspirational leadership, began to look to themselves. Early in May, at the Haughs of Cromdale, Buchan's fledgling army was surprised and scattered – the 'Rout of Cromdale'. This debacle marked the end of the rising; though it had been doomed to fail from the moment an unknown soldier in Leven's regiment fired his fatal shot.

While Dundee had been flying the Jacobite standard, in Scotland even weightier events had been unfolding across the Irish Sea. In March 1689 James had returned from France to Ireland, there to lead a great rally of his supporters and mount a serious challenge to the Williamites. The late Professor Hayes-McCoy has pointed out that Ireland was to be the base for a Jacobite recovery, and Scotland the back door to England.[32] This is undoubtedly correct, and war was to continue until the final defeat of these hopes after the battle of Aughrim in 1691. That which has been identified as the key encounter is the Battle of the Boyne, fought the year before, when both sides recognised the strategic importance of Dublin. James at that point controlled the city, and William of Orange sought to wrest that control away. The battle was not a major tactical defeat for the Jacobites, who, though worsted, did not incur crippling losses. James lost perhaps 1,000 men from his substantial army; the Williamites as many, if not slightly more.[33]

Strategically, the gains were significant, since not only Dublin but also the whole of Leinster and a fair portion of Munster fell. Though the Jacobites kept the field for a further year, their hopes, after the Boyne, began to wither. French troops, so vital to the continuance of the struggle, were largely withdrawn, but the fighting persisted with a series of stubborn rearguard actions. However, with the final fall of Limerick in October 1691, hostilities in Ireland were effectively ended, and James' hopes lay in ruins. The surrender of Limerick and the Rout of Cromdale between them sounded the death knell of the Jacobite cause. In retrospect, this period was the best that James, his son and grandson would ever experience in terms of a real prospect of success. The Jacobite movement as a political affiliation was only getting started, but its heyday had already passed. Never again would the House of Stuart be able to raise such a major challenge.

As the fighting raged in Ireland, French and Anglo-Dutch forces also clashed at sea. In June 1690 the French Admiral Tourville had beaten Torrington off Beachy Head. This might have been dangerous had a French army been poised to swoop from the Channel ports. Fortunately for the Williamites, no such force was then in being; the moment passed, and Tourville had to be content with a relatively minor spoiling raid on Teignmouth. Rumors of an incipient invasion persisted, and there were few enough troops available on the south coast to serve as a viable deterrent. Jacobite sentiment was, however, muted in the extreme, and the usual precautions were taken against recusant gentry. This was unfortunate for James, unlucky his cause had failed to prosper in either Scotland or Ireland, for this was a rare interval when the French Navy could command the Channel.[34]

Within a year, this had changed: the English were putting more and more ships into the fight, and the French reverted to privateering, to avoid fleet actions. Louis in 1692, determined to try again to land an army in support of James. This, perhaps, though often over-looked, was a moment of great danger for the Williamites, and one of real hope for James. In May, the two fleets collided off Barfleur. This time, the Anglo Dutch, under Russell, having achieved numerical superiority, bested Tourville.[35] It had been close and confused, but despite Killiecrankie, the overall strategic victory rested with William and Mary; the Tory clans, including clan Iain Abrach had tacked their banners to those of the losing side.

CHAPTER 3

The Great Feud:
'The Greed of the Campbells'

'Perhaps no nation goes better armed.'

William Sacheverell

'… A hereditary capacity for aggrandisoement like the Hapsburgs or
the Brandenburgs … an insatiable lust for land.'

Contemporary Observer

' 'Feud' – Prolonged mutual hostility, esp. between two families,
tribes, etc. with murderous assaults in revenge for a previous injury.'

Oxford English Dictionary

In the uncertain times of Toom Tabard's reign,[1] before Edward I of
England's fatal intervention, the tone of future relations between
Campbells and MacDonalds was established when the MacDougalls
(clan Donald's cousins who were to lose out so completely in the wars
of Independence) murdered Sir Colin Campbell. The crime was committed between Loch Awe and Oban, on the String of Lorne. Quite
why Sir John MacDougall found it expedient to summarily do away

with Big Colin is unclear, though the latter was ostensibly engaged on behalf of the Crown in brokering an accord with MacDonald of Islay. The Campbell knight may well have been the victim of the ongoing struggle for regional hegemony being waged between the MacSorley factions, between MacDougall and MacDonald.[2] It is fair to say that subsequently relations did not improve.

CLAN DONALD

By the seventeenth century, Clan Donald, following the collapse of the Lordship and the internecine bloodletting of the Age of Forays, had lost much of its previous unchallenged hegemony to the Campbells and other aspiring names such as MacKenzie, to whom traditional allies such as the Mathesons defected. MacDonalds also quarreled with MacLeans and fought them in the wonderfully named Battle of the Western Isles 1586, which left three score of Clan Donald lifeless.[3] Fifteen years later, MacDonald of Sleat was in action against his former brother-in-law, Sir Rory MacLeod, the latter being worsted in the fight at Siol Tormoit.[4] The Sleat branch of the clan in due course became called Clan Donald North, to distinguish them from the Dunyveg branch, Clan Donald South, the *Clan Iain Mor*.

These originally took their name from John Mor Tanister, who was murdered in 1427, a sibling of Donald of the Isles. His power had been centered around Dunyveg on Islay, but by right of his wife, he had acquired estates in Ireland, that part of Antrim known as the Glens. Thus the chiefs of Clan Iain Mor became MacDonalds of Islay and Antrim. When the Lordship fell, the Dunyveg branch, despite two generations of chiefs falling to the axe, swelled to partly fill the vacuum. In the closing decades of the sixteenth century, they were riven by fissiparous disputes which resulted in the Irish element breaking away, metamorphosing into the MacDonnells of Antrim. In 1620 Randal MacDonnell was elevated to the earldom of Antrim.

It should be remembered that the Irish connection was always a strong one, and the fact that the English ruled in Ireland and James VI in Scotland proved no effective bar. For centuries the Isles had been exporting fighting men to Ireland – hardy mercenaries who formed their own class of Gaelic elite, the Galloglas (or Gallowglass). Manpower for the Irish rebels fighting the Elizabethan expansion in Ulster fed in from the Western Highlands and Islands. Swift Hebridean galleys manoeuvred expertly around the English standing squadron, the Ulster patrol, whose thankless and nigh on impossible task it was to limit the traffic. If intercepted, the clansmen would cheerfully offer their swords to the Crown. Links were vibrant and enduring. The culture of the Gael at this time, even as the social and political fabric of the clan 'system' began to unravel, was dynamic. Music and verse, both of magical quality, proliferated. As the wars in Ireland increased in tempo, numerous of the clans became directly involved on either or both sides – usually depending upon who was paymaster. *Clan Iain Mor*, under the leadership of Angus MacDonald of Dunyveg, became dangerously embroiled in bitter feud with the MacLeans, led by Angus' brother-in-law, Lachlan Mor MacLean of Duart.

This was no small business: both sides recruited allies, struggling for possession of the Rhinns of Islay – even going so far as to buy in mercenaries. MacLean found gainful employment for Spanish survivors gathered from the wrack of the Armada. James VI could not afford to ignore such an affront to his power, and the King was mindful both of the need to exert his full authority over these quarrelsome subjects and keeping an eye out for his best interest in the matter of the English succession. Angus was temporarily tamed by 1591, though two sons were kept as surety. One of these, James (latterly to be knighted), used his time in Edinburgh well and acted as a brake on his father's intemperance, which had tried the king's patience so sorely that he was looking at ways of resolving the dispute in MacLean's favour.

As measures intended to curb the wilder spirits were progressively introduced, men like Angus became something of an anachronism, to the extent that Sir James finally usurped his father's role (after setting fire to his lodgings and seeing the old man badly burnt). As James sought to show conformity, MacLean moved in a bid to exert his authority over the Rhinns and expel any remaining MacDonald tenants. Sir James attempted conciliation, but, when this failed, resorted once more to arms. A battle was fought in August 1598 by Loch Gruinart. Sir Lachlan Mor with several hundred of his adherents were cut down in a victory for Clan Donald. Undeterred, the MacLeans were soon back on the offensive with a new confederation.

Sir James offered generous concessions to the crown, humbling himself in order that his claims on Islay might be recognised. However, the King, favouring the notion of Lowland colonies being established, and of experimenting with Lewis (forfeited by MacLean) temporised. Another factor was the Campbells, who were only too happy to keep the pot bubbling, since that which weakened Dunyveg benefited them. But they too were not immune from internal squabbles, the cadet branches vying for control of the seventh earl of Argyll, then a minor. At least one senior figure, Campbell of Calder, was murdered during the course of this dispute (1592). That Clan Diarmid was adept at using disputes amongst its neighbours to its own longer term advantage cannot be denied; but the propensity of such neighbours to engage in such murderous quarrels, regardless of external intermeddling, was a continuing boost to Campbell ambition.

Clanranald claimed their descent from Somerled's son Ranald (d. c.1207), and their country lay in Moidart, Arisaig and Lochaber. They were out with Montrose and again for Dundee where their chief, like MacDonald of Sleat, led 500 clansmen onto the field at Killiecrankie. During the bad old days of the Age of Forays, they had pursued vigorous vendettas against the Frasers, Grants and Gordon Earls of Huntly. One chevauchee had sparked a further clan fight: the Battle of the Shirts,' when Clanranald, with MacDonald of Keppoch and the Camerons, slogged it out with the Frasers. Several hundred combatants were involved, and it was said that only a handful from either side lived to tell the tale – Lord Lovat and his heir were amongst the dead on the Fraser side.

MacDonalds of Glengarry are descended from Donald, one of the five sons of Ranald, progenitor of Clanranald. Glengarry sided with Sleat in an abortive bid to resuscitate the Lordship, which foundered before the walls of Eilean Donan and led to the chief enjoying a sojourn behind bars, being released on the death of James V in 1542. A feud with the rump of the Mathesons was resolved in Glengarry's favour and they marched with Clanranald to fight in the Battle of the Shirts in 1544. Their continued advancement brought them into conflict with the MacKenzies, and led to further skirmishes. During one of these in 1581, the MacDonalds engaged in a spot of congregation burning, the victims, as they were immolated, were treated to a rant from Glengarry's piper who joyfully circled the burning church![6] Aeneas, the ninth Chief, was out with Montrose and suffered for his allegiance after the disaster at Worcester; nonetheless Alastair Dubh led Glengarry broadswords at Killiecrankie.

The Keppoch MacDonalds trace their line back to a younger son of John of Islay by his second wife, Margaret Stewart, daughter to Robert II. In the late fifteenth century, following the dissolution of the Lordship, the sept quarreled with the MacLarens and subsequentley-fought a battle against them. On being worsted, the McLarens sought aid from Stewart of Appin and a re-match was fought. This time the odds were more even, and during the day's long and bloody battle, both Stewart and Keppoch fell.[7] As late as 1663, as noted previously, MacDonalds of Keppoch were settling their internal differences with the thrust of a dirk: the twelfth Chief, Alexander and his brother were murdered near Invergarry.[8] The clan was out during the civil wars, and again in 1689. The MacDonald's of Ardnamurchan were a junior branch, being descended from Iain Sprangach, third son of the fourth chief of Clan Donald, and the third to lead the small clan may have been amongst the fallen at Harlaw. In the reign of James IV MacIain of Ardnamurchan ruthlessly supported the crown against those of his name, prizing opportunism above blood; amongst others, he put to death Sir Alexander MacDonald of Lochalsh after the latter's defeat by the MacKenzies.[9] Despite this trimming, the clan were eventually subsumed by the growing power of Clan Campbell, and their lands were occupied. A mini Diaspora ensued, with many merging into Clanranald.

CLAN IAIN ABRACH

In this proud if disunited heritage, Clan Iain Abrach[10] were a relatively minor sept, though their lineage was as good and ancient as any. The very nature of their forbidding glen cut them off from their Campbell neighbours to the south in Glenorchy and through prosperous Breadalbane. Iain Abrach was never an easy neighbour. Violent and lawless, they routinely pillaged their contemporaries, drove off the sturdy cattle, retreating over the Black Mount to their dark fastness. When the Lordship ended and Clan Donald's centuries-old hegemony was broken up, the Glencoe men found they had become mere vassals. At first their feudal superiors were the Stewarts of Appin, latterly Campbell of Glenorchy and Argyll. It would be these landlords and neighbours whose accounts, and not infrequent complaints, that composed a rather one-sided picture of the MacIains: invariably pejorative, and a litany of raiding, stealing and depredation. This pattern was established by the end of the fifteenth century, and exacerbated by their role in the rescue of Donald Dubh, heir to the defunct title and held a prisoner by Argyll since childhood on the Isle of Innischonnell. In a classic commando style raid the MacDonalds assailed the castle and set the captive at liberty.

Glencoe men were frequently to be found supplying muscle to forays by Glengarry or Keppoch, sometimes with and sometimes against Stewart of Appin or the Camerons. They might cheerfully foray against the Campbell lands in Glenorchy, but, as we have seen, did not scruple to abet in the harrying of Clan Gregor, acting as caterans. John MacDonald, eighth chief, had entered into a bond with Colin Campbell of Glenorchy, and the clan had followed Argyll's banner in his vendetta with the Ogilvies of Glenisla. A feud broke out, which was prosecuted with such gleeful savagery that Lord Ogivly, left in dire straits, complained bitterly to the Privy Council over the depredations he had endured to the extent that 'only with great difficulty and sore advertisement did he, his wife and his bairns escape'.[11]

Surprisingly, clan Iain Abrach never suffered the full rigor of legal sanction, such as was directed against the luckless MacGregors. Their affronts were committed under the banners of greater men and, as caterans, they had their uses. Besides their distant, secret and inhospitable glen was scarcely worth coveting. In part this remains surprising, given the litany of complaints: reif [plundering], houghing [inflicting injuries], and purpose to murder, hership [despoliation and cattle thieving], spulzie [wasting] and stouthreif [thieving generally], not to mention murder. Cutting throats did not appear to cause the MacIains any qualms. In fact they were noted for their violence in an age of extreme violence. They were credited with a significant tally of Stewarts and the massacre of Colquhoun prisoners after Glenfruin by Clan Gregor was attributed to MacDonald allies. Aggressive as they were, the traffic was by no means one sided: 'Mad' Colin Campbell of Glenlyon strung up three-dozen Glencoe men who fell into his hands after a failed raid, and Stewart of Appin ambushed the MacDonald chief, together with his brother, and dispatched them both.[12]

Given the prevailing anarchy and general mayhem which obtained during the Age of Forays, it has to be borne in mind that a small clan must needs fend for itself. The ability to punch its your weight might be a decisive factor in retaining life, limb and lands. The Western Highlands were a very great distance from Edinburgh, and the Privy Council's interest in the collective misdeeds of the clans was limited, their ability to intermeddle often more so. Besides, the uncertainties of the age produced a legion of landless caterans, desperadoes and outlaws, readily available for hire or private mischief. In a couple of instances MacIains were prepared to answer the summonses of the Council and explain themselves. No punitive consequences are recorded, which suggests the history may not be as relentlessly one-sided as it might appear at first glance.

'King Campbell'

Archibald Campbell, tenth Earl and first Duke (1701) was, if he
lacked friends, more circumscribed and cautious than his immediate
predecessors, both of whom had ended their lives on the block (or
the Maiden[13]). In 1661 his grandfather Archibald, the Marquess of
Argyll, was executed for treason. The former paladin of the Covenant
and nemesis of Montrose. His passing dismayed few, and it was two
years before his son, also Archibald, Lord Lorne, recovered the title
and became ninth earl. Despite having impeccable royalist credentials, he also had been condemned and imprisoned, and it was only
his friendship with John Maitland, Earl of Lauderdale, rising star
in the Restoration firmament, that secured his release and advancement. His wings clipped by James, as Duke of York, intervening in
the feud with the MacLeans, he finally lost his head after his abortive
rising in 1685. The tenth earl therefore came into a dangerous and
uncertain inheritance, he might be MacCailean Mor and master in
his own glens, but that had not saved either parent or grandparent.
Wise men learn the lessons of history.

His mother was a daughter of the fourth Earl of Moray, and he
did not permit the matter of his father's killing interfere with his
efforts to win the favour of James VI & II. It was to no avail: even
Archibald's easy charm and a ready willingness to convert to Popish
ways could not melt the King's disdain. He seamlessly transferred his
loyalty to the Williamite cause wherein his father's treason might be
dressed as martyrdom. William, after all, needed friends. Something
of a hedonist he married Elizabeth Tollemache, daughter of Lionel,
third Baronet of Helmingham. However, his dynastic duty done and
line secure, he soon found the company of a string of nubile mistresses more agreeable. The last, Peggy Allison, was probably the
love of his life. His portrait by Nicholas Maes shows a bland, full
face with careful eyes above a long nose; his weaknesses indicated
by a sensual and perhaps petulant mouth. Argyll was essentially a
trimmer, a man who put expediency above conscience and personal

interest uppermost, schooled in the bitter politics of survival. That MacDonald of Glencoe or any other of that name should find sympathy in one whose forbears, through two generations, had died their traitors' deaths steeped in enmity, was highly unlikely.

Campbell of Glenorchy was the junior branch, though theirs was an ancient, and they would argue honourable, line. Sir Colin Campbell, first of Glenorchy, was the eldest son from his father's second marriage and is credited with the original construction of great Kilchurn Castle on Loch Awe (though it may have been his wife who began the building whilst her husband was crusading). A knight of Rhodes and sometimes crusader, he was active in hunting down the regicides after the murder of James I in 1437. In consequence, James II conferred on him the Barony of Lawers. It was this Sir Colin, 'the Black' who enlarged his fief at the expense of the Macgregors, a trend enthusiastically maintained by his descendants, most notably the determined 'Grey Colin' sixth Laird, who hired Appin Stewarts and the Glencoe men to act as caterans, harrying both Menzies and the Gregarach. A list of depredations which the Council deplored but could not or would not curtail. Grey Colin was succeeded by 'Black Duncan of the Cowl' or 'Black Duncan of the Seven Castles', an even more ruthless character, who consolidated his expanding grip on Breadalbane with an iron hand, scattering the glens with his keeps. In his glowering portrait he has the look of a grim-faced *condotierre*: hard eyes in a long face with a square black beard beneath a bulbous nose and mean gash of a mouth.

This admirable tradition of unscrupulous garnering of lands fell into disuse. The eighth, ninth and tenth lairds spent more than they amassed and succeeded only in saddling their amply patrimony with significant debt. Thus John Campbell, the eleventh laird and latterly first Earl of Breadalbane and Holland, came like Argyll, into a difficult and encumbered inheritance, loaded with the burdens of indebtedness rather than treason. His mother was Lady Mary Graham, a daughter of the first earl of Airth. Embodied with all the hubris and venality of his name, he was astute, slippery and a noted dissembler. Though his rise was steady and marked, its passage and the means employed won 'Grey John' few friends.

It was in October 1672 that he foreclosed on the estates of his debtor George Sinclair, sixth Earl of Caithness. Later, upon Sinclair's death, he assumed both the dead man's titles and his widow – marrying to secure his position and also avert the need to pay the lady an annuity! In 1680, finding that the Caithness men were resisting his encroachment, he sent a battalion sized force to enforce his rights and rout the Sinclairs. Such high-handedness did not go unchallenged and the bastard son of the fifth earl was successful in the courts. By way of compensation, Grey John was elevated to the Earldom of Breadalbane and Holland, Viscount of Tay and Pentland, Lord of Glenorchy, Benderloch, Ormelie and Wick. Grey John had arrived, and yet never, in terms of his own vaunting hubris, completely, since his nephew Argyll had always masked his rise, still head of the senior branch of the Clan Campbell.

Resplendent in ermine, he stares calmly from the portrait by Sir John de Medina, sporting his magnificent and admired wig, calm, inscrutable, with studied gravitas. It is the face of a man who knows his place in the world and will strive continually to attain it, with perhaps just a hint of bitterness and resentment, which the sitter may have tried to mask. For all his constant scheming, Grey John would always be second fiddle '… cunning as a fox, wise as a serpent, slippery as an eel'.[14] In the grim tradition of his sept, Breadalbane had not received much in the way of fatherly love – a dereliction he had repaid by assuming management of the estates and reducing his parent to the status of mendicant pensioner. It was not until 1686 that the tenth Laird finally obliged by dying and Grey John, who had passed his half-century, came fully into his own.

'He is an object of compassion when I see him'. Thus did Grey John describe his cousin Robert Campbell, fifth Laird of Glenlyon. A long and lovely glen, said to be one of the sleeping places of the Fianna, guarded by their dozen towers. It was not until the closing years of the fifteenth century that Glenlyon came into the hands of a Campbell sept, although, true to family tradition, the newcomers quickly asserted themselves and brushed aside any who might claim prior title. The third laird was 'Mad Colin', who is said to have suffered a brain injury at an early age.[15] If so, the damage affected his temperament. Both vicious and aggressive, he could claim the honour of stringing up three dozen of *Clan Iain Abrach* who fell into his hands. As these were all taken in the course of an abortive foray; such summary justice probably raised few eyebrows at the time. The fifth Laird succeeded at a very early age, on the death of his grandfather, and was barely into his teens when the MacDonalds, returning from the satisfying business of chastising Clan Campbell in the name of Charles I, took up Glenlyon. This they accomplished with their usual zeal and efficiency, stripping the verdant pastures bare, emptying every byre. Economically, this was a disaster.

Though his mother was the formidable Jean Campbell, Grey John's aunt, he inherited little by way of firm resolve. To the ruin inflicted by Clan Donald he added the twin vices of cards and strong liquor, being unsuccessful in the former and with little apparent head for the latter. His adult life was a long, dismal roll of mounting debts and angry creditors. His seat was Mad Colin's hold of Meggernie and, despite his mounting burden, he spent lavishly on improving the property, transforming the grim fortalice into a pleasant country house. Such rash expenditure only served to exacerbate his position. He was finally forced to sell off all the standing timber in the Glen, a trace of the Old Caledonian Forest. His tenants, driven to desperation, went so far as to offer him half their beasts to placate his more frantic creditors. By 1684 he was obliged to sell most of what remained of his inheritance to the earl of Tullibardine, retaining only his wife's small estate of Chesthill.

Breadalbane was the last of his friends to abandon him. Pride in the name compelled Grey John to keep forking out on his indigent relative's behalf. If Glenlyon's own profligacy was not sufficient to ensure his ruin. Clan Donald, once again, obliged. Returning from Killiecrankie they again paid their compliments to Glenlyon and ravaged the place with a satisfying thoroughness; Chesthill was pillaged and left bare. Any hope the Laird might have entertained of keeping his head above water, even if only just, vanished in the dust of the MacIains. They hammered the final nails into his fiscal coffin with dire certainty. So it was that Robert Campbell of Glenlyon was left with no recourse in his fifty-ninth year, other than to seek a commission in Argyll's Regiment of foot.

Despite his dissolute ways, he still cut something of a cavalier dash. Had he served in the civil wars he would have made the perfect companion for such hard-drinking officers as George Goring, for whom the notion of an addiction to cards and the bottle carried no hint of opprobrium. He was cultured, educated, charming when sober and urbane. His portrait, by an unknown artist, shows a long pale face with an abundance of the Campbell blond waves. There is a likeness to Argyll: the pale, oval face, almost girlish, shapely sweep of long nose, and small, slightly effeminate mouth. He is shown in the martial attire of the period, a cuirassier's blackened harness, (which he would be most unlikely ever to have worn in earnest), with a generous fall of lace at the neck.

As they spilled over Rannoch Moor from that foray after Dundee, driving lifted cattle and sheep, slung with a clattering of stolen gear down to pans and utensils, the men of Clan Iain Abrach might think themselves well-pleased and laugh at Glenlyon's loss. For some, this loss would prove their obituary.

THE FLOWERING OF ENMITY 1644 – 1690

There is a prevailing perception that the Massacre of Glencoe was largely a Campbell affair, and one motivated entirely by clan hatred and a desire for revenge – the working out of a blood feud. Magnus Linklater refers to relatively recent utterances by a senior Campbell figure, who described the killings as a piffling incident with the trifling loss of some thirty-two illiterate tinkers, cattle rustlers and general miscreants.[16] This may have been uttered, rather ill-advisedly in jest, or at least cloaked in jest, but the Massacre of Glencoe did in no small part arise from tribal hatreds. That said, even the most biased of Clan Donald hagiographers would have to concede that clan Campbell had some grounds for ardent dislike. It was the civil wars and the intoxicating time of Montrose and MacColla, 'The Year of Miracles', that afforded Clan Donald a golden opportunity to wreak havoc upon their principal rivals, as unexpected as it was savage.

It was in the autumn of 1644, after Montrose had won Tippermuir and Aberdeen and fought *MacCailean Mor* to a standstill at Fyvie, that the Royalists struck westwards against Argyll. This was economic warfare at its most basic, a grand chevauchee through the hitherto sacrosanct glens of Clan Campbell. There was nothing swashbuckling or romantic in this: it was naked terror, of the blade and flaming torch. MacDonalds set to the work with great enthusiasm, whipping through Argyll like a hurricane, emptying fields and byres, stripping homes bare, leaving only the acrid smell of smoke in their wake. Any who resisted or simply got in the way were cut down without compunction, and by the time the orgy of destruction consumed Inveraray nearly a thousand inhabitants, mainly Campbells or their dependents, had been murdered. And it was pure murder: these were not an enemy force under arms but, for the most part, what might now be termed ethnic cleansing. As their chief fled from his burning capital by galley, the miserable survivors watched the rape of their country. Mass was celebrated in the ashes to rub further salt into the gaping wound. That Clan Campbell might resent this and carry the scars for a generation and more is only natural.

Clan Iain Abrach may or may not have directly participated in the taking up of Argyll, but Alasdair MacIain, eleventh Chief, had brought his broadsword to swell the Royalist muster by November 1644, and provided a guide to see the army safely over the Devil's Staircase and toward the Great Glen. A Campbell brigade some 3,000 strong was mustered to follow, big with vengeance, the formidable pairing of Montrose and MacColla, who now produced, through the harsh, swirling blizzards of a Highland winter, one of their most impressive manoeuvres, which culminated in the charge at Inverlochy. This was a double blow to Clan Campbell under the command of Auchinbreck, who, with hundreds of his name, lay piled on the shore or slopping in the bloody shallows of Loch Leven. Happily, Argyll himself had kept his galley to hand and once more fled across the water.

Nearly a year later, in October 1645, the Year of Miracles had gone by; MacDonalds of Glencoe again harried Glenorchy, adding further corpses to the heap and stripping the desperate inhabitants of what little they had left. Such depredations could be claimed as the usages of war, but the reality was pure plunder and malice. For those stripped of animals and shelter winter would bring famine and death, as simple as that. Such total despoliation created a virtual death sentence for those not immediately put to the sword. Indeed, to do so in such circumstances might almost have been accounted a kindness. In December it would appear that an agreement or band was drafted by the Royalist officers, many from the gentry of Clan Donald, who confirmed their commitment to a policy of destroying the power of Clan Campbell for good. Any pretence that the campaign was being pursued to attain objective military aims was thereby dispelled. This was a feud, a bloody vendetta that Alasdair MacColla was only too happy to lead.

That December witnessed the rape of Breadalbane. Isolated strongpoints, if well-garrisoned, could hold out, but the Royalists indulged in a tornado of destruction. MacDonald, MacNabs and MacGregors; these had cause to hate Clan Diarmid, but one atrocity cannot justify another. Pillage, murder and rapine were the orders of the day and none is recorded as having demurred. Even the baptismal font of the Kirk of Kenmore was lifted. Whole townships were left ravaged and destitute, their houses torched and smoldering with the charred remains of their menfolk, and byres emptied and bare. The Laird of Glenorchy was forced to borrow the huge sum of £5,000 to try and help his tenants begin to rebuild; if this was not a genocide it would suffice. What happened after in Glencoe, whilst repugnant, has to be considered in the light of what went before:

> About twenty people surrounded our house; shouting, "Get out of here"...
> My father came out and asked them what they wanted. They took my
> father and killed him. They shot my brother while he was coming down the
> stairs. Then they shot my grandfather and two uncles in the front yard.[17]

Historians of Clan Campbell are adamant that the band drawn up was an incitement to indiscriminate mass killing. Sir James Lamont, a Royalist and signatory to the agreement, described the document 'bearing in plain terms of combination among us for the ruin of the name of Campbell.'[18] In the words of the clan's writer 'a most cruell horrid and bloody band for rooting out the name of Campbell'.[19] None of this could truly be said to be in pursuance of a legitimate war aim or aims: the country ravaged had no strategic significance in the wider struggle, nor was the King's cause well served by such overt brigandage. Any assertion that his clan and Irish allies were nothing more than a pack of barbarians received a significant boost, handing the Presbyterians an inexpugnable argument.

One atrocity followed another. Campbell captives were immolated in a byre by Lagganmore; a hundred of the Lamonts were then killed by Clan Diarmid at Dunoon. David Leslie withdrew the offer of being quartered after MacDonald of Sanda surrendered Dunaverty. Few on the Royalist side would forget the deliberate targeting of female followers caught foraging by Presbyterian horse before Kilsyth or, most telling of all, the cold blooded murder of Irish prisoners taken at Philiphaugh, men who had been offered clemency but were shot instead. Even worse and as mentioned previously, several hundred of their dependents taken in the rout were deliberately drowned, their heaped, sodden corpses left on the riverbanks. This was a legacy both sides would long remember.

By now the predators of Clan Iain Abrach had developed a taste for Campbell beef. In June 1646, with Keppoch MacDonalds, they forayed against Sir Robert Campbell's lands around the western shores of Loch Tay. This time they did not go unchallenged; Campbell gentry were gathered at Finlarig to celebrate the marriage of Campbell of Glenorchy's daughter, and, their anger fuelled by whisky, they set off on the Hot Trod. The raiders were led by Keppoch's son Angus Og, and the Campbells doubtless thought they would simply attempt to make good their escape and hang on to lifted beasts. Below the crest of the hill of stones *Sron a'Chlachain,* as the men of Clan Diarmid struggled up the slope behind, the fumes still clouding, Angus Og launched his company in a well timed downhill charge, swift, cohesive and bloodily successful. Most notable of the Glencoe men was the formidably brutal Big Archibald MacPhail, something of a local celebrity, who having beseeched the Almighty to either lend favour to Clan Donald or, if that was too much, kindly remain neutral, laid on with gusto. In a few minutes, three-dozen Campbells fell; a score more carried their hurts bleeding back to Finlarig. Big Archie boasted that he had ruined the groom's wedding night with a well shot, if reprehensible, shaft from his bow![20]

Angus Og had not scored his minor triumph without loss. After the fight, which raged mainly in the Corrie of the Bannocks – the stream flowing outwards known thereafter as the Bloody Burn – the MacDonalds had their wounded as well as their cattle. A second body of Campbell militia, better armed and presumably sober, was on their trail. A running fight ensued in which the bridegroom, Menzies (not, as John Prebble mentions, overly discommoded by Big Archie's ungentlemanly arrow) inflicted a mortal wound on Angus Og. Such was the magnitude of Clan Campbell's losses in the course of these Royalist incursions, that it took them a decade and more to rebuild – and that with the aid of some £50,000 worth of Parliamentary subsidy. If what had been attempted was not genocide then it was certainly within the modern definition of ethnic cleansing. Clan Campbell, in its inexorably ruthless rise, had made few friends and a legion of enemies. Their conduct, particularly toward the MacGregors, was savage. In this, of course, they had previously been abetted by MacDonalds of Glencoe.

Within the decade, MacDonalds returned to Breadalbane, as men of Clan Iain Abrach with Keppoch raided Glenlyon; 'the Raid of Colin's Cows'. As the raiders withdrew by the narrows of Glen Meran, a young female captive called MacNee, hamstrung some of the cows, slowing the party sufficiently for the Campbell posse to come to contact. Another confused and vicious little melee followed; the MacDonalds barely scraped free, with more than a few hurts. The girl called MacNee they simply killed, though the memory of her courage lived on in the song.[21] By this time, 1655, the eleventh Chief of the MacIains had been dead for five years, succeeded by his son, another Alasdair, twelfth of the name and destined to be forever associated with the massacre of his people. A veritable giant, red-haired and flamboyant, he was a figure worthy of the Fianna, distinguished not only by his height and breadth but also by his curling mustachios, the charm of French manners and a willingness to plunder at will. Though he might appear like a figure straight from the pages of G.A. Henty, the majority of his contemporaries, particularly the inhabitants of Breadalbane, considered him to be nothing more than a common bandit and *braggadocio*, a vicious anachronism.

When Bonny Dundee called out the clans, it must have seemed to many of them that the glory days of the Year of Miracles might return and the Campbells might be treated to another drubbing. MacIain led 120 broadswords from the Glen to the muster on the field of Dalcomera in the Great Glen. Here the chiefs, blazing peacocks in their gaudy finery, acclaimed Claverhouse, the very epitome of a Highland general. The twelfth Chief of Glencoe, though he might not boast the roll of tenants enjoyed by Keppoch or Glengarry or the imposing Lochiel, still had his two strong sons to flank him, a piper to quicken the blood and a tail of defiant young blades. Apart from his great height and martial bearing, MacIain sported a fine buff leather jerkin, booty from some distant foray and a hefty brass-barreled blunderbuss.[22] One of the Jacobite commander's staff was his young standard bearer, James Philip of Almericlose, who was inspired to epic verse by the Homeric company attending his general:

> Nixt with a dareing look and warlike stride
> Glencoe advanced: His rattling amour shone
> With dreadful glare: His large, broad, brawny back
> A thick bull's hide impenetrably hard,
> Instead of Cloaths invest, and though along
> Twice fifty of gigantick limbs and size
> The warrior led, fierce, hardy, wild and strong,
> Yet his vast bulk did like a turret rise
> By head and shoulders o'er the surly crew.
> Round, in his left, his mighty shield he twirled,
> And in his right, his broadsword brandished high,
> Which flashed like lightning with affrighting gleams.
> His visage boisterous, horribly was graced
> With stiff mustachios like two bending horns,
> And turbid, fiery eyes, as meteors red,
> Which fury and revenge did threaten round.[23]

At this point the chief was in his sixties, still impressive and resolutely active. The portrait painted by the besotted Almericlose evokes images from the *Iliad,* and that was no doubt intended. Robert Campbell of Glenlyon might have offered a somewhat less glowing testament. For, and as we have seen, following the defeat of the Jacobite clans in the smoking streets of Dunkeld MacIain, leading his and Keppoch's men, he again descended on Breadalbane. Grey John had cannily vacillated; expressing good intentions to both sides, the death of Dundee had assisted in his final, circumspect choice, a belated espousal of the Government side. This defection cost him dear; politically expedient, it offered the MacDonalds license to plunder, and as ever, they availed themselves fully of the proffered gift. They took up their traditional killing grounds with a will, slighting Breadalbane's tower at Achallader, burning, harrying and stealing as they joyfully progressed. Even though Glenlyon had papers from Colonel Cannon confirming immunity, they did him no good; his glen was thoroughly sacked. What could move was stolen, what could not was destroyed.

His losses, by his own subsequent account, totaled 36 horses, 240 beasts, 993 sheep 133 goats and all his gear.[24] In cash terms he had lost £8,000 Scots.[25] For a man already in dire straits, such catastrophic loss was the final straw: he was effectively destitute.

For the MacIains and their chief this was a return to the good old days, the Age of Forays, when force was the only law that obtained. Times had, however changed, whether or not they appreciated or acknowledged the fact. In the short term the Privy Council might damn all MacDonalds as murderous renegades, and clansmen might snort derisively, believing themselves to be inviolate in their own glens. But they lived at the threshold of the Age of Reason, the Whig supremacy, the Act of Union was not two decades distant. Their brutal rapacity and narrow hubris condemned them in the eyes of all but a handful of their contemporaries. Most viewed them as outlaws, a throwback to a dark and dismal past, a brake on the flowering of the rule of law in the Western Highlands. Something would have to be done. If MacIain had been a more sensitive man, he might have felt the chill breeze of history at his back as he drove his newly acquired herds home.

Tantalizingly, the magistrates in Inveraray did once manage to get their hands of MacIain, though they failed to keep hold. To any from Clan Donald, the Campbell capital, now splendidly rebuilt after their earlier demolitions, was hostile territory. The townsmen had no cause to love them, many would have lost relatives, property or gear. It was more than that. Inverary was a Lowland town, a magnate's settlement foisted onto the Highland landscape. None of the septs of Clan Donald could boast a township with fine, loftily gabled buildings, inns and taverns, a pattern of streets, offices and shops, hub of ducal power and thriving seat of enterprise. Inveraray summed up all that Clan Campbell had gained and all the MacDonalds had lost.

In the autumn of 1673, MacIain had dealt with a summons from the bench, which required John Dow Beg MacDonald of Achnacone to answer an unrecorded indictment. Instead of John Dow, the chief dispatched a lesser tenant, Donald MacRankin from Achtriachtan, as substitute.

Their worships did not share the joke, if any was intended, and they dealt harshly with the luckless Donald, who was scourged and suffered his tongue being bored with a hot iron.[26] MacIain, John MacDonald, tacksman of Achtriachtan, together with a third Glencoe man, John MacAllan, were all fined in absentia. There is no evidence to say the indemnities were ever paid. John Prebble takes the view that the matter may have concerned a serious alleged offence, on account of which MacIain found himself, half a year later, in chains and incarcerated in Inverary Tolbooth.

MacIain, together with various gentry of Glencoe, was accused of murdering two men of the glen. What sparked this bloody episode is as unclear as the notes recording the alleged offence. Several of the chief's cousins were named among the assassins, and the size of the group suggests something more than a petty local feud. Given MacIain's grip on his people, it would seem impossible that such an outrage should occur without his authority or connivance. It is clear the Argyll justices took this view. The matter was, of course, a serious one, punishable by hanging. What is equally unclear is how the Campbells came to lay hands on the old fox at all. It is unlikely in the extreme that he came voluntarily or quietly. There has to be the suggestion that he was snatched by main force or abducted from some other place.

Having finally got their hands on this most elusive of local predators, who had avoided their reach for at least quarter of a century, how galling that he should contrive to slip his bonds, slip the hounds and return safe home, unrepentant and un-chastised. By April 1674 the chief was home again, and the bench left fuming. The court had limited options; under the terms of the General Band,[27] Sir James MacDonald of Sleat, yet more distant on Skye, was deemed surety for MacIain and received a peremptory letter from the Council in Edinburgh. This correspondence alludes to the fact of MacIain's escape, possibly in the company of John MacDonald of Achtriachtan, and refers to accusations of several murders and depredations. The Council goes on to point out to Sir James his legal obligations. More practically, they simply require him to cooperate with Argyll in pursuing the alleged criminals. In the event, nothing further seems to have occurred and the matter was apparently dropped.[28] In any case the Campbell chief was soon distracted by his feud with MacLean. This bitter and savage dispute dragged on for six years. MacIain did proffer assistance to MacLean, but generally seems to have wisely kept his head down. None of the Glencoe men marched with the Highland Host in 1678.

At some point there would have to be a reckoning. The Tory clans, like the Native Americans of the late nineteenth century, were a people running out of their time. MacIain, for all his bluster, was no fool, but the day was approaching a deal faster than he could have anticipated.

CHAPTER 4

The Gathering Storm
1690 – 1691

'Next came Glencoe, terrible in unwonted arms ,,,'

James Philip of Almerieclose
(translated from the Latin by Rev. Alexander D. Murdoch;
Scottish History Society, 1888)

'Cold, cold this night is my bed,
Cold, cold this night is my child.
Lasting, lasting, this night in my sleep.
I in my shroud and thou in my arm.
The shadow of death creeps over me.
The warm pulse of my love will not stir
The wind of the heights they sleep-lulling.
The close-clinging snow of the peaks they mantle.'

Gaelic Verse

' 'Insurgent' – rising in active revolt … a rebel, a revolutionary.'

Oxford English Dictionary

Cromwell had built the first fort at Inverlochy during the Protectorate, and its governor had been his loyal subordinate John Hill. Now ageing, Hill was to return to Loch Linnhe and supervise the building of a new fort of the same name. It is likely the old soldier greeted his commission with joy; he had no idea of what might finally be asked of him.

FORCES OF THE CROWN

The army, in the main, was by no means a popular institution. British forces had swelled dramatically during the wars following the restoration of Charles II, and despite the many laurels, opinions varied. Tories feared the military as an instrument of intimidation and repression under the Whigs. What is more both sides of the house became alarmed at the expenditure involved. Armies are an expensive undertaking, and whilst expenditure during Chares II reign had been pegged at under £300,000 per annum this rocketed under William III. Between the late autumn of 1688 and the closing months of 1691 the bill had reached £3, 481,585 6s 7 ½d, a colossal sum! Charles, after 1660, had quickly recognised the need for a form of standing army, though he felt the need, conversely, to dismantle Cromwell's great war-machine. During this period the military establishment comprised two separate forces: the English establishment, and that which served in Ireland, controlled from Dublin. Though the latter was the smaller, it was less vulnerable to the politician's axe. This arrangement was not provided for by statute until 1699, and the initial Irish division was some 12,000 strong. These troops could, of course, be used as a pool of reinforcements when emergency threatened the mainland.

By the date of Charles' death in 1685 the peacetime establishment had swelled to 7, 472 serving in marching or field battalions, with a further second tier of 1,393 deployed in garrisons.[1] Monmouth's Rebellion provided the pretext to increase this total to nearly 20,000. The Glorious Revolution and wars in Flanders, Ireland and Scotland demanded even more substantial forces: some 73, 692 at the outset, rising to 93,635 by 1694.[2] At the Restoration, the Irish Establishment, mainly composed of old Cromwellians, stood at 7,500. Under James this force was both expanded and radicalized, with Protestant officers being replaced by Catholics. At its height in 1690, the Jacobite Irish could field a force 45,000 strong. Compared to this, the Scottish establishment was tiny: in 1685 it could muster only 2,199 soldiers.[3]

A standing army was not a concept recognised by the English courts or polity. Even the Articles of War first codified in 1663 had no force at law, and could only be employed effectively as a regulated code of conduct which dealt with disciplinary matters within the armed forces. If a civilian element were to be involved, then the matter would have to be processed through the legal system in the usual way. Each annual Mutiny [Army] Act was sure to have a rough ride at the hands of the opposition. The shade of Cromwell was regularly alluded to and, in order to get legislation through, the administration had to fuse parsimony with dissembling. The prevailing system abetted this practice for the army, in some ways resembling a form of private enterprise, with advancement, in the main, being secured by purchase – a system regarded as archaic even at the time of the Glorious Revolution. A colonel was provided with funds from the public purse to raise, equip, feed and clothe his men, subject to the normal audit procedures, usually undertaken externally, and inspections from within the establishment undertaken by senior officers. At this time the War Office was but a small department, and much of the day-to-day administration was undertaken by the regimental agents, essentially civilian contractors. Britain (apart from the creaking militia) did not suffer any form of conscription, so recruitment into the ranks depended on the zeal of the colonel, the depths of his pockets, and the wiles of the recruiting sergeant.

Military life in the late seventeenth century is portrayed as the last resort of the desperate, or a dumping ground for felons. This is however, unfair, agricultural unemployment, the lure of adventure, and the need to escape domestic entanglements might equally serve to motivate recruits. Work on the land might be both seasonal and uncertain. Instructions on the matter of recruiting forbade the inclusion of Catholics, foreigners, those too young, too old, feeble in mind or body. Expediency, however (and as ever) proved a great leveler. The magistrates were also happy to provide recruits whose choice in the matter was strictly curtailed. At this time there was no fixed period of service: a man would remain wedded to the colours 'for life', or until age, wounds or disability compelled his discharge. It would be fair to assert that the majority of those who came in were young men, aged between 17 and 25 years, although more than a sprinkling were older, and that unemployment was the single prime motivator. Though men would die in battle or succumb after to their wounds, many more would fall victim to disease and neglect. Colonel Hill's garrison at Inverlochy was to be plagued by a high death toll. Men lost not to the swords of clansmen, but to sickness, poor diet and the indifference of a distant administration.

Officers might regard their men as a commodity, yet many belied the image of the hard drinking, flogging variety (though corporal punishment was still considered necessary for discipline and the lash freely administered.) Marlborough's battles had yet to be fought and to justify an innate sense of superiority in the British soldier. He was a volunteer, even if compelled occasionally by desperation. He could load and fire his musket faster and to far greater effect than his continental adversaries. His remuneration at eight pence a day was modest in the extreme, and subject to stoppages for necessaries. Even his subsistence monies, in theory guaranteed not to fall below half that, was subject to deductions levied by the Paymaster-General. It is hardly to be wondered at that many soldiers maintained additional part-time employment. A professional standards authority, the Board of General Officers, was some way distant at this time, and was not constituted until 1714. Marlborough would introduce a drill manual 'New Exercise of Firelocks and Bayonets' in 1708, but in the 1690s the army did not specifically require its young officers to exhibit any level of academic qualification or professional competence, apart from the specialist units such as artillery or engineers.[4]

This is not to say that leadership skills were lacking; in fact, quite the opposite. Most officers learnt their profession well, and purchase did not cancel out merit. It has been estimated that, in the early eighteenth century, most foot captains had served for nearly twenty years before taking command of a company.[5] Since the days of Edward I in the late thirteenth century, campaigning in Scotland held little lustre. English officers, in the late seventeenth century, would far rather do their service in Flanders, fighting conventional foes in a war of massed battalions than endure the cold, misery and outpost skirmishes which 'frontier' warfare in the Highlands might entail.

Britain was primarily a naval and maritime power. Once peace was declared, new regiments raised for the recent war were disbanded and the older survivors reduced, often to the bone. Drill mainly consisted of a basic exercise of arms, the grander movements by brigades could not be attempted, even battalion-sized manoeuvres only occurred once a year in the course of the spring review. Battle in the late seventeenth century was the kingdom of black powder (gunpowder). The propellant for both artillery and small arms is a particularly noxious mixture. When discharged it gives off vast clouds of cloying, sulphureous smoke, blinding the combatants after the first volley. Men were obliged to bite off the paper cartridges they carried, to dribble powder into the pan of their muskets, and then to charge the barrel, ram down ball and paper wadding. They would very quickly be blackened and begrimed by the greasy residue. To add to this they could expect to be maddened by thirst, blinded by smoke and deafened by the hurricane of noise.

Round shot from the great guns, bouncing or 'grazing' before impact, would punch through files, knocking men over like skittles, shearing limbs, spreading a noisome mess of entrails, fragments of bone, brain tissue and great gouts of blood. The soft lead musket balls, flattening on impact, would inflict gaping wounds, driving cloth and fabric into the cavity, the cloying stench of black powder competing with the stink of blood and ordure. Many men opened their bowels or emptied bladders as the fight began. It is unlikely that recruits had earlier been apprised of any of these elements by the recruiting party! British fire superiority, created by long, rippling volleys, was effective against slow moving regular formations and against the French, whose Gallic élan frequently triumphed over discipline. Against fast moving Highlanders it was markedly less effective – even a steady fire was not sufficiently intense to mow down the attackers before they closed to contact. Consequently, the practice against Highlanders was often to fire massed battalion volleys for maximum effect and the front rank would, after discharging their muskets, kneel with fixed bayonets to present a steel tipped hedge.

The principal weapon of the infantryman was the William III Land Pattern flint musket, forerunner of the more famous 'Brown Bess'. At the time of Glencoe, most foot battalions were armed with flint guns, long barreled, still with a wooden ramrod or 'scouring stick' and of .85-inch calibre. Around fifteen pounds in weight, and firing a 1¼ ounce ball, from 4½ drams of black powder, the musket was loaded by biting off the end of the paper cartridge, as described above, and, after priming the pan, tipping the balance of the powder down the barrel. This was followed by rolling in the ball and compressing the load with the remains of the cartridge used as wadding and tamped down with the ramrod. The recoil was fierce and got fiercer as firing continued, residue of powder progressively fouling the barrel. Though slow to load and vulnerable to damp and wind, the flint musket was durable and functional. Each man was, to a degree, his own armourer, carrying spare flints (a flint would be worn out after thirty or so rounds), and other replacement parts. His cartridges, ready made up in their paper cases, were carried in a leather container, the 'cartouche' or cartridge box, with the individual rounds slotted into a drilled wooden 'magazine' within.

Flint had almost completely replaced the venerable matchlock as a means of ignition. The mechanism, hence its name, relied for its effectiveness on a sharpened flint held between the jaws of the cock; this was controlled by a spring. Drawn back once to safe or 'half-cock', where it would not give fire (hence the expression 'going off at half-cock'), then again to full, ready for the firing. Once the trigger was depressed, releasing the spring, the flint struck sharply against a steel or frizzen, which was hinged over the pan containing fine powder. The sparks fell onto the pan, igniting the primer, which flashed through the touchhole to ignite the main charge. A competent musketeer might fire two rounds in a minute.

A socket bayonet with its triangular 17 inch blade was fitted and drill, at this time, more resembled the stately moves of the pike, than the now more familiar practice which was later introduced and based more on the Prussian model. On the command 'charge your bayonet', the barrel and stock were grasped in the left hand, in front of the lock, and the right hand placed behind the brass butt plate with the weapon then thrust forward on the next command, 'push your bayonet'. As this was now a socket bayonet and not the dagger-like plug variety, which had served Mackay so badly at Killiecrankie, the musket could still be loaded and fired with the blade attached. It was not ideal, however, as the length and the angle of the socket made loading and ramming considerably more difficult. Conventional bayonet drill was also of limited effect against clansmen. The superiority of their seemingly archaic arms at close quarters, and their long familiarity in the use of them, could see them batter and hew their way through a line of bayonets with horrifying speed.

Regiments bore the name of their colonel, a system that would have been instantly recognisable to the combatants of the civil wars half a century earlier. Disbanding of regiments, which inevitably followed the conclusion of hostilities, was usually carried out strictly on account of seniority. A typical battalion of foot comprised a dozen companies, eleven of which had three score soldiers whilst the last, the grenadiers, recruited an extra file of ten. The full complement was thus forty-four officers with 780 NCOs and other ranks. On the payroll also were the surgeon's mate, quartermaster and solicitor, drum major and deputy-marshal. Each company was commanded by a captain, and served by a lieutenant, ensign and two sergeants or corporals. Only the grenadier company had a second full lieutenant as opposed to ensign. Three or four companies might march under the control of the colonel himself, who drew wages of 10s a day, the same daily rate as a captain.

When preparing to engage, the battalion deployed from column into line, ranks marching in step, instruments playing, foot covered by horse and guns on their flanks. The files dressed by beat of drum, sergeants using their leveled halberds to direct and, where necessary prod. Once lines were formed, officers and NCOs took their stations. A firefight might commence at, say, 60 – 70 yards maximum, quite frequently at even closer distance. The fire, with its choking, blinding corollary of smoke, was both deafening and blinding and, though wildly inaccurate, could do significant hurt to massed ranks opposed. Normally, pikes would stand in the centre, in five ranks, with musketeers in six on each flank of the block, firing by ranks. The function of the pikes was to give protection against enemy blocks and cavalry. During the course of the Nine Years War British foot battalions displayed steadiness and resolve, earning plaudits from the King on the bloody ground of Steenkirk and Landen. William was a constant, if not always successful, general.

Heavy lead balls were flattened by the rush of air to inflict ghastly funnel shaped wounds. Great palls of filthy discharge obscured the field, air heated with stabbing flames and the hot blood of men, their faces rendered demonic by powder residue. After both sides had given several volleys, one would advance with the bayonet. Only rarely did the survivors of the enemy regiments stand to receive the rush. Grenadiers were very much the elite, introduced around 1678. Their weapon, as the name implies, was the grenade, a circular bomb, roughly the size of a cricket ball, ignited from a projecting fuse, lit by a slow match wound around the thrower's left wrist. The projectiles were hurled in volleys, a mini-bombardment before the files closed to contact. Grenadiers were chosen for their steadiness and stature, being essentially shock troops, used for assaulting prepared fortifications. During the long Williamite Wars in Flanders, their skills and resolve were much in demand.

For the rank and file, life beneath the colours was by no means an entirely attractive occupation. As a rule, the men were accommodated in the damp and cold of canvas encampments, or billeted out in inns, taverns or on hapless civilians who much resented the practice. Purpose-built barracks were still a relative rarity, though more plentiful in Scotland. Billeting, aside from souring relations with the populace, was inefficient as the men were distributed in penny packets in a slew of dwellings. Ale and spirits, together with cards and dice, were likely to be his principal diversions. Many soldiers were married, and the 'army women' were not necessarily the cohort of harlots that they were frequently portrayed. The women, in fact, performed a whole series of vital functions: as cooks, laundresses, sutlers and, in an age before the establishment of army medial services, nurses.

An enlisted man's clothing consisted of a greatcoat, with coloured cuffs and facings, worn over a sleeved, woolen doublet or waistcoat with breeches and dark coloured gaiters. There was little concession to seasonal variations. The ordinary or 'hatmen' companies wore plain brimmed hats, whilst the elite grenadiers sported the more ornate and distinctive mitre cap. By way of equipment, the soldier was furnished with his cartridge box, worn from a stiff leather belt slung over the left shoulder. Around his waist was another broad buff leather belt, from which were suspended his bayonet, together with a short sword or hanger. To complete his marching kit, he would carry a form of knapsack, a linen bread bag and a tin canteen. Plate amour for body defence had by now virtually disappeared, only the officer's decorative steel gorget surviving. From 1660 the ratio of pikemen to musketeers had steadily diminished, the puissant pike by 1690 was virtually as obsolescent as amour. Though the pike was vanishing officers retained the half pike or spontoon, sergeants carried halberds.

Though many officers were humane and exhibited a genuine concern for the welfare of their men, discipline was both strict and punitive. The lash was considered the fittest remedy for a whole range of offences. The number of strokes awarded might be considerable, fifteen hundred for certain offences. These would be administered in batches to allow the recipient some chance for recuperation. For lesser offences a man might be sentenced to solitary confinement in 'the black hole' on a bread and water diet. Despite the severity of the regime, desertion was by no means uncommon; the bullying of unscrupulous sergeants, the poor diet, bad accommodation and the sheer, grinding tedium of garrison duty all undermined a soldier's will to continue. The more enterprising officers and men cultivated diverse interests and 'business' activities, to ease both the financial strain and the tedium.

Officers were usually, in the broad sense, 'gentlemen' of good if not necessarily wealthy stock. Most would be younger sons or otherwise impoverished. Following family tradition was common; but the burgeoning professional classes and the clergy also contributed their sons. Increasingly, as the eighteenth century progressed, the percentage of officers coming from Scottish or Anglo-Irish families increased. Despite this, promotion from the ranks was by no means unheard of, such promotion having been earned through ability and good service. For most, the vehicle for entry was purchase, and the practice was not regulated until after 1720. The acquisition of a commission was a financial investment. It inevitably cost more to buy into a fashionable regiment, and price was influenced by the unit's proximity to London. When an officer was moving up he could sometimes effectively trade in his existing commission against the higher rank and supply the difference in cash. Alternatively, he could sell his present commission and pay the full rate for the other. Should an officer fall in battle or be cashiered, then the nearest below him in seniority would be made up at no cost (such a 'free' commission however held no residual 'trade in' value).

Obviously the modern world views such a system, with its implications of elitism and privilege, with disdain. To the politicians of the day, however, it had the considerable recommendation of being self-financing and it implied that control of the armed forces at battalion-level remained in the hands of men of property. The expediency of wartime also prompted the practice of giving commissions to any who could, subject to the right level of patronage, deliver a set number of recruits – free enterprise in action! The fiscal risk attaching to the raising of the volunteers naturally fell on the officer concerned, and he might be forced even to buy in recruits from an agent or 'crimp'.

Argyll's regiment was raised after April 1689, and was thus the first regular Highland battalion to serve the British Crown. Its formation pre-dates that of the 42nd Foot (Black Watch) by half a century. This was no mere militia but a regular muster comprising ten foot companies, raised from the Campbell glens, officered by gentry and tacksmen of the name. Given King William's urgent need for fresh troops this was a significant boon. Furthermore these were not, as John Prebble observes, raw or untrained in war but Highlanders born to arms, serving under their own chiefs, united by the bonds of blood, community and loyalty. Their grandfathers had spilled their blood for Argyll and the Covenant and these young men were keenly aware of that tradition. Equally, they were aware who had slain their forbears at Inverlochy and wasted their homes since.

Some 600 men would form the battalion and whilst Argyll was Colonel, in practice the duties of commanding officer would be exercised by a Lieutenant Colonel. In the first instance this was Sir Duncan Campbell of Auchinbreck, a tried veteran whose relative had fallen trying to stem the rot at Inverlochy. A Lowland officer, Robert Jackson, a staunch Williamite with a family connection, succeeded him in 1691. His major was to be Robert Duncanson of Fassokie in Stirling-shire and of whom we shall hear a great deal more. Duncanson was a career soldier from a family with a long history of service to Clan Campbell. He would find himself entirely at home, for most of the company officers shared the name including of course the oldest of the company commanders, Robert Campbell of Glenlyon. Their names and destinies would become inextricably linked. Service to the Crown would, for the majority of officers, NCOs and private men (termed 'sentinels'), be allied to private quarrel. These men were bred to hate Clan Donald, but even had they not been their treatment at the hands of Keppoch, Glengarry, Clanranald and Glencoe would not be of the sort that engenders amity. Officers raised their companies in the old way, by levy from amongst their tenantry, thus maintaining the bonds of communal obligation and tradition. Each then would be fully able to recite the catalogue of wrongs inflicted by MacDonalds since 1644, and, to be fair to them, this was not unimpressive.

As Argyll's was to be a regular foot battalion and no mere militia, saffron and plaid, broadsword and targe were to be laid aside for musket and, initially at least, pike. A third of each company of threescore would trail the pike whilst the rest formed the musket block, the shot. Though their ardour was not in question. It was recognised that the clansmen could not comport themselves like civilized soldiers of the King without the benefit of drill, and lots of it. Thus, in its wisdom, the Privy Council withdrew sixteen experienced NCOs from Bargany's Regiment to instruct and beat the drill book into these new recruits to the King's colours. One of these, Sergeant Barber, was to feature in the events of 13th February 1692. Firstly, officers and men were constrained to swear the oath of obedience. Oaths, to a Highlander, were an important and binding matter, not to be trivialized or trimmed. The terms were uncompromising: all ranks must obey the Crown, and its Commander-in-Chief for the time being, and carry out all orders given. There is no qualification or test for conscience; the concept of the 'Just' order does not enter into the terms of the oath, blind obedience is all that is required. In due course, some of the soldiers would be called upon to examine their own consciences in the matter of strict obedience to orders.[6]

Obliged as the Privy Council were to the Duke, parsimony, as ever, ruled, and Argyll was obliged for the first year of their service to fund his men from his own capacious pocket, a burden he was not over-keen to shoulder. The price of demonstrating his unshakeable loyalty to the Protestant throne was amounting to a deal more than he had envisaged! This outlay was very considerable: the wages bill alone was £16,000 a year,[7] and it was two full years before the full muster, now of thirteen companies, was completely uniformed and accoutred. They wore the blue bonnet and Argyll's badge; their coats were faced in yellow, matching their stockings, below grey breeches; the only trace of plaid was the pattern on their waistcoats. On their feet they wore soldiers' boots of stout leather. The Duke was well pleased with his new battalion when he saw it paraded at Perth, as he should be, ordered ranks of scarlet, yellow and blue, each bearing his crest; the burnished gorgets of the officers in their well-tailored uniforms. In line his Grace's own company took place of honour on the right, with Glenlyon's on the extreme left, his being the most recently raised. If anything disturbed the Duke's equanimity, it was probably the sight of the importunate Glenlyon who, aged nearly sixty, was forced to take the King's shilling in a last ditch effort to stave off some of his more pressing creditors.

Perhaps fortunately the battalion mustered too late to fight at Killiecrankie but was deployed, under-strength as it then was, in mopping up operations. Fighting as marines, they took a Jacobite supply vessel off Kintyre and engaged in the highly satisfying business of wresting back territory from the MacLeans who had impudently re-occupied ground previously lost to Argyll. From his grace's perspective and from that of his name, this was agreeable labour – pursuing avarice and revenge under the royal banner, in redcoats and ostensibly 'wedded to Brown Bess' but with the clan slogan on their lips. Campbell of Airds was able, with his company, to pursue an ambition to take back Castle Stalker, garrisoned by the Appin men, though this proved a tougher nut and was not handed back until some nine months later. All the same, wearing the redcoat brought distinct advantages.

THE FORT AT INVERLOCHY

Colonel John Hill is one of the very few who, on the Government side, emerged from the grim recounting of the massacre with any measure of integrity left intact. That he did finally accede to the order for the killing and is thus complicit is perhaps less damning than might at first appear to be the case. By the spring of 1690, Hill was an ageing warhorse, a survivor of the Commonwealth who retained the ideals of those halcyon days, with a residual penchant for sermonizing. No portrait of this old soldier survives, and he would doubtless have looked down his disapproving nose at the thought of such vanity, but we may imagine him as a lean, spare man who carried his years well and was determined to do his duty. He was quite remarkably enlightened where his dealings with the chiefs were concerned, and if he tended to paternalism, he also advocated reason and forbearance, matched firmness with fairness and a willingness to listen. At a time when the growing divide with the Lowlands was polarizing attitudes, and in the febrile climate following Dundee's rebellion, his was the voice of decency and restraint. In terms of the restored garrison at Inverlochy, his was a sound appointment.

One man who was far less restrained in his attitudes was General Hugh Mackay of Scourie. Younger than Hill, and born at the outset of the great civil wars, he was first commissioned in 1660 into Dumbarton's Foot (now Royal Scots) and saw action in Europe, serving the Venetians on Crete, before fighting under Turenne in the Low Countries. He was latterly instrumental in serving the Williamite faction, and was rewarded with the Commander-in-Chief's baton. That he should be out of love with the Jacobite clans is hardly surprising, given the humiliation of Killiecrankie and the deliverance of Dunkeld, which did not alter the cardinal fact that a royal army had been decisively routed. It was his contention, as Commander-in-Chief, that the Highlands could only be held down by the establishment of a series of strong points and major garrison forts. This included re-building Cromwell's old outpost on the shores of Loch Leven, which was furnished with all materials necessary for the building of a Citadel at Inverlochy, in order to better reduce the Highlanders, as well as to keep them in order.[8]

At the outset, the King was disinclined to authorize what would be a considerable capital project with significant implications for future revenue commitment. His attention was firmly focused on Flanders as the main cockpit of the titanic struggle with Louis XIV. If William was not a great general, he was a considerable strategist, stiffened by deep resolve and an iron will. Beating the French was his life's work, and if he did not see it achieved, this would not be from want of commitment. In this grand crusade, the military affairs of Scotland were of minor consequence. Nonetheless, the lessons of Killiecrankie were clear. The Tory clans, properly led and, God forbid, succoured by the French, could continue to pose a major threat. This threat must, for the stability of the regime, be eliminated. This is not to say that his attitude was coloured by the contagion of the *mi run mor nan Gal*. He was indifferent, not hateful. During his absences abroad he left Queen Mary a fairly free hand and she, as a Stuart, retained some vestige of matriarchal care for her wayward clan subjects.

That the threat was still potent was illustrated by the ill-conceived rising orchestrated by Colonel Cannon and Alexander Buchan. That this was something of a damp squib, brushed aside by Livingstone's bold charge at Cromdale, did not detract from the sense of renewed alarm.[9] Far more serious events were astir in Ireland, and the King was obliged to concede to the merits of Mackay's plan. The construction of a new fort at Inverlochy had already been mooted by the Convention Parliament in July, 1689: 'It is believed that it will the sooner be more effectuate, by reason of some Remains of Fortification that yet continue there, since the time the English were in those Parts and made Inverlochy the chief garrison, and headquarters in all those Highlands, which kept all the savage inhabitants in those countries in great awe, and forc'd them to live regularly, as their Lowland neighbours used to do.'[10] This initial proposal liked not and it was not until the spur of fresh troubles in Ireland added a sense of urgency that the expenditure involved received the royal seal of approval.

Colonel John Hill was no stranger to Lochaber: as a Major he had served in Monck's original garrison. He had also served with some steadfastness in the preceding civil wars and brought this quality, together with common sense and fairness to his responsibilities amongst the clans. It would not be too far fetched to liken his attitude to that of a Victorian District Officer stationed amongst the hill tribes of the north-west frontier, a stern but honorable approach, laced with a measure of compassion and a penchant for conversion. Hill, like so many other former Cromwellians, found himself something of an anachronism at the Restoration; but Monck, who had made the transition to Royalist with admirable élan, and secured his elevation to his Dukedom of Albemarle, may have been influential in securing his loyal subordinate a position in Ireland. Hill became a married man, a father of two unmarried daughters and, latterly a widower.

For three decades he remained in regular if undistinguished service across the Irish Sea, rising to become Constable of Belfast, a city he sustained against Jacobite forces after the Revolution of 1688, even emptying his own slender purse to buy off some of the wilder elements. That he might hope, even in his sixties, for some fitting reward was not unnatural, and the city fathers wrote a glowing testimonial '... he did appear zealous for the interest of their now Majesties King William and Queen Mary, in giving advice and direction to the inhabitants how to behave themselves with the enemy ... .'[11] The Burghers had good cause to be grateful to Hill, but their gratitude did not extend to reimbursing him! Nonetheless, he was able to use this favourable reference as a calling card to those now in authority, and remind them that, despite his years, he retained sufficient vigour for a fighting command. And who indeed was better qualified to act as governor at Inverlochy? None presently in service could demonstrate such sound credentials.

From his lodgings in the Scottish capital, Hill maintained his career offensive, penning his observations on the state of the Highlands and the best mode of governance and, in truth, he was almost certainly the best man for the job. Key figures such as Lochiel would remember him with approbation, and the overall situation in Lochaber had changed but little in the intervening years. He pointed out that the temperament of the chiefs was such that they were motivated more by local self-interest and pride than by the wider political context, and that, should the French be able to land forces unopposed, the threat from the west could become very potent indeed. The potency of that threat would be amply demonstrated in 1745 – 1746, when a Highland army, barely more than a strong brigade, could march from Glenfinnan to Derby, routing a Government army and then march back they way they had come, brushing aside their pursuers and trouncing another army at Falkirk. As the weeks passed and spring followed winter, Hill was still in correspondence but without his commission or any sign of it. He was not ignored, but neither was he advanced. These were anxious weeks for an old man with dependent daughters, no trade but his sword, and no fortune to sustain his old age.

Amongst those who Hill might count upon as supporters he could name the Secretary of State for Scotland,[12] George Melville, fourth Baron, first Earl Melville, and George MacKenzie, Viscount Tarbat and first Earl of Cromartie. Melville had assisted Monmouth in his suppression of Conventicles, but showed distinct moderation. His Whiggish leanings drew down a dangerous taint of complicity with the Rye House plotters[13] in 1683 and he was obliged, with his son, to decamp swiftly to the Netherlands. He returned with William and Mary, being useful in the decision of the Convention Parliament to offer them the crown of Scotland, a usefulness that procured him his high office after 1689. His pronounced Whiggish sentiment stood him in good stead and procured lucrative offices for his son, the earl of Leven, but his rise naturally attracted jealous enemies: Grey John, Argyll, the powerful pairing of the Dalrymples father and son, the Marquis of Annandale and William Carstares, the King's chaplain. Though Dundee's rebellion had achieved nothing, the romance of Killiecrankie ensured that Jacobite sentiment remained strong, with a rash of clubs and cabals, some probably largely ineffectual, but a few, such as the 'Kiliecrankies' and the 'Club', exerting real influence.

Tarbat was an urbane and charming schemer, learned and highly-cultured and, though he affected indolence, was both capable and ambitious. He was, moreover, a Highlander, and understood the mentalities of the chiefs. He had served the Stuarts, though narrowly missing a fatal fall and was relieved of his offices in the wake of the Revolution. The same charm he had liberally employed to oil his path with the former regime was seamlessly applied to currying favour with the new. William was in need of good men and pragmatism, as ever, won the day. Melville had need of the MacKenzie, for both realised the speedy and effective bringing to heel of the rebel clans was their passport to continued success in office. Both were therefore pleased to hear from Colonel Hill, who appeared ideally suited to the task.

Both Melville and MacKenzie were of the wholly sensible opinion that any cash which is be provided to sweeten the chiefs defection from the House of Stuart should, rather than being freely disbursed as bribes, be spent buying out the reversions of the existing feudal superioritie, lifting this onerous burden from the backs of those further down the Highland social pyramid. Colonel Hill was to receive unexpected and perhaps not wholly welcome support from Grey John, who now threw his hat into the ring. The two men were mutually antipathetic. Hill, like most of his contemporaries, mistrusted Breadalbane, but the earl now suggested it should be he who was appointed (and placed in funds) to negotiate with the chiefs! For the moment William temporized. Breadalbane's scheme was entertained but un-funded; Mackay's demands for an iron fist were listened to but not acted upon, and John Hill was kept waiting.

With the pressure building in Ireland, events in the early summer of 1690 began to move in Mackay's and Hill's favour. The Rout of Cromdale was a resounding little victory, if insufficient recompense for Killiecrankie. With William busily engaged in his preparations for a major campaign in Ireland, it was a strategic necessity that the back door in Scotland be firmly closed. Mackay's scheme was favoured, Breadalbane temporarily frustrated, it looked as though the old Roundhead might yet have his day. If Hill could have foreseen what his appointment would entail, he might have been a deal less sanguine. The welcome news came whilst he was near Inverness staying with his old friend Forbes of Culloden. He was soon on his way to Inverlochy to rendezvous with Mackay and oversee construction of the outpost he was to command.

On 14th May, the convoy sailed from Greenock for Loch Leven. The ships carried men and materials, some eight companies of foot. Mackay was planning to march a much larger force, some 7,000 strong, into Lochaber to consolidate the Government's grip, and by 3rd July, the juncture was finally affected – work on the new fort could proceed. The old Cromwellian citadel had been thrown up by the mouth of the River Nevis, south of the site of the original medieval castle,[14] and Mackay found he did not much care for the location: 'The situation of the old fort did not please me, being commanded from a near hill, but I could not change it, there being none else to fit.'[15] This being the case, he set to work with a will, and the shell of the new strong-point was thrown up in less than a fortnight: 'In eleven days I got it at its full height, the matter of twenty feet from the bottom of the fosse, pallisaded round, with a 'chemin couvert' [16] and glacis, a perfect defence.'[17] In plan, the new works markedly resembled the old,[18] the enceinte being formed by an irregular pentagon, finished with a triangular bastion at the south east and four lesser, two-pointed bastions forming each of the remaining corners. Midway along the southern elevation the main gate was protected by a three-cornered ravelin, with a sallyport through the north wall, possibly a Cromwellian survivor.[19] To the north the works were flanked by the miry ground leading to the river, whilst the west faced the expanse of Loch Linnhe. The additional ground works were added to the south and east where an approach was practicable.

John Hill would have no difficulty in recognizing the fort in its refurbished form. It seems likely that the destruction by the clans in 1661 may have been a less thorough slighting than may be imagined, and that substantial traces remained. Finished with twelve pieces of ordnance borrowed from the naval escort, the fort was certainly defensible. It was, however, still somewhat makeshift, an earthen redoubt topped by timber palings, devoid of masonry and any internal structures. The garrison was accommodated under canvas, not perhaps an undue hardship in summer but a wholly insufficient expedient for a grim Lochaber winter. Hill was to find his governorship a great trial, ignored by a parsimonious administration and beset by difficulties. If his garrison did not suffer from enemy action, want and disease stalked the lines and ensured the new graveyard with regularly furnished with new arrivals. Supplies of wood to build barrack piles did arrive but no nails were sent; the winter clothing Mackay had requested did not arrive. The companies of Highland irregulars, Menzies' and Balnagowan's were quickly thinned by a rash of desertions, and rumblings of mutiny hung in the air like gathering storm clouds.

Mackay did his best to support Hill, but supply, arrears of pay, lack of materials and the indifferent quality of the troops sent out would dog the old man's difficult tenure. Already, with the works scarce complete, the Lowland companies of the Cameronians, orchestrated by their vociferous preacher,[20] and disheartened as they were destined to remain, were muttering. The fort was only intended to hold a single company of foot, and when Mackay marched, Hill was left with a garrison comprising Highlanders, including four companies from Argyll's. It was a most difficult and inauspicious beginning. When the King, from Waterford, finally authorized the raising of Hill's new regiment, this was a rather hurried compromise, the first drafts being mustered from the rump of Glencairn and Kenmure's. This was inauspicious as the latter had been the first to give ground at Killiecrankie. Winter brought hardship, despair, desertion and death from sickness. Hill himself was gravely ill, and likely to join the swelling muster in the cemetery. By a supreme effort of will he kept going, trying, by superb example to hold his tatterdemalion garrison together – an exhausting and thankless task. Colonel John Hill was one servant of the Crown who thoroughly earned his meagre stipend, his expenses from Belfast still outstanding, in the amount of some £400, a very considerable sum to a man without private means.

Such dire neglect was no fault of the acerbic Mackay, who, before he handed over his baton, had written to the Duke of Hamilton with the clear assertion that the fort was, ' ... the most important in the kingdom at present, and that which at length will make such as would sell their credit or service at such a dear rate to the King of no greater use, nor more necessary to him, than a Lothian or Fife laird ...it [must] by no means neglected though other things should be postponed.'[21] The General was undoubtedly thinking of Breadalbane when he referred so dismissively to those seeking to exploit the situation. Grey John was no partisan of Hill's; the fort at Inverlochy did not suit his purposes, either in the short or longer term. His principal seat was the formidable bastion of Kilchurn, the hold originally built at the northern end of Lochawe by his ancestor Sir Colin. It was to here Grey John had cannily retired whilst the events of the Glorious Revolution and Dundee's rising unfolded, disabled, as he blandly asserted, by a persistent attack of gout. His contemporaries will have construed this according to their prejudices yet Kilchurn was not merely a fortified residence but a major plank in his own scheme for policing the glens. He had earlier mooted the notion of a full battalion of clan levies as a form of tribal police commanded, unsurprisingly, by himself as Colonel, with a suitable nominee to lead in the field. To his end he had begun converting Kilchurn into a garrison fort, adding a new barrack pile along the northern internal elevation.[22] That this grand design should be thus thwarted, did not like at all.

GREY JOHN AND THE TREATY

If Hill was experiencing constant difficulties of supply and muster, he was at least not overly-troubled with partisan activity. Colonel Cannon was still skulking though to little effect. The loser at Cromdale had little hope of raising another following, though Glengarry was notoriously entertaining King James' agent, Sir George Barclay, at his seat barely a score of miles from the walls of Hill's fort. This was probably mere bravado, for there was no sign of any resurgence or hint of aid from France. If the chiefs were quiescent, they were not yet ready to bend the knee to William of Orange; they retained an air of truculent neutrality. For all of Hill's fair dealing, none of the chiefs had submitted; stubborn pride and opportunism kept them at home. A few men of middle rank, including John MacDonald, tacksman of Atriochtan, had come in, seeking letters of protection. These Hill had been pleased to issue, and though they did not bind those above, nor compromise their honour, this was evidence of a certain level of realpolitik amongst those of middling sort. One surprising caller was young Keppoch, who suggested to the governor that the administration, by distributing largesse, might win over some of the key names, whose authority would then serve to sway the rest. Hill was indefatigable in maintaining his correspondence, and he placed particular reliance upon Tarbat, who, as he in turn wrote to the King, knew precisely where the investment should be made:

> One thing all the clans desire which is as much to your advantage as theirs, which is that these [feudal] superiorities be bought from the Highland lords, so that [the chiefs] may hold their estates immediately of you; and having them as immediate vassals, keeping a little garrison in Lochaber, and a man of ability, being no Highlander, to be your lieutenant-governor there, you will indeed be master of the Highlands as ever King of Scotland was.

This was extremely sound advice. For as long as the lesser gentry were vassals of the magnates, they would be bound to respond to their summons, and the great men of the Tory clans would always have recourse to an available pool of manpower. Remove that obligation and ensure these men owed allegiance direct to the British Crown and the potential was vastly diminished. Such a step would also decrease factionalism and the propensity for inter-clan feuding, which, as the Campbell/MacLean fracas had shown, remained latent.

Mackay had made no secret of his disdain for Grey John, an antipathy which Hill shared. He was just that sort of local magnate whose influence could be at best duplicitous if not wholly pernicious, and he was nothing if not constant in his relentless ambition.[23]

Now Grey John was back on the offensive. If he could seize the initiative and resurrect his scheme for buying off the chiefs and suborning their loyalties, then the fort at Inverlochy might be made redundant. It might yet be Campbell militia which patrolled the Highlands. Tarbat's proposals held nothing but impoverishment for Breadalbane. If he was shorn of his feudal superiorities then his local power base was infinitely diminished – that would not do at all. For all his trimming, Grey John was no fool; he it was who had first, in this 'Proposals Concerning the Highlanders,'[24] suggested to the King that troublesome clansmen would do well in red coats – a suggestion that would have to wait for over half a century to mature. He knew the chiefs and their following. He understood the whirlpool of loyalties and ancient feuds to a degree no Lowlander could ever hope to emulate.

By the spring of 1691, when it was obvious that the founding of the fort at Inverlochy had no produced any dramatic wave of capitulations, Grey John effortlessly moved onto the offensive. He journeyed to London and offered his advices to Queen Mary, who had full capacity whilst William campaigned in Flanders. The Queen and Council were sufficiently impressed to refer the proposal to Parliament, which voted funds accordingly, not the whopping £20,000 Grey John requested but some £8,000 less – still a very sizeable sum. With the coin ringing sweetly in his coffers, Breadalbane returned to the Highlands, summoning the chiefs to a conference at his castle of Achallader. This was an interesting choice, as the place had received the hostile intentions of the Tory clans during the rising, and had, at least in part, been slighted. Perhaps Grey John felt the chiefs might find this partial ruin more congenial than grim-faced Kilchurn, too potent a symbol of Campbell might.

Hill was effectively by-passed, to his fury and chagrin. To a conscientious officer, loyal and untainted by historic leanings and partisanship, such dealings were deeply offensive and threatened to undo the work he was so patiently building. This was the very opposite of what he and Tarbat proposed: far from curbing the magnatial powers of the great chiefs, such unrestrained brokering, funded from the common purse, could only add luster to 'King' Campbell's crown. This, of course, was precisely what Grey John had in mind when the conference convened on 30th June. If Hill had severe doubts over Breadalbane's probity, the Tory clans hated him with deeply instilled venom. He was the very symbol of Campbell hubris and avarice, one whose lands and fortune had, over generations, been built on the ruthless despoliation of lesser names. His duplicity was plain: he flirted with the Jacobites in the Highlands but gushed loyalty in London. No man was less worthy of their trust.

On the other hand, the jingle of gold coin is a great seducer, and the chiefs were aware of their growing isolation. No prospect of hope came from the exiled court at St. Germain. Barclay and Cannon were active but could offer nothing. The Stuart cause had run out of credit, and there was no Bonny Dundee waiting in the wings to ignite the fire that might have burned so brightly in their collective breast before Killiecrankie. Thus Lochiel came to Achallader, as did Keppoch and Glengarry, MacLean of Duart, Stewart of Appin and MacIain of Glencoe. With them were two Jacobite officers, Barclay and General Thomas Buchan. The chiefs came, in not as penitents, but as free princes in their own glens, each with his tail of spirited household men, according to his rank. The pipes played, saffron and plaid blazed defiant in the early summer sun. Breadalbane stood uneasily if fluently astride two worlds. Like them he was monarch in his own glen, with pipers and bards aplenty to recite the deeds of Clan Diarmid. Indeed, as a Highland chief he was greater than any, having more acres and more strong keeps to his name. Yet he was also ostensibly a Whig grandee, with the King's gold in his vault and Parliament's authority in his pocket. He represented the new whilst retaining the trappings of the old. If the ironies of his situation struck him, he did not smile but applied the full fluency of his silvered tongue to win over these proud Gaels, hereditary enemies of all who bore his name.

THE MASTER OF STAIR

It was Charles II who is said to have remarked, with uncanny percipience, that there was no trouble arising in Scotland but that a Campbell or Dalrymple was behind it. Now both appeared to be in alliance, for Melville's sun had begun to set and his fellow Secretary John Dalrymple, latterly first Earl of Stair, was set to rise. John's father James, first Viscount Stair, was an accomplished Scottish jurist from South Ayrshire. His family had long association with the Reformation, even numbering medieval Lollards amongst their ancestors. He held a commission in the Bishops Wars, prior to beginning an academic career as professor of mathematics, logic, ethics and politics at the University of Glasgow. After a gilded tenure of seven years he transferred his energies and his brilliant mind to the law. He rose in the opinion and counsels of his contemporaries, being dispatched several times to negotiate with the exiled Charles II following the Regicide. Though he refused to take the oath of allegiance to the Commonwealth, his honesty and patent abilities impressed both Monck and Cromwell, and his refusal to trim did not act as a bar to his further advancement; indeed, it appeared Monck relied heavily on his good advices. He did not lose out when the King came back but received a knighthood.

Again, when called upon to swear to the unlawfulness of the Covenant, he demurred. Though Charles valued him highly enough to propose a compromise form of the oath. He subsequently acted as a commissioner when the matter of Union was raised in 1670. In January 1671, he was appointed as Lord President of the Court of Session;[25] he also sat as MP for Wigtonshire and was a constant voice for moderation during the persecutions of Lauderdale's administration. He was unpopular with James, Duke of York, and was barred from the chancellorship, which would otherwise certainly have been his. His eclipse was not wasted, for he used the time of his disfavour to complete a seminal work on the Scottish legal system. Finding himself persecuted through allegations leveled against his wife, he wisely withdrew to voluntary exile in the Netherlands. He may have had some involvement with Argyll's failed bid, and proceedings were begun but discontinued. His son the Master of Stair had smoothed relations with James and succeeded the moderate Tarbat as Lord Advocate.[26] A new star was rising.

John Dalrymple had been one of Argyll's defence team when he faced an accusation of treason in 1681. He was as intellectually gifted as his father, and his ambition was not limited by scruple. He had none of his parent's reforming zeal and appears to have derided both Covenanter and Papist alike, urbane, fastidious and relentless. He did not lack moral or physical courage, though he despised Dundee and his Highland following. To such a man as Stair who, until his dying day was to prove a great and untiring champion of the Union, (which he would prefer to see as his life's work) the Highlanders, with their backwardness and outlandish posturing, were an obstacle to progress – a race of Hottentots who must be brought onto reservations or disposed of. He would never understand why his name would become inextricably linked to the Massacre of Glencoe or why its shadow would haunt him to the grave.[27] The MacDonalds of Glencoe, who were to become the focus of his very concentrated hatred, were a tribe of mindless savages, barbarians and thieves whose removal was entirely fitting in a civilized society. With this sentiment, it has to be said, most of his Lowland contemporaries would have heartily concurred.

In the course of his seemingly inexorable rise, he made few friends and very many enemies. His conceit was such he did not require the approbation or amity of lesser men. His experiences under James II when he had suffered Dundee's malice, twice being imprisoned, offended his dignity and fastidiousness and confirmed his contempt for those who espoused factionalism. Despite his difficult beginning, he won the King's favour and was elevated to high office. He had no love of conventicles any more than he felt for the Mass, his lack of bigotry and penchant for expediency won him few friends on either side of the religious divide. His portrait, by Sir John de Medina, shows a cultured and unswerving gaze, and not unattractive features; his intelligence is plain and there is no hint of humour or self-deprecation though he was perfectly capable of both. When William of Orange landed and the last Stuart king fled, Dalrymple moved with oiled precision to secure his own place and ease the passage of his new employer, neatly sidestepping his swelling cabal of opponents who had hoped to unseat him through the taint of Jacobitism. As ever, he was ahead of them.

It was due to his influence and guidance that the Scots' Parliament offered the crown to William and Mary, and talk of Union arose. Nothing at this stage transpired, but the cornerstone of his longer-term manifesto was laid down, and, to give Stair credit, he never subsequently wavered from that objective. He emerges with little credit from the business of Glencoe, yet his influence overall was by no means wholly pernicious, and we must view his conduct towards the MacIains in the light of what he perceived as high purpose. It was obvious that the Highland problem would have to be resolved before Union could be accomplished. The English, perhaps even less than the Lowland Scots, would not be anxious to welcome a motley of savages into this wider and emerging polity. There was no longer a place for the Highland clans and a lasting, not so say final, solution for their continued intransigence would have to be found.

William, it has to be said, had shown scant enthusiasm for his and the Queen's northern realm; it was the Scottish commissioners who travelled to London for the coronation ceremony. Even this truncated ceremony was not without incident when the King demurred from that clause in the oath requiring him to 'root out all heretics etc.' Dalrymple was immediately on hand, not to say on cue, with a bland reassurance. Soon he was both Privy Councilor and, again, Lord

Advocate; he was omnipresent and indispensable, the King's adviser on all matters pertaining to Scotland. In January 1691 he had been appointed as Joint Secretary with Melville; in reality' the latter was now second fiddle, a cypher. For the moment, of course, responsibility for the unsatisfactory state of affairs north of the Highland Line could be laid firmly at Melville's door. The cost of the standing garrison was considerable and the troops could, in the King's view, be more gain-fully employed fighting in the real war across the North Sea.

From February, the shape of royal policy begins to emerge, clothed in the language of avuncular reason. Undoubtedly formed by Stair, it mixes carrot and stick:

> The King desires peace and concord amongst his subjects, those who have wandered may rejoin the flock without reprisal but, [and this was to be significant] … if any continue incorrigible or so foolish as to be imposed upon by vain suggestions to make their native country the stage of war and desolation, it will be your care [Melville's] to discover their designs and secure such persons that they be not in a capacity to ruin themselves and others.[28]

Velvet language as yet, but the germ of threat emerges. The King has been patient, but patience is finite, and vacillation is no longer an option. Given the expense of maintaining forces in the Highlands, and given that it was viewed as a part of the nation's consider-able outlay on the French Wars, this was inevitable. Stair would be concerned to ensure that any censure remained with Melville – yes-terday's man – whilst any laurels accrued to him. The Master was on the rise; patience and compassion were fripperies he could ill afford.

Behind Stair's careful use of words lay a rather starker reality: William was indeed running out of patience the antics of a bunch of clansmen were making a fool out of him in front of the rulers of Europe. It was derision he could not bear to weather, as such a per-ceived failing diminished his credentials as arch-opponent of French imperialism – something which Stair was well aware of. If Melville felt insecure, tidings of mutinous murmurings reached him from Sir Thomas Livingstone, now C-in-C Scotland. Hill was dangerously ill again that winter, the rigours of his thankless office and a Highland winter having taken their combined toll. Through sheer willpower the old man pulled through, never abandoning his absolute devotion to duty.

Spring brought little relief; supplies continued to be meager and tardy. Livingstone was pressing for a series of active patrols against the recalcitrant chiefs (an unhelpful command, which Hill wisely ignored) and, of course, Grey John was back in the game. In failing to heed the C in C's orders, Hill had an unexpected ally in Stair, alarmed at the cost of further alarums whilst the Treasury was emptied to finance the war in Flanders, a war that was progressing slowly and generally unfavourably. Whilst Breadalbane prepared for his summit at Achallader, Hill, somewhat recovered in the spring again, wrote to Melville, intimating he had disdained to use force, as his superior had urged, but had instead drafted a form of oath which he felt would, in time, be acceptable to the clan chiefs as more tacksmen came in to swear:

> I hope I have taken the better way, which is easier, viz., I sent them the form of a very strict oath, and that withal a draft of one much easier, which is never to take up arms against King William and Queen Mary and their Government, nor to suffer any of their friends, men, tenants and servants to take up arms ... [29]

This was a reasoned and logical approach, wearing down the prickly sensibilities of the great chiefs and allowing reason and moderation to sway the outcome; but Hill, in his crumbling and half-starved garrison fort, did not have £12,000 in gold to bargain with. In Grey John's case, the additional constraint of integrity did not obtain. Precisely what did transpire after 30th June in the discussions held in the smoke-damaged keep at Achallader is not entirely clear, perhaps, given the disposition and propensities of the facilitator, this is scarcely to be wondered at. Breadalbane's own account was that he was able to procure a truce with the chiefs to endure until October. During the intervening months he would ensure the monies to be paid to them were disbursed accordingly. The Jacobite officers would be furnished with safe-conducts to permit them to travel to the exiled court and solicit James' acquiescence.

THE OATH OF ALLEGIANCE

The settlement offered was generous to the chiefs. They would receive their reward based upon a suspension of hostilities rather than a binding oath of allegiance to the crown. Keppoch concurred, though Glengarry stormed off, not out of loyalty to the Stuarts but in a fury that his share of the bribe was less than he had anticipated. He began fortifying his house, digging ditches, outworks and planting palisades. Lochiel, however, did also sign (he and Grey John were in fact related through the former's mother – a Glenorchy Campbell).

Breadalbane was loath to publicly admit that his treaty was fatally flawed, in that the chiefs were agreeing to a temporary truce only and that they remained bound by the oaths they had previously sworn to James, at Dalcomera and Blair Castle. Parliament's gold was buying a respite, not a solution. Until they were released by the exiled Stuart they were not bound to affirm any lasting and binding commitment to William and Mary. Such an outcome would have done little to increase Breadalbane's standing had it become known; £12,000 would be expected to buy a good deal more than a few paltry months grace. In this perhaps he could have been misjudged. The act of bribery was subtly conceived and gold is always a great persuader. Bringing Lochiel on-side was a master-stroke, and in the circumstances, Grey John probably did as well as any man might.

One who was most emphatically excluded from the rising edifice of Breadalbane's Achallader Treaty was MacIain of Glencoe. He had attended, but no feelings of amity arose. Grey John specifically singled out Glencoe intimating that any monies paid would be handed over net of compensation for the clan's recent depredations. This put MacIain in an impossible situation, and high words followed. The chief dismissed Breadalbane as a schemer. The Government would forget the blood of redcoats spilt at Killiecrankie, but Campbell would be paid for his cows. Both were acts of war – there must be a full indemnity or none. He stormed out, cursing the hatred of Clan Diarmid. In part this can have come as no surprise, he cannot have expected Breadalbane to easily overlook the rape of his glens, the ruin of his kin. He would have done better to have trimmed; though, as Grey John would have calculated, this would have been too great an affront to his dignity.

Such a quarrel and Glencoe's exclusion cannot have been accidental. Breadalbane was not the man to allow passion to cloud self-interest; on the face of it, his row with MacIain imperilled the success of his venture. No doubt he felt safe on counting on the avarice of the other chiefs to dispel any family sentiment. There is no suggestion that any of Clan Donald took up the quarrel, and so, if he gambled, he won. MacIain was now isolated from the rest and this was no random mischance. We have no record of Breadalbane's strategy; the realities of this were locked behind an inscrutable mask. Of all the MacDonalds, he had cause to hate Glencoe most: they had been a savage and rapacious thorn in the side of the Breadalbane Campbells for several generations. Pillage, rapine, slaughter and destruction followed them as night follows day. If this pestilential sept could be excluded from a general amnesty, kept aside, locked in their dark glen, then done away with to show the stick behind the carrot, then both his and the King's purposes might best be achieved. We may surmise, and it is no more than a theory, that the idea for the Massacre of Glencoe begins here.

In August, William III raised the tempo with a proclamation, drafted in Flanders and dated the 17th of that month. Those who had been under arms against the Government were required to swear an oath of allegiance, and this was no mild form of undertaking such as

John Hill had circulated:

> The persons who have been in arms before the time foresaid, and shall
> plead and take benefit of this our gracious indemnity, shall swear and sign
> the oath of allegiance to us by themselves, or the sheriff clerk subscribing
> for such as cannot write, and that before famous witnesses, betwixt and
> the first day of January next to come, [i.e. 1st January 1692] in presence of
> the lords of our Privy Council – or the sheriff – or their deputes – of the
> respective shires where any of the said persons live.[30]

With the stick came the carrot, taking up Tarbat's point and offering
to acquire the feudal superiorities, though this notable inducement
was played down when the notices were nailed up across the shires.
Only the threat remained; quite plainly any who failed to submit
would be outlawed and there was no mention of a need for any prior
consents. The matter was plain: submit, swear or face the consequences, and, whilst the latter were not defined, the clear implication
was that theses would surely be severe.

CHAPTER 5

Prelude: 'To Maul Them in the Long Cold Nights'

'This is by the Kings speciall command, for the good and safty of the Country, that these miscreants be cutt off root and branch.'

Major Duncanson's Order to Robert Campbell of Glenlyon
12th February 1692

'I hope the soldiers will not trouble the Government with prisoners …'

Sir John Dalrymple, Master of Stair writing to
Sir Thomas Livingstone C in C Scotland

' 'Atrocity' – An extremely wicked or cruel act, esp. one involving physical violence or injury.'

Oxford English Dictionary

INVERLOCHY

29th December 1691 was a miserable, cold and wintry day in the fort at Inverlochy. A drear wind, howling from the north-west whistled through Lochaber and beat upon the waters of Loch Linnhe, which shifted gunmetal grey beneath snow-laden skies. And snow there was, drifting against the palisades and filtering through every crevice. Sentries huddled in mute misery on the crude ramparts and doubtless, in the manner of sentinels down the years, cursed their lot. It was an unenviable one, and that of the governor, John Hill, his health uncertain, alone in his cold and Spartan quarters, little better. His command, so long sought, had proved a curse. That spring, recovering slowly from an earlier bout of the same illness that beset him now, he had written despondently to Tarbat:

> I find ill-wishers grow upon me ... and some great men. They say I am old, and would, I think, have me to reduce all the Highlands myself, which, if I could do, there would be as little need for them as there is for this garrison. I would his majesty would give me any other place where I could be serviceable to him and let some emulators take this, and then I might be quiet.[1]

Who these armchair strategists were he did not elaborate, but we can safely assume he had little time for Breadalbane or Stair. The governor was an honest man and a decent one who had striven against mighty obstacles: an indifferent and cynical administration and the truculence of the clans to bring order without bloodshed. At this point, mercifully, he did not fully comprehend what was to come.

He had probably not much liked the business of the oath – it smacked too much of the stick, whilst he preferred the patience of the carrot. He fervently believed the Highlands had never experienced better governance than in the days of the Protectorate, and, though the experiment in republicanism had not endured, it had for a while at least produced impartiality and order. The chiefs would fret under the fetters of an Anglo-Saxon invader, but they must grudgingly acknowledge the even-handed efficiency of his justice. Lochiel, particularly, was an active collaborator and on excellent terms with Monck. Unwelcome as the Cromwellian presence might have been, it did engender good Government, something missing from the Highlands since the fall of the Lordship. Discipline might be an unexpected intruder, but soon they learnt that being able to sleep in their beds without fear of throats being cut brought advantages. The fort at Inverlochy, whilst representing an unparalleled intrusion, was also a ready and profitable market for the Camerons.[2]

Restoration, whilst welcomed, brought an end to good governance. The clansmen might be monarchists, but their notion of monarchy was a weak central administration whose failings afforded them free rein. The execution and attainder of Argyll, whilst celebrated, did not bring about the hoped for demise of King Campbell, for there was an early recognition that control of the Highlands was best entrusted to strong local agents and the Campbells – as vigorously touted by Lord Lorne, the first earl's son – were the proven implement of crown authority. The civil wars had left a bitter legacy. MacColla's campaigns, though adding luster to his martial legend, had achieved little beyond the ruin of his name and the deaths of thousands. The harryings of Argyll had been merciless and savage. Hill was aware he now commanded in a very different climate to that which he had obtained under the Commonwealth. Schemers like Grey John undermined his authority, and the chiefs, bound by their undertakings to James, were reluctant to come in. His patience would bring rewards; already, lesser tacksmen of Glencoe like Inverrigan and Achtriachtan carried his letters of protection in their pouches.[3] His policy was more that of Monck than Mackay.[4]

Toward dusk he found he had a visitor, none other than MacIain of Glencoe, with a slew of nimble ghilllies trotting behind his garron. It was over a generation since Hill had last seen the chief of Clan Iain Abrach, but the old man was still physically impressive, his great height and breadth undiminished and his bearing which was as proudly erect as ever. His mane of hair and famous mustachios might now be silvered, and the strong face lined, but he was every inch the epitome of the Highland chief, monarch in his own glen and not in the habit of bowing. Now, in this grim winter's dusk, the MacDonald announced he was attending to swear the oath. In one breath, the Colonel's spirits must have leapt to see this, most recalcitrant of Gaels, now ready to bend the knee – any joy tempered by irritation that MacIain was speaking to the wrong man. Did he not realise how close the deadline? Did he not understand the consequences of delay and did he not comprehend that the oath must, as plainly advertised, be sworn in front of a sheriff? A civil, not a military appointment, and the nearest courthouse was at Inveraray. This was the rub, of course: MacIain would not willingly journey to the Lion's den. Last time he had done so was as a prisoner and he had removed himself before, in the grim parlance of the day 'his neck felt the weight of his boots'. Inverary was the Campbell capital, a Lowland bastide thrown up in the Highlands, proof in stone and mortar that King Campbell had conquered Kintyre and Argyll.

Whilst Hill plainly understood MacIain's dilemma, he also comprehended – perhaps even more plainly – the peril in which the chief and his people now stood, and was aware of the mutterings, the desire to apply fire and sword. The only remedy Hill could conceive was that the MacDonald must swallow both pride and apprehension and get to Inverary as quickly as possible, before the year's end. This would, given the vile weather and the state of communications, be no easy matter. The best the old soldier could do was to write a letter of commendation to the Sheriff-Depute, Sir Colin Campbell of Ardkinglas. Hill had considerable respect for Ardkinglas, whom he knew to be an honest and reasonable man, a competent and conscientious law-officer. As his pen scratched across the cold parchment in the darkening austerity of his office, Hill entreated the sheriff to receive a lost sheep – one who had attempted to take the oath within the stipulated time but might yet fail due to his ignorance of the full import of the proclamation. He entreated that MacIain's submission be accepted even though he might be a day or two late. Thus the governor, quite sensibly, set more store by the fact of MacIain's submission than by the absolute technicalities of the date. Others would prove less accommodating.

Above: 1. The Coire Gabhail – it was up this steep defile that the MacDonalds' of Glencoe are alleged to have driven stolen cattle. The narrow path is steep and precipitous, even allowing for a smaller, hardier and more nimble breed of cattle, the likelihood seems remote.

Right: 2. A view over the landscape of the upper glen; harsh upland terrain of bog and scree, ground out over millennia by the glaciers; a landscape of legend and myth.

Left: 3. The main road now traverses the glen, otherwise little has changed; over this landscape in the teeth of the biting blizzard dazed survivors fled. That exhaustion and exposure should take their toll is hardly to be wondered at.

Below: 4. This is the glen in spring, where but a few moments before a warming sun had been shining, until sleet laden showers chased between the lines of mountains, the land reverting to the chill and frozen winds of winter.

Right: 5. The nineteenth-century shepherd's bothy is dwarfed by the steep slopes behind. Basic as such dwellings are, they represent a significant increase in levels of comfort and sanitation from the altogether cruder crofts that would form the townships in 1692. No trace of these now remains.

Below: 6. The ostensible cairn upon which each successive chief of MacDonald of Glencoe was installed.

7. A further view of the approach to the **Coire Gabhail** amidst the grandeur of the 'Three Sisters', Stob Coire Nan Lochan stands behind. The author has, in the past, seen the elusive wildcat on these slopes.

8. The defile leading to Coire Gabhail – the landscape has barely changed since the late seventeenth century.

Right: 9. A view across the placid waters of Loch Achtriachtan; the township of that name has disappeared. On the night of the massacre it was a scene of horror.

Below: 10. The Devil's Staircase – modern signpost at the Glencoe end.

11. The Glencoe end of the Devil's Staircase – it was down this precipitous pathway that Hamilton's weary companies trudged through the fierce snow.

12. The rampart of mountains on either flank provide the glen with its topographical identity and protected the MacDonalds as surely as fortress walls; but walls also contain as well as shelter and trap fugitives like driven game.

13. Light thickens in snow-laden air, such conditions would mirror those that obtained the day preceding the night of the Massacre.

14. Eilean Munde – the traditional resting ground of the chiefs of Clan Iain Abrach; the chapel is long decayed, the atmosphere, however, survives intact!

15. The Gateway to Fort William – this no longer stands where once stood the fort but has been moved to form an impressive entrance to the town cemetery.

16. The inscription on the gate: 'This arch was erected in 1690 over the main entrance to the Fort and re-erected here in 1896 where Sir Allan Cameron of Erracht in 1793, raised the 79th or Cameron Highlanders, a Regiment which distinguished itself on many a hard fought field for King and Country'. Thus, by donning a red coat the recalcitrant rebel becomes the cutting edge of Empire.

17. Rannoch Moor – storm clouds gather; a view the Glen Orchy Campbells would doubtless have been familiar with, as attackers and cattle disappeared from sight.

18. The approach looking over the Black Mount, home to the MacDonalds, summer shielings. Now only the mournful cry of the curlew and the roar of traffic on the highway disturbs the calm.

19. The lower ground looking eastwards up the glen; here were the townships, winter grazing and cultivation.

20. Inverlochy Castle – originally a Comyn hold in the thirteenth century, the castle featured in the action at the Battle of Inverlochy in 1645, the MacDonalds' most spectacular and bloody success against their rivals Clan Campbell. Argyll himself wisely, if uninspiringly, watched the action from his galley and sailed serenely clear of the wrack of his army; the bulk was less fortunate.

21. The Meeting of the Waters Glencoe – spectacular and wildly romantic the tumbling waters collide, cold and clear.

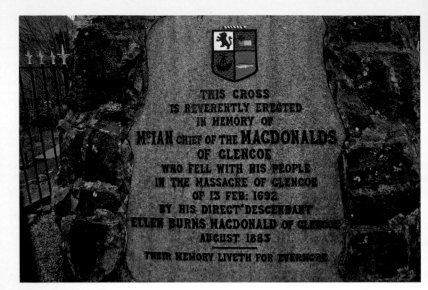

22. Memorial by the present Glencoe village: 'This cross is reverently erected in memory of McIain Chief of the MacDonalds of Glencoe who fell with his people in the Massacre of Glencoe of 13th February: 1692 by his direct descendant Ellen Burns MacDonald of Glencoe August 1883 – Their Memory Liveth For Evermore'.

23. The memorial with the glen behind. This is really the only feature to commemorate the massacre and a simple annual remembrance is held on the anniversary.

24. Pap of Glencoe viewed looking northwards from the Monument.

25. Glencoe viewed from the area of the Monument.

Sir Thomas Livingstone was a disciple of Mackay's insofar as he favoured punitive action. He had little time for Breadalbane's schemes, wished to slight Glengarry's impudent works and bring the recalcitrant chiefs to heel by main force. Hill had wisely turned a deaf ear to this bluster – Monck had never suffered a Killiecrankie! During the summer of 1691, Stair had been content to allow Grey John's plots to bear fruit; bribery was cheaper and more reliable than military force. At this juncture Sir John was happy to work in partnership with Breadalbane. At best this was a marriage of convenience, two grasping pragmatists who recognise a mutuality of interest, which, however transient, coincides at a particular time. Grey John was indeed useful to the Master, for Stair had no real grasp of matters in the Highlands. He was a Lowlander and his first hand knowledge was confined to the unhappy experience of the Highland Host. These malcontents, skulking in their dark glens, were nonetheless a collective throwback to a bygone age, vain and foolish savages who did not possess sufficient wit to comprehend that history had passed them by. More tellingly, they represented everything Dalrymple detested. Their barbarous tongue, outlandish dress, propensities for tribal violence, their presumed Popery, perceived hubris and insularity offended him mightily. For a man who, had it not been for the events about to unfold, might best have been remembered as chief architect of the Union, they represented everything his fastidious logic rejected. We see, as the determination to inflict punishment hardens, he becomes almost obsessive in his desire to inflict harm upon the Tory clans, narrowing to a specific focus on MacDonald of Glencoe.

To what extent this policy was insidiously shaped by Grey John is uncertain, although, at the outset, his influence must have been considerable. And it was the Campbell who had so ostentatiously quarreled with MacIain, by excluding him from the Achallader accords, and thus immediately separated the Glencoe men from the rest, pushing clan Iain Abrach to the margin and singling them out. Dalrymple did not have sufficient knowledge of the topography to identify Glencoe as a suitable killing ground, only that here was one clan, small, isolated, self contained, and locked within the bowl of the glen, whose sheltering peaks might yet become tombstones.

During that febrile summer, however, Stair, moved more by a shortage of cash and the pressing needs of the endless war in Flanders, was obliged to rein in his Commander-in-Chief: 'His Majesty ordered me to write to you not to meddle with them [the clans] at present, for you know how little the Treasury can spare.' What Grey John had been anxious to keep hidden was the fact that the agreement reached at Achallader was nothing more than a cease-fire, and that the hard facts attendant upon a lasting solution – an oath of submission (subject to acquiescence by James) and the subsequent handing out of cash to the chiefs – were all missing. The report he delivered to the Queen in London and then, in person, to the King in Flanders painted an altogether rosier picture, suggesting a definite and lasting accord. This suited Stair's present purpose, and he was happy to lend his influential support. William was not troubled with the matter of James' dispensation.

Nor did the truce itself endure in the Highlands. Within weeks Glencoe MacDonalds, with Stewart of Appin, beat up craft carrying provisions to Inverlochy. Hill reacted with vigour, the guilty parties had barely settled to toast their success when they found themselves clapped in irons. Amongst the haul was Alasdair Og, MacIain's hot-tempered younger son. Had King William been in London, their fate might have been uncertain but Queen Mary, conscious of her ancestry, and the blood these mettlesome swashbucklers had shed for her father and grandfather and anxious to maintain the truce, ordered their early release. Hill might possibly have approved, but fortune, possibly in the form of Glengarry, was that August, to hand him a promising windfall – the true text of what had been agreed at Achallader and which had never reached the ears of King or Council. What was revealed was at best duplicitous and, at worst, treasonable.

'THE PRIVATE ARTICLES'

Grey John's treaty was hedged with a handspan of private caveats:
• Should the Jacobites invade, or if there was a domestic insurgency, the chiefs were released – the agreement was void.
• If King James refused to release them from their earlier obligation the treaty would lapse.
• Two of James' agents were to be granted passage to St. Germain to seek the necessary consent.
• If the Williamites intervened in Flanders then all the chiefs present, including Breadalbane, would declare for James.
• That if William and Mary should refuse these terms then Grey John would lead a thousand Campbell broadswords beneath King James' banner.[5]

Obviously, the joint monarchs could not refuse the terms, as they had not seen them. Breadalbane's conduct was worse than improper, devious or deceitful, it was clearly seditious. Hill wasted no time in penning furious correspondence to the Duke of Hamilton, who immediately acquainted the Privy Council with the facts of Grey John's nefarious conduct. Surprisingly, this received corroboration from the Earl of Kintore, who had had separate confirmation from another source. The Council wrote indignantly to the King. Hamilton was no lover of either Breadalbane or Stair and such an opportunity was not to be missed. Grey John, ably informed of domestic matters by his agent and lawyer Colin Campbell of Carwhin, took fright, strenuously spluttering outraged denials. Stair, as ever was unruffled; the Campbell still had his uses and keeping the chiefs in line was the current policy objective. Correspondence then passed between Grey John and Colonel Hill; the former hurt and indignant, the latter firm and unrepentant. By the autumn the spat had blown itself out – William was not minded to concern himself over Breadalbane's double-dealing. The ultimatum to the chiefs had already been issued though the original draft included the assurance that the £12,000 sterling would be disbursed to buy out feudal reversions. Of individual cash incentives to the chiefs themselves, nothing more was said.

At this point the King appeared magnanimous. Even MacIain and Achtriachtan were pardoned for the rather mysterious murder that had prompted the former's incarceration and daring escape from Inverary. One key player yet to be consulted was James, lately King of England and Scotland. Two Jacobite officers, Sir George Barclay and Duncan Menzies of Fornooth, had been nominated to seek the exiled Stuart's instructions. After some delays, both envoys were on their way by high summer. John Prebble, no royalist, apportions a measure of the blame for Glencoe upon James. His prevarication and obstinacy, which, as he slipped into old age, grew more pronounced, proved a significant barrier. Summer turned to autumn and the 1st January deadline grew ever closer.

For John Hill, ageing and ailing, the cynicism of his superiors was a constant challenge. The old Cromwellian might have seen much of the world, yet he remained an idealist, committed to the notion of doing the Lord's work in a patient and honest manner. If Hill was denied greatness, he never lacked for decency. Conviction, faith and the obligation of service kept him striving, however high the odds mounted. That his efforts would be spurned, his honour besmirched and his humanity compromised might have been factors a less punctilious man could have foreseen. Hill could not. In theory, his burden had been eased by the appointment of a deputy, James Hamilton, who was further appointed as Lieutenant Colonel to Hill's regiment. Hamilton's antecedents are unsure, but it appears he owed his current roles to the Master's influence, and that there was a deeper obligation on his part occasioned by some prior disreputable conduct.[6]

This is all very vague, but Hamilton was everything Hill was not, and we may safely surmise the Governor found the arrival of a subordinate far less of a boon than might be anticipated. Hamilton emerges as ambitious and utterly unscrupulous. Stair, with his keen perception, had divined that Hill was too upright a man to be his perfect creature, and that he required a more pliant ally at

26. Lochleven – the castle, which occupies an island site in a strategic position on the Edinburgh-Stirling-Perth axis, is associated most popularly with Mary Queen of Scots. It was strengthened by Robert I and David II. Originally more strongly placed than its contemporary remains would suggest: the water levels in the loch dropped considerably after canalisation works in the nineteenth century.

27. Dumbarton – this great hold atop its volcanic plug has an ancient lineage, being the capital of the Strathclyde Britons. It fell to the Norse and then came into the possession of the King of Scots, remaining a royal stronghold. Its importance declined after the close of the civil wars, but the defences were upgraded in the later period as a further deterrent to the Jacobites.

28. The Old Tolbooth, Edinburgh – the original gaol was built in 1480 and re-built some eighty years later, adjacent to the Signet Library. Many Highland chiefs would find themselves familiar with its interior, and it housed many celebrated prisoners before finally being demolished in 1817.

29. The Marquis of Montrose – James Graham, Marquis of Montrose (1612 – 1650), is regarded as a great commander of the civil wars. Though tactically brilliant, his failures of intelligence and reconnaissance led to near misses and eventual disaster. During his 'Year of Miracles', the clans moved to centre-stage in the greater struggle being waged throughout the Three Kingdoms.

30. The Execution of Montrose – after his final defeat at Carbisdale on 27th April 1650, the Marquis fled the ground and, after some days' wandering, unwisely accepted shelter from Neil MacLeod of Assynt. Ardvreck castle proved a 'deadly refuge' when MacLeod, in defiance of the accepted laws of hospitality, betrayed his guest. The jubilant Covenanters degraded their captive who maintained a quiet dignity throughout. Tried on 20th May he was hanged the day after, thus bringing to an end a dramatic and romantic career.

31. Glencoe – a nineteenth-century view of the glen. This was at the time when, the Clearance having effectively initiated a process of de-population. The romantic revival ushered in by Scott saw the remote Highlands transformed into a romantic landscape peopled by heroic figures of myth. As ever, the reality was somewhat different.

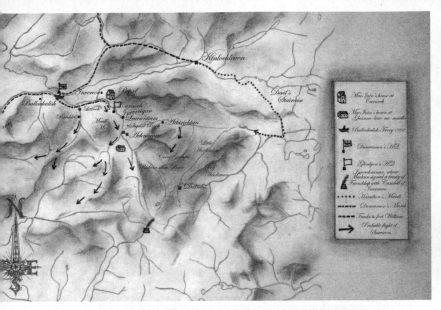

32. Map of Glencoe showing the topography of the glen: principal settlements, the routes by which the companies of Argyll's regiment approached on the morning of the massacre, and the escape routes taken by the survivors.

Inverlochy, one perhaps already indebted, whose previous 'lapse' ensured a willingness to atone through unquestioning compliance. Hamilton was careful to pay lip-service to Hill's seniority, but he frequently corresponded privately with Dalrymple – telling Stair what he assumed he wished to hear. He reported the regiment was in fine form, something of an overstatement as Hill's battalion remained under-strength, under-equipped, under-paid and under-fed, addicted to drink and desertion. As Secretary, Sir John would doubtless prefer to imagine the garrison as being ably mustered and 'battle-ready', a contrary view would vex, and thus was avoided.

As days shortened and winds quickened, growing fresh with the first intimations of snow along the line of peaks, the chiefs' faith in Grey John, never strong, began to dissipate. James had issued no dispensation; there was no sign of any cash, and Grey John's credibility, at best limited, began to ebb. Stair provided the troubled earl with weak assurances. Grey John was his tool, as was Hamilton; the duplicity of Achallader merely forced him deeper into the Master's clutches. The King was not presently disposed to disburse the promised bribes but, be assured, the cash was available. Winter began to close in on the Highlands; high ceilings were closed up, and clansmen clustered around their hearths in the townships. There was no word from France and consequently no oath taking. Achallader and any optimism the sham-treaty might have engendered vanished with the summer haze. It was a time of deep uncertainty.

One significant event occurred at the beginning of December. If the Highlanders missed its import this was perhaps unsurprising, but it brought a very significant shift in the political landscape, which was to set in train the events that led up to the Massacre. In that month Stair finally disposed of his rival and Joint Secretary Melville, and assumed sole responsibility. This was significant, for praise or censure would now be his alone; he could no longer deflect blame onto his fellow minister. Policy toward the chiefs could be labeled historically as Melville and, for as long as his lordship continued in office, the failure of inaction could be laid at his door. This happy escape was no longer available, and something had to be done. Nothing had been heard from the decaying exile at St. Germain, none of the chiefs had come in, and most remained under arms. Grey John's gambit had failed, his flawed initiative had run out of steam, compromised by and mired in its author's proven duplicity. As the pressure on Stair increased, so did his impatience with these recalcitrant savages impeding his rise. Contempt had matured into hate, a bitter bile-filled loathing for these Popish throwbacks, whose very existence was an affront to reason and progress. Patience was a luxury he could no longer afford.

It was not as if he had not been patient. As far back as June he had cautioned Breadalbane that the King's patience was not inexhaustible:

> If they [the chiefs] will be mad, before Lammas [1st August] they will repent it, for the army will be allowed to go into the Highlands, which some thirst so much for, and the frigates will attack them; but I have so much confidence of your character and capacity to let them see the ground they stand on, that I think these suppositions are vain.[7]

In September he had written in an equally reasonable tone: 'The best cure of all these matters is, that the chieftains do it [take the oath] as quickly as can be, which will take off the trials of suspicion against the rest.'[8] Two days later, having provided his assurance as to the availability of funds, the best evidence of sincerity was the bringing of the matter quickly to a conclusion: 'I hope your lordship shall not only keep them [the chiefs] from giving any offence but bring them to take the allegiance which they ought to do very cheerfully, for their lives and fortunes they have from their Majesties.'[9]

A GOOD MAULING

With the creeping chill of winter came a hardening of the Secretary's willingness to rely upon reason and persuasion. By December he was writing to Hamilton in more ominous tones, considering falling back upon Livingstone's earlier enthusiasm for punitive action: 'for the winter time is the only season in which we are sure the Highlanders cannot escape us, nor carry their wives, bairns and cattle to the mountains … .'[10] Given that the responsibility for resolving the Highland question now rested soley on Dalrymple and he could not afford to fail, it is not surprising, considering the apparent lack of progress and the failure of Breadalbane's scheme, that force might again arise as the preferred or indeed only option. This is still some distance from the expressed intention to destroy any single clan as an example. We must now enquire as to where this notion did in fact originate. Most likely it was not Stair's alone. His detailed knowledge of the clans was insufficient, that the axe should fall upon MacDonalds of Glencoe had to be the suggestion of another. Hamilton was equally poorly versed, if closer to the seat of the problem; besides, he was an instrument, not an advisor, his role was to do not to instigate. The concept had to come from Grey John. What man had greater motive to hate clan Iain Abrach, the sept so clearly excluded from the Achallader accord. The Master's correspondence to Breadalbane, penned on 2nd December, would clearly suggest some prior consideration.

Dalrymple focuses his anger against Clan Donald and Lochiel, though next day he appeared slightly mollified by assurances received from Tarbat that Glengarry was ready to come in:

> By the next I expect to hear either that these people are coming to your hand, or else your scheme for mauling them, for it will not delay … I am not changed as to the expediency of doing things by the easiest means and at leisure, but the madness of these people and their ungratefulness to you makes me plainly see that there is no reckoning on them, but 'delenda est

Carthago'. Yet who have accepted, and do take the oath, will be safe. But deserve no kindness ... *Therefore look on and you shall be satisfied of your revenge*[11] (author's emphasis).

This final phrase is significant, for it refers plainly to previous discussion and would imply some urging on Breadalbane's part, as well as showing that the Campbell is motivated by personal vindictiveness. Though the correspondence does not state against whom this was directed, MacIain, given what had gone before, has to be the prime candidate.

At the same juncture, the Secretary wrote to both Hill and Hamilton though his instructions are really being directed at the latter – enquiring whether this is the proper time to 'maul' the clans and what amount of force is required.[12] As far as we can tell Dalrymple, was proposing some form of general punitive action against all those who had not come in, equal to the ancient legal concept of Letters of Fire and Sword. A further incentive to move swiftly was the availability of forces. Hill's own regiment was at Inverlochy, though, guided by Hamilton's rosy reporting, Stair would perhaps have been mistaken if he viewed the battalion as a finely honed instrument of war. Argyll's regiment was also by the fort, their condition significantly better; Leven's was stationed in the Highland capital, and Buchan's was detailed to join with it. William had need of these reserves in Flanders and, if they were to be deployed to resolve domestic difficulties, then best it was done swiftly, so as not to try the King's patience.

There can be no attempt to absolve Stair from the horror that was to come, but his impatience can easily be comprehended. When the Achallader accord was entered into, it might be expected that the truce would swiftly lead to a settlement, a note of urgency significantly underlined by proclamation of the oath. He had manouvered relentlessly to attain his high office, unscrupulously undermining his rival Melville. Success brought with it a heavy burden: Williamite Government was established, but far from secure. The Jacobites in

Scotland had been confounded but not dealt with, the shadow of Killiecrankie still lingered. If the clans were to find another paladin such as Dundee then what might they accomplish, at a time when resources were diverted to Flanders, Stair's task was to secure the back door of the Highlands and, in December 1691, this was very far from certain. For the moment his ire was directed principally at Glengarry, 'that being the only popish clan in the kingdom, and it would have been popular to take severe courses with them'. With the final waning of the old year and no good news from Paris or the Highlands, Stair could now see no alternative but to engage in harsh measures. The warning order he sent to Livingstone during the first week in January was calmly explicit:

You know in general that those troops posted at Inverness and Inverlochy will be ordered to take in the house of Invergarry, and to destroy entirely the county of Lochaber, Lochiel's lands, Keppoch's, Glengarry's, Appin and Glencoe. If there be any opposition the troops [Leven's & Buchan's] will need to join; if not, they may act separately which will make the work shorter. I assure you their power shall be full enough, and I hope the soldiers will not trouble the Government with prisoners. The slighting the offered mercy, and depending still upon foreign assistance, will justify all the severity which can be used against those who can neither be obliged nor trusted ... It's true, it's a rigid season for the soldiers to work, but it's the only time they cannot escape you, for human constitutions cannot endure to be long out of houses. A few days will do all that's at present either necessary or possible.[13]

This then was what January presaged: a short, sharp, winter campaign through the disaffected glens. That Stair instructs he does not wish for captives should not be taken as an incitement to killing. He is not authorizing indiscriminate slaughter. This is to be punitive action within the law, and one for which there was ample precedent. He intends the clans to suffer severe economic hardship and loss, with their people driven into the hills. That many will die there he accepts as the wages of their own folly. This is harsh treatment, but a far cry from what was eventually proposed and put into effect. Matters in fact had taken a very distinct turn, however: On 21st December an utterly exhausted Menzies of Fornooth had knocked on the door of Campbell of Carwhin. For nearly ten days he had been constantly travelling, from Paris to London and thence to Edinburgh. King James had at last consented to release the chiefs from their prime obligation and they were at liberty to swear the oath. The exiled monarch's vexatious sloth had left very little time for his adherents to put their lives and fortunes beyond the Government's anger:

To our trusty and well-beloved General-Major Thomas Buchan, or to the officer commanding our Forces in our ancient Kingdom of Scotland.

JAMES R.

Right trusty and well beloved, we greet you well. We are informed of the state of our subjects in the Highlands, and of the condition that you and our other officers there are in, as well by our trusty and well-beloved Sir George Barclay, brigadier of our Forces, as by our trusty and well-beloved Major Duncan Menzies: And therefore we have thought fit hereby to authorize you to give leave to our said subjects and officers who have hitherto behaved themselves so loyally in our cause to do what may be most for their own and your safety. For doing whereof this hall be your warrant. Saint Germain this 12th day of December 1691, in the seventh year of our reign.[14]

It was 22nd December when Menzies climbed wearily back into the saddle and rode westwards. He could go no further than his own home in Perthshire before he collapsed from exhaustion. Carwhin, who, like Fornooth, appreciating the desperate urgency, had written to his colleague Alexander Campbell of Barcaldine, Grey John's local agent, entreating him to convey this momentous news to the clans. Menzies had dispatched gallopers who made contact with Lochiel on the 28th. The Cameron wasted no time in posting to Inverary, where he hastened to take the oath. As he passed Inverlochy, he gave word to Hill and may, from Ballachulish, have sent a runner to MacIain, which would explain his attendance next day at the fort.[15] Indeed there was no time to lose, the columns of marching men were already in motion down the great glen, and companies from the Whig clans were being mustered. The chiefs would be fully aware of these preparations and of their import.

INVERARY

When the twelfth chief of Clan Iain Abrach left Inverlochy on the 29th, he had reason to be doubly apprehensive. To take the oath now he had no choice but to enter the lion's den of the Campbell citadel. Given the circumstances of his last visit and the taking up of Clan Diarmid lands since, the prospect was scarcely an attractive one. He knew also that Williamite forces were on the move and that Glencoe was likely on their list of preferred destinations. Time was very much of the essence and time was short, exceedingly short: the chief was an elderly man and he had a long journey that was fatiguing in summer, and an ordeal in the depths of Highland winter.

As the small party, who had already battled along the track by Loch Linnhe to reach the fort, retraced their steps in thick, snow-laden dark, the wind, at least partly, was deflected by the great mass of high ground to the west commanding Ardgour. Loch Leven was crossed safely, and MacIain probably sent at least one of his tail eastwards up Glencoe to carry news of his intentions. To reach Inverary, the party, seeking the shortest route, would normally proceed inland along the southerly course of the Laroch Burn running between the peaks of *Ben Vair* and *Meall Mor* then down Glen Creran to the ferry at Connel. In this dismal season, with piling snow drifting in the upland passages, this was out of the question, and the safer route hugged the coast through Appin.

By first light on what was effectively the second day, 30th December, the party had attained Duror where the road cuts inland to miss the small Ardsheal Peninsula. It was a cold and bleak dawn, with a strong wind cutting like a knife. Even the fleet ghillies were bent double. By noon they had got no further than the inn at Creagan, where a warming dram eased some life back into stiffened limbs. So fierce was the gale that the ferry passage over the mouth of Loch Creran could not be attempted, and they were obliged to head north for several miles to the head of the loch by Glasdrum, then southwards again to Dallachulish and South Creagan. If MacIain hoped to cross Loch Etive that day he was disappointed. So vile the weather, so savage the winds and deepening drifts that darkness was upon them by the time they had stumbled to Barcaldine, miles short of Glen Etive.

If the chief felt fortune was against him, he was about to be proved entirely correct. As ill-luck would have it, a company of the Argyll men was garrisoning the tower there and their sentinels surrounded the MacDonalds. This detachment was a commanded party under Captain Thomas Drummond, with orders for Inverlochy. Capturing men of Clan Iain Abrach was a signal boon on a cold winter's day, and the captain took pleasure in humiliating his unwilling guests; MacIain and his tail were treated as prisoners of war, his letter of protection from Hill ignored and the party detained all that night. In the cold light of another freezing dawn, Drummond had time to reflect he had no real grounds for holding the MacDonalds, and he would do his best not to give offence to the Governor of the fort. With ill grace he consented to release MacIain, but it took precious hours of patient negotiation before the officious officer of grenadiers would let the ghillies go. The best part of the day was lost and the ice-bound hills were again shrouded in darkness by the time the exhausted group stumbled wetly into Taynuilt on the southern shore of Loch Etive. They did so as the old year was ending and with the chimes of midnight any hope of attaining Inverary and taking the oath within the deadline slipped away.

Their trials were not at an end, far from it. Next morning the weather had, if anything, worsened. The blizzard raged like a demon as they struggled, knee deep, up the Pass of Brander, the slopes of Ben Cruachan lost in the swirl. At the head of Loch Awe they stumbled past Breadalbane's fortress of Kilchurn, a very tangible reminder that this was Campbell country with 'King Campbell' writ in stone, although the more philosophical aspects probably passed them by. Another long, bitter night shivering in soaking plaid – on 2nd January 1692 the chief of Clan Iain Abrach and his floundering tail of ghillies finally descended Glen Aray to the very heart of their enemies' territory. Here was food and shelter, warmth of fireside and solace in a dram. Ill-fortune, however, continued. Their companion, Sir Colin Campbell of Ardkinglas, was not in town: he was away feasting the New Year with kin and might not return for several days, and, in his absence, there was none who might administer the oath.

Here was a double blow. MacIain was already late; technically he was outside the King's mercy, an outlaw. This was bad but to be so in the very bosom of his foes was hazardous in the extreme. There was nothing for it but to lie low and pray for Ardkinglas' early return. To stir abroad in the streets of this alien place was to invite trouble. Men still blowing the fumes of Hogmanay are more apt to begin a quarrel and any from Clan Donald were an obvious target. The chief and his people stayed in their lodgings, careful to avoid notice. It was a miserable and anxious time, as precious days slipped away into January. On the 5th, Sir Colin returned to find an anxious MacDonald fretfully waiting. This was totally unexpected, and the sight of the giant chief of Clan Iain Abrach attending his chambers must quickly have dispelled any residual fumes from the sheriff's clear, legal mind.

He looked at his impressive supplicant, read Hill's letter probably several times, enquired of MacIain how the devil he came to be so late in offering his submission and wondered precisely what it was he should do for the best. His quandary was entirely understandable: Technically he had no authority to administer the oath. MacIain was out of time and, by the letter of the law, that quite simply was that. Equally, and like Hill, Ardkinglas was a decent man who valued the governor's opinion and understood the need to promote a peaceful outcome. He wavered, thinking he must turn MacIain away, but the chief was desperate. He was no longer young; the stress and exhaustion of the journey would have taken their toll, probably he also divined that the sheriff was a fair-minded man trying to do what was right.

The Gael can always mount a fair show of earnest emotion; MacIain produced both entreaty and tears. If he could but take the oath then all his clan were come in; any who demurred would answer to their chief and could languish in Campbell gaols or be sent to serve the King in a red coat. Ardkinglas required a night's deep consideration, but on 6th January he permitted the twelfth Chief of the MacDonalds of Glencoe to swear the oath of loyalty to William and Mary. An optimistic observer might have concluded the whole business of the clansmen's submissions to now be satisfactorily concluded. They would have been quite wrong.

EDINBURGH

As MacIain and his tail slipped quietly out of Inverary, doubtless heartened both to be heading home and with their urgent business safely concluded, Sir Colin sat down to pen three items of correspondence. The first to another Colin Campbell, Sheriff-Clerk of Argyll, presently in Edinburgh; next to Hill; and finally, a report on recent events to the Duke of Argyll himself, now in London. Though well schooled in the arts of survival in a harsh and hostile world, MacIain was not a lawyer and it was into the hands of lawyers that his fate and that of his people now passed. Had he understood this and been aware of what passed in Edinburgh, his return to his pleasant seat at Carnoch would have been anything but joyful.

Ardkinglas' correspondence, together with the engrossment of the sworn oath, duly passed over the desk of the Sheriff-Clerk. Dutifully, this Colin Campbell passed the document on to Sir Gilbert Elliot and David Moncrieff, themselves clerks to the Privy Council. It was now their turn to be vexed: the oath was duly sworn but this had clearly taken place after the deadline, so its validity was necessarily in question. Being bureaucrats, they preferred to wash their hands of the matter and returned the deed to Campbell, declining to agree its worth. Uncertain, the Sheriff-Clerk approached his kinsman John, Writer to the Signet[16] who sought an opinion from Lord Aberuchill, a Campbell lord of Session and council member. It might be easy to suppose these Campbell lawyers bore malice against Clan Donald, but this would be unfair; after all the oath had been submitted by their kinsman Ardkinglas, a senior and highly-regarded figure. The matter was highly difficult and contentious: Aberuchill himself sought advice from fellow members including Lord Stair, Sir John's father and the leading jurist of his day. There can be no doubt that these senior lawyers pondered the matter deeply, understanding the burden of their deliberations. Finally, and probably correctly, they concluded that the oath, as presently given, was inadmissible and that, in the circumstances, a royal warrant was required before MacIain's submission could be judged acceptable within the law.

It is hard to argue against the weight of legal argument; the proclamation issued by the King was emphatic as to the date by which the oath must be sworn. No officer of the court or indeed the council themselves had power to amend; sanction for such an extension would have to come directly from the throne itself. The document was thus struck out and was never seen by the council as a whole. In this we need not detect anything sinister: the members felt they were acting correctly in the circumstances and what was about to ensue was not within their contemplation. We need not impute any base motives to Lord Stair. That the Master was his son would not have affected his judgment of the matter – the elder Dalrymple had, throughout his long career, shown himself to be a man of punctilious probity, absolute integrity, and possessed of a first-rate legal brain. It is doubtful any lawyer of his day would have questioned his view. Sir John Dalrymple was a man of altogether more opportunistic stamp, and he had just been furnished with a pretext for punitive action of the most extreme sort.

CHAPTER 6

Preparations:
'A Great Work of Charity'

'See that this be putt in execution without feud or favour, else you may expect to be dealt with as one not true to King nor Government …'

Duncanson's Order

'Pray, when anything concerning Glencoe is resolved, let it be secret and suddain …'

Sir John Dalrymple, Master of Stair, writing to Colonel Hill, commander of the garrison at Inverlochy

' 'Massacre' – Murder (esp. a large number of people) cruelly or violently.'

Oxford English Dictionary

It would seem, in January 1692, that the policy of forbearance championed by Hill and Tarbat was bearing fruit. King James, from his lonely exile, had given consent to the clan chiefs taking the oath, a tacit admission that his cause, if not dead, was apparently moribund in the Highlands. This should, we might assume, come as a considerable relief to the Master of Stair, whose preparations for a punitive, winter campaign were already well underway. Dalrymple was a fastidious and cautious man, well aware of the present constraints on the treasury. The submission of Lochiel in particular and the 'lost sheep' of Glencoe should have come as a boon, for it was by means of such he could now claim to have pacified the Highlands, a 'result' which had eluded his predecessor Melville. We must ask a question that is crucial in the story of the bloody and wicked events that were to follow, and that is, why was he still determined on military measures that, as January wore on, became quite clearly more draconian in scope?

Mauling the MacDonalds

The central question at this point is what, or perhaps who, convinced Stair that force, brutal and overwhelming force, was the only viable option and remained in some part necessary, despite news of the submissions. Lochiel, Appin, Keppoch and Glencoe had all come in, only Glengarry with his fortified tower remained obdurate, but Invergarry was no Masada even if a siege in winter was difficult, slow and expensive. The Master had the Lowlander's contempt for the 'Macks', but nothing in his career would suggest a violent or vindictive disposition. He it was who despised extremism in all its forms, the paladin of reason. How was it he came to develop such a hatred of Glencoe, a place he had never seen and a people of whom, at first hand, he knew nothing? If we are searching for Mephistopheles then we are left with only one candidate, Grey John Campbell of Glenorchy. He had cause aplenty, the knowledge plus the will. It is surprising that Stair would permit himself to be so influenced, but Breadalbane was clearly deeply insidious and knew just how to tap into the well of instinctive local resentment.

On 9th January the Secretary wrote again to his Commander-in-Chief:

> For my part I could have wished the Macdonalds had not divided, and I
> am sorry that Keppoch and MacIan of Glencoe are safe ... I would be as
> tender of blood or severities as any man, if I did not see the reputation of
> the Government in question upon slighted mercy, and the security of the
> nation in danger by those who have been obstinate to that degree that, if
> we believe them rational, we must think they depend upon such assur-
> ances of help that we can never oblige them even to their own advantages
> from this Government and therefore it musty make sure of them.[1]

It has to be conceded, as John Prebble stresses, that a measure of the blame
for Glencoe must lie with the exiled Stuart. Had he consented in the late
summer or early autumn then any pretext for severity would have lapsed
and the chiefs could have taken the oath in a timely manner. Even those
still under the shadow, MacLeans, MacDonald of Sleat and, of course
Glengarry, could have been brought in without the need for powder and
shot. Dalrymple had expressed, when writing to Livingstone, some pious
concern for the commons, that these should not suffer unduly on account
of the obduracy of their betters: 'I am most concerned ... for the poor
commonality. I do well know if nothing be done to disable them, they
will join with their lairds and chieftains whenever these appear ... I think
they should have some ease and feel the advantage of having their King
their master'.[2] The common people of Glencoe were soon to discover to
the full what advantages lay in having the King as master.

At that season both Argyll and Breadalbane were in London, and a
number of meetings took place between these three principal actors. On
7th January the Master had dined with both Campbell gentlemen, and it
was Argyll who, at some point, provided the welcome news that MacIain's
submission was late; thus a postscript to the letter to Livingstone: 'Just
now my lord Argyll tells me that Glencoe hath not taken the oath, at
which I rejoice. It's a good work of charity to be exact in rooting out that
damnable sept – *the worst in all the Highlands*',[3] (author's emphasis).
This bile sounds like a good Campbell rant and neither Argyll nor the

slippery Breadalbane would weep for Clan Iain Abrach, and yet Grey John was becoming increasingly uneasy. He may have felt two stirrings of alarm. The first that matters were passing out of his control, and the second that, should events turn unfavourable, he would be blamed. In this his instincts had not lied, he would be proved correct on both counts: He wrote peevishly to Barcaldine, 'All methods have been ordered before I came here … l haven't meddled in it …'. This certainly reads as a vanguard for exculpation, and it may be Argyll's counsels that were now pre-eminent, if so, then he plainly preferred the course of violent retribution. Dalrymple's apparently obsessive hatred of Glencoe may make more sense if we consider that both the leading Campbells were pouring poison in equal measure.

This unholy triumvirate, which certainly up to some point included Grey John even if he was increasingly a passenger, provided a powerful lobby to move the King from his previous moderate stance. It may be that William was secretly a good deal less accommodating in his attitude to these lost sheep of the Highlands than public utterances would suggest. After all, these insurgents had come near to shaking his throne under Dundee. Several were still under arms and defiant; by swearing so late the chiefs had made the act appear as a studied insult (in fact they were, of course, bound by their previous undertaking). A new flurry of correspondence ensued: to Livingstone on 16th January new orders were given: 'If McKean of Glencoe and that tribe, can be well separated from the rest, it will be a proper vindication of the public justice to extirpate that sept of thieves'.[4] On the same day the Master wrote in more detail to the Commander-in-Chief: 'For a just example of vengeance I entreat this thieving tribe in Glencoe to be rooted out in earnest'.[5] On the same day similar instructions were sent out to Colonel Hill, but with an ominous postscript:

> The Earls of Argyll and Breadalbane have promised they shall have no retreat in their bounds. The passes to Rannoch would be secured, and the hazard certified to the Laird of Weem to retreat them. In that case Argyll's detachment, with a party that may be posted in Island Stalker, must cut them off .[6]

Again, on 30th January to Livingstone:

> I am glad that Glencoe did not come in within the time prescribed. I hope what's done may be in earnest, since the rest are not in a condition to draw together to help. I think to herry their cattle or burn their houses is but to render them desperate, lawless men, to rob their neighbours; but I believe you will be satisfied it were a great advantage to the nation that thieving tribes were rooted out and cut off. It must be quietly done, otherwise they will make shift for both the men and their cattle.[7]

Before proceeding further, we must consider the Secretary's intentions. Does this correspondence constitute an order to massacre the MacDonalds of Glencoe? The language appears to be express: Clan Iain Abrach is to be 'rooted out in earnest' and 'rooted out and cut off'. How are we to interpret the use of the verb 'to extirpate'? This is defined as 'to root out; destroy completely'[8] but that is an English version. In Scots the meaning is subtly different and provides a refuge for Dalrymple against what would now be a charge of genocide. In the past, as we have seen, for the Government to issue a Commission of Fire and Sword was an available if harsh remedy. This was the sentence handed down upon the MacGregors, and it may be this is what was intended. Nothing in Dalrymple's career shows him as delighting in slaughter, and we cannot say he is revealed as being by temperament a cruel man. In Scots 'extirpate' meant to deprive the clan of lands and status, to render all broken men, despoil their lands and property, lift their stock and drive them from ancestral ground. It was, within current definitions, more type 'B' ethnic cleansing than type 'A'.[9]

Most writers on this subject, including both Buchan and Prebble, are in no doubt that Dalrymple favoured a full genocide, yet I must beg to differ. I feel that the case against the master is at worst, and in Scots' law, 'Not Proven'. In English law it would have to be argued whether he had the specific intent that the Glencoe men be put to the sword. Here was a statesmanlike figure, one who deplored extremism;

and what, in political terms, was to be gained by a massacre? Such slaughters had achieved nothing in the past, and Dalrymple was not the man simply to acquiesce to becoming the Campbells' accessory in an act of private murder. That he intended an example there can be no doubt, but whether this amounted to mass-murder is open to questioning.

Livingstone, in writing to Hamilton on the 23rd, had intimated that the garrison at Inverlochy – and by implication its officers in particular – would be judged by their conduct in the matter of Glencoe. The Commander-in-Chief had made no secret of his preference for radical solutions. What we perhaps have is not a conspiracy but an escalation of expectation as to outcomes; a military man might interpret 'rooting out' in a different way to politicians. For the Campbell earls anything that diminished Clan Donald was to be welcomed, particular vengeance falling on Glencoe even more so. If Breadalbane now begins the largely unsuccessful process of seeking to extricate himself from the mire he has probably engendered, it is because he sees the business escalating beyond his original intent.

John Buchan also asserts the Master had to be aware[10] that the deed must involve treachery if it was to be 'quietly done'. Again I think this is an assumption too far; the Secretary was a politician, distant from the events and lacking in personal knowledge. He was aware the Glencoe people could be targeted because their territory was so enclosed and their overall numbers few. The clansmen's ability to remove themselves, their families and kin from danger at short notice, meant that suddenness and surprise were vital – that much is self-evident. Nowhere, however, in the instructions, is there any exhortation toward murder under trust. Dalrymple's conduct is reprehensible and unnecessarily vindictive. He allows himself to be influenced by those who are motivated, as he is well aware, entirely by self-interest and ancient hatreds. Breadalbane undoubtedly represented MacIain's behaviour at Achallader as being symptomatic of a determined insurgent, intent on remaining outside the King's peace; but Stair was too old a hand not to see through Grey John, given that no other of his contemporaries was disposed to trust in him.

If we accept Buchan's order of culpability, (1) Grey John, (2) Stair and (3) King William III, we must examine the role of the sovereign in instructing an act of genocide against his own people. And the MacDonalds were the King's subjects; he was ruler of both England and Scotland, even if he was disinclined to evince much interest in the latter. It was known MacIain had taken the oath, and even if the substance of this was made void by its lateness, the sentiment in equity was not. William had pressing matters to occupy him in Europe, and it was by Flanders that his capable mind was most occupied. Though he later sought to distance himself from Glencoe, affirming that his knowledge of the business was but vague, then that was simply the royal prerogative in action. Prudent men kept their own counsel on the subject. In fact Stair had briefed the King most thoroughly.

By the middle of January the list of available targets was decreasing. Finding himself isolated, Glengarry had belatedly agreed to come in, and Livingstone's orders of the 16th empowered him to treat with the chief. His submission would be accepted, his Jacobite 'guests' Cannon and Buchan would be allowed to depart, their passports assured, and the castle at Invergarry would be surrendered without a fight. William signed the orders at both top and bottom, implying strongly he was fully acquainted with the content. To give him due, the King could not be expected to be personally fluent in Scottish affairs. He had competent ministers such as Stair and influential magnates in the shape of Argyll and Breadalbane. Both of these had good reason to be shown as zealous in the Williamite cause: the former was the son and grandson of attainted traitors, and the latter's loyalties were far from unquestionable. There has to be a certain degree of appealing symmetry in affirming one's own loyalty through advocating the destruction of local opponents. It is quite probable that the King's later assertions were in fact partly true: he acceded to the advice being given because he believed that to be the correct advice. Stair was not seeking to mislead, rather to have his urgings confirmed – always and merely the good servant and not a principal.

CHAIN OF COMMAND

I am more of the persuasion, unfashionable as it may be, that the Massacre of Glencoe occurred because of a chain of misguided events, rather than a concerted conspiracy. Put quite bluntly, from the King's perspective, murdering a single small tribe of his own subjects was politically undesirable, worse, it would be stupid and damaging. Such action would serve only to fracture the brittle accord with the rebel clans, the ink of their submission barely dry. Both sovereign and Secretary must see that this course would be tantamount to handing the Jacobites a major coup; it was bound to be entirely self-defeating. Both King and minister were cynical, self-serving and capable of total ruthlessness; neither was stupid or deliberately cruel.

John Forbes had collected instructions for the Governor of Inverlochy in Edinburgh, and had hastened westwards in the biting weather to deliver them to his colonel. Stair had, on the 16th, written to Tweeddale expressing similar sentiments, though without giving precise detail. Indeed, there was no need; the detailed planning was a matter for the chain of command. Livingstone would pass the orders on to Hill and Hamilton, the former of these would then give out orders to his subordinates in the usual way. On the face of it, what was ordered now was little different from what had been envisaged and put in motion before the rash of submissions. Hill, as may be imagined, liked not his fresh orders. These ran contrary to the policy he had pursued since the date of his appointment, and came at a time when the fruits of his patience were beginning to ripen. Furthermore, it was obvious that he was being consulted as a matter of form, and that Hamilton was taking executive charge. We have no inkling of the nature of their relationship, but we may assume it was devoid of warmth. His Lieutenant Colonel was precisely the type of ruthlessly amoral, self-serving martinet Hill despised. His preferment, whilst an insult, was also cause for alarm. Hill knew his subordinate was unlikely to be overly troubled by matters of conscience.

Hamilton's major difficulty was this: if he was to put in hand a scheme that ensured the quarry was caught unaware, then the attack had to be delivered from within the lair. Any external advance would be detected and, regardless of care, the high passes from the glen could not all be blocked. Put simply, if there was any warning the MacDonalds would flee; such actions were second nature to them – retaliation was more the norm than the exception. Stair in his instructions to Livingstone had made it plain that the manner in which matters were put in hand was entrusted to the soldiers: 'I am confident … you [Livingstone] will see there are full powers given you in very plain Terms, and yet the method left *very much to your own discretion*',[11] (author's emphasis). Equally, Stair was aware of Hill's propensity for accommodation, and the instructions penned to him caution him from too liberal a path:

> Until we see what is done by the Chiefs, it is not time to Receive their Tenants, or admitting them to take the Oaths, or hoping for Pardon, till they give Evidence they are willing to pay their Rents to you, and to take Tacks for their former Duties; who will not doe so, and were in the Rebellion, must feel the dismal consequences of it.[12]

So much for the safe conducts Hill had issued in good faith to Achtriachtan and Inverrigan, since these were not valid currency. Glencoe was now specifically targeted, and there can be no question that Stair was ignorant of the oath taking. This would be one thing, but that he chose to rely upon the technical letter of the law shows a degree of objectivity plainly unwarranted by the circumstances.

Within the fort at Inverlochy, Hamilton cannot have acted in a vacuum. He would have been obliged to consult with Forbes and the regimental officers. Even if Hill was effectively marginalized, he cannot have been entirely unaware of what was proposed. It was plain the Commander-in-Chief was expecting matters to be undertaken swiftly but the detailed planning has to be Hamilton's. Here was a man already under something of a cloud, who owed his second chance to the good wishes of the Secretary and, presumably, the Commander-in-Chief. He must not fail. The business of Glencoe was his marker for full restoration and advancement; being over-fastidious about the manner of execution would not avail. It is at this point that Buchan asserts the two dissenting officers (Farquhar and Kennedy) who voiced their protest, although John Prebble puts this later, on the very eve of the Massacre, when orders were given out at platoon level. The latter is more persuasive. The planning in the initial stages would involve senior officers only; the more who knew, the greater the risk of a security breach which, in the way of all military operations, could be fatal. Junior officers, with the rank and file, could be given their orders on the day.

In their final form, the written orders which Hamilton issued to Duncanson at Ballachulish on 12th February were unequivocal, as such orders had to be, and their clear intent has damned the memory of both ever since, created an irremediable stain upon their honouring and, by implication, that of the British Crown:

> Sir,
>
> Per second to the Commander in Chief and my Colonel's Orders to me for putting in Execution the Service commanded against the Rebels in Glenco, wherein you, with the Party of the Earl of Argyle's Regiment under your Command are to be concern'd: You are therefore forthwith to order your affairs so, as that the several Posts already assign'd you, be by you and your several Detachments fallen in action with, precisely by seven a Clock to morrow Morning, being 'Saturday' at which time I will endeavor the same with those appointed from this Regiment [Hill's] for the other Places. It will be most necessary you secure those Avenues on the South side that the Old Fox, nor none of his cubs get away. The orders are that none be spar'd from 70 of the Sword, nor the Government troubled with Prisoners. That is all until I see you.
>
> From
> Your humble servant,

JAMES HAMILTON

Please to order a Guard to secure the Ferry, and the Boats there; and the Boats must be all on this side the Ferry, after your Men are over.

For their Majesties Service, for major Robert Duncanson of the Earl of Argyle's Regiment.[13]

Now the Secretary's general instruction to take severe action against the MacDonalds has been translated beyond a mere police action, however salutary, into something very much worse. This order is unequivocal, as orders given in the field in anticipation of detailed operations must be; indeed, the words are a model of clarity, and Duncanson cannot have had any doubts (nor did he) as to the nature of the action proposed. Whatever was in Stair's mind was now interpreted as an order to kill, with special admonition that MacIain and his sons must be got rid of and that no person under seventy years of age be spared. In effect this is an order to slaughter everyone. There is no mention of sparing women and children, though the usages of war would imply this. What was to be enacted amounted to genocide, or ethnic cleansing, or just plain mass-murder. There is no vestige of doubt, nor any exoneration for the senior officers involved. Hamilton must, however, have believed he was carrying out his orders from the Commander-in-Chief and through him from the Secretary.

He would, therefore, claim the defence that he was, at all times, only obeying his direct orders. This is a moot point, and such a defence was not found invalid until Nuremburg and when it suited the victors to do so. If he interpreted these orders too zealously then he would be culpable, but it is unlikely he would so conduct himself unless he was convinced this was what was required. Thus either he was wrong, or his was more right than the ambiguity of the earlier correspondence might outwardly suggest. On Monday, 1st February, as John Forbes huddled in his cloak, seeking passage across the ferry at Ballachulish, he witnessed numbers of troops crossing from the far bank, men he identified as being from Argyll's. This scene John

Prebble memorably describes in the opening pages of his magnificent account. He refers to the men carrying musket and pike, though I suspect the latter were probably phased out and that the men all carried firelock and bayonet. Their officer was Robert Campbell of Glenlyon, and Forbes must have been struck by the incongruity of a man in his seventh decade serving as a mere captain. He was still both tall and upright though, at close quarters, the toll taken by years of drink and debauchery was written on his features, burnished with the toper's habitual bonhomie. The weather was raw and the soldiers wrapped their plaids around them as stinging wind whipped across sullen waters, frothing the wavelets.

Intelligence of the soldier's coming started through the lower reaches of Glencoe like wildfire, vigilance was the code to centuries of survival in a mainly hostile world. By the time Glenlyon had formed his men into a marching column and began moving westwards, a body of the clansmen, under John MacDonald, were already forming. These MacDonalds were, however, unarmed, or at least appeared to be. There was no apparent reason for punitive action, and at that time men of Clan Iain Abrach were wary more than overtly hostile; the sight of a red coat was not one generally to be welcomed in Glencoe. Matters proceeded quite civilly; Glenlyon was all hearty and disarming. Though he was one whom the clan had savagely despoiled, and whose present service was occasioned by the desperation arising, he was also kin. Glenlyon's mother had, as her third husband, wed Stewart of Appin and her granddaughter, Glenlyon's niece, was now John's sister-in-law, being married to Alasdair. The captain explained that his company was detailed to take part in operations against Glengarry, should any now arise, but that Inverlochy was full to bursting and there was no room either under roof or canvas for his company. Thus the men were to be billeted in the locality, and Glencoe was to be their host. Glenlyon apologized for the imposition, but orders were, of course, orders – a statement that would ring mighty hollow in less than a fortnight.

FREE QUARTER

Even without the history of bad blood between Clan Iain Abrach and King Campbell, no rural or, for that matter, urban population relished acting as hosts to their Majesties' forces. Frequently, as in the instant case, these men brought few or no supplies with them, and people living on or very near subsistence had little to spare. It was winter and the MacDonalds were bunkered down in their settlements. The quartering of troops was not something they were accustomed to, an alien presence in their private glen. To this was added the fact that these men were of their ancient enemy, one they had only three summers ago heartily despoiled. John MacDonald would be acutely aware of Glenlyon's situation, his clan being one of the prime causes, and painfully aware that scarce two winters ago the man's family had nearly starved due to the MacDonalds. He had little choice, however: one of Glenlyon's subordinates Lieutenant Lindsay, also kin, had the signed orders. Glenlyon's other officer was Ensign Lundie [Lindsay] and, as senior NCO, Sergeant Barber, with James Hendrie as junior. Drummond was not at this point, present to lead his grenadiers. It is likely that his own junior officers, Lieutenants Kilpatrick and Campbell, were commanding their platoons.[14]

If the majority of Glenlyon's company were Campbells or other Highlanders, they at least shared a common language with their hosts and a common culture. Past hatreds might abound, but the laws of hospitality provided the cement that could bind them together. Drummond's grenadiers were, in the main, from Lowland stock; the sergeants were Walter Purdie, Walter Buchanan and Walter Bruce, the three Walters. They and their men came from outside this Gaelic network, excluded by speech and custom. Whilst the chief and his sons could switch from the Irish tongue to English or French with equal facility, the commons could not, thus to them the Lowlanders were foreigners. The logistics of quartering 120 men amongst the necklace of crowded townships were complex. The men would be spread through the communities, perhaps three or five per dwelling depending on space and capacity. At a stroke the population was increased by at least a third and, aside from some claret to assuage the sensibilities of the gentry and aquavit for the commons, their knapsacks were largely empty.

Afterwards, survivors would say that they had been uneasy from the start. Alasdair Og for one was unhappy, as was his wife. Glenlyon might be of her blood, but there was something 'not quite right' about his demeanor. He was an impressive figure, urbane and cultured, a lively guest until too far gone in his cups when braggadocio took over. Everyone in the glen would be aware of his circumstances, reduced to a mere company commander at his age, hounded by creditors and with no rents coming in from his shrunken estate thanks to the thoroughness of his hosts' earlier despoiling. For many of the clansmen there was deep unease. Whatever the circumstances, having two full companies of their hereditary foes planted in their midst was an unnerving experience, and their fears of course, were to prove fully justified.

It is most unlikely that any of the rank and file knew of their full purpose in coming to Glencoe, but it is impossible that their officers and probably the NCOs did not. Glenlyon did well to appear nervous, and there may have been looks which passed between him and his junior officers, who appeared rather lumpen next to their captain's beaming joviality; perhaps their acting skills were less well-honed. Sorting the men's billets would have taken the whole day. Sgt Barber took a commanded party to Achnacone, the senior tenant and gentleman. Glenlyon declined MacIain's offer and lodged instead with Inverrigan, the latter doubtless feeling the comfort of Hill's letter in his pocket. He might as well have used it to light his pipe. It may in fact have been that the chief was not residing in his seat at Carnoch but was staying in his summerhouse. This seems unlikely, though he would be nearer to both of his sons, since his subsequent murder clearly took place at Carnoch.

If foodstuffs were relatively short, the soldiers lived better than they would expect on the stale and miserable fare doled out by a grudging administration. In the glen there was salted fish and some venison; there was gaming and song, old tales to be told around peat fires through long evenings and sport upon the haughs during the day; there was aquavit and ale. Hospitality was a sacred obligation in the Highlands and whatever unease that may have been felt, or was later recalled as having been felt, would have been dispelled by the ancient bond of shared bread and board. To the clansmen his was an absolute trust, that it should be profaned by violence offered to the host by his guest was unthinkable.

During the first dozen days of February the earlier foul weather had ameliorated. Snow lay in a deep blanket over the peaks, swamped corries and high passes alike, but the days had turned mild, wind shifting more westerly. In the sheltered bowl of the valley floor, there was green sward and tumbling waters, air fresh and keen. Every morning the men would practice drill, lining up on the level ground to bear the abuse of ranting sergeants determined to make soldiers from farm boys – some of the NCOs had been drafted in from other units for this very purpose. Besides, drill kept idleness at bay, kept young men looking to their front and not at the lissom shapes of girls and the power of coy glances. For the men of Glencoe this might be an additional cause for concern. Their daughters saw few of the opposite sex outside their own kinsmen, and these strapping lads, even in hateful Campbell plaid, would have offered a welcome diversion. We have no record of any dalliance, but it would not be unnatural, and one might speculate whether some were born later that year, as the clan sheltered in skulking misery, who might claim the blood of clan Diarmid.

Lieutenant Lindsay was quartered with MacIain and we may speculate as to why Glenlyon preferred Inveriggan. True, this was more central, a wiser choice of location for the commanding officer, and besides, as John Prebble suggests, he might have found the Chief's house too well furnished with spoils from his own. It would be unusual indeed in Glencoe to hear the drums beat out reveille each dark morning, but as the days passed, an air of informality prevailed, and afternoons were given to sports, wrestling and fierce little games of shinty as ferocious as training for war. Pleasant exertions washed down by a reviving dram. For the soldiers, this was a good deal more agreeable than life at the fort. By evening fires the pipes would sound, their wild, romantic dirges, old and haunting songs filled the darkness and guttering light of pine-knots shone on the faces of singers and listeners. This was a life of hardship, of suffering, of mortality and occasionally of violence, but it was the old way, things as they had always been, and these hours were to prove more precious than the singers knew.

Not all were acquiescent, however; a file of tenants gathered to petition their chief to drive the redcoats out, and received a stiff telling-off for their pains. MacIain knew well neither he nor they had any choice in the matter. He could not, of course, be aware that his submission had been held invalid, but he understood this tribulation to be a test of his new found loyalty to the Williamite crown and he could not afford to be found wanting. Glenlyon, addicted to play and the bottle, found ample time to engage in both. Of a morning he would take a dram with his niece Sarah, Alasdair's wife, and spend his evenings at cards there or at Inverrigan, drinking with reckless abandon through the hours of darkness. Whether we ascribe this behavior simply as his customary debauchery, or whether he was blotting out what he knew must ensue, remains a matter of speculation. We should wonder, however, what goes through the mind of a man who, if he is morally bankrupt and a sot, sits at play with a young man to whom he is related, and others around their own fires, knowing, at some point in the very near future, it will be his express duty to murder each and every one of them, possibly including his own niece. A man would have to be very wicked indeed not to feel a chill at such a prospect, and Glenlyon, for all his weaknesses, was not a cruel or vicious man.

Armies through history have been at pains to prevent heir men fraternizing with the foe, and the Christmas Truce of 1914 emerges as a notably poignant example. Once a man has broken bread with another, seen his wife and bairns scampering, slept beneath his roof, shared the comradeship of sport and listened to his music, then it goes against all nature to do him violence. Killing is best done in hot blood against a faceless enemy, when fear and the red mist, the habit of discipline, files of comrades and the sergeant's orders, familiar in their blaspheming, drive a soldier on. Base murder, done in cold blood is another thing completely, and most men rebel; uniform is the badge of honor, of élan and of tradition, not the cloak of an assassin.

Glenlyon was a frequent dinner guest at the chief's house. MacIain was noted for his genial hospitality, for the splendors of his well-stocked cellar and groaning table. The commons might tighten their belts, but it was important for the status of the clan that a chief was seen to offer the very best to his guests. Lindsay and Lundie were also regular attendees, though unable to match their superior's practiced and well-fuelled geniality. Another guest who may have viewed the soldiers in a pejorative light was the bard Murdoch Matheson, an agent of Seaforth, his feudal superior. The young man, already celebrated, had stopped off on his journey back from Inverlochy.[15] Matheson was right, and his instincts were to be fully vindicated by events. Hamilton had prepared his plan thoroughly. Glenlyon with his own and Drummond's companies were positioned within Glencoe, Duncanson with a further four companies of Argyll's foot lay at Ballachulish; Hamilton himself would lead further companies from Hill's over the Devil's Staircase from Kinlochleven to seal the eastern end of the glen.

There was a single stumbling block to the final execution of the plan, and this was Colonel John Hill. Isolated by his inferior's plotting, Hill was nevertheless in command: no action could legally be taken without his agreement and, significantly, his signature upon the orders. On 4th February he had been relieved to report Glengarry's submission and could not now believe there would be any recourse to force; no need remained. The orders he received from Stair, however, in the middle part of February, removed any hopes he might have entertained he must be as earnest in the matter as he could be, '... be secret and sudden ... be quick.'

Now the old soldier faced his gravest test, a grossly onerous burden for an honorable man, one who had given a lifetime of service, and to whom the crown, in every sense, was heavily indebted. To be used as a tool of oppressive tyranny after all his patient endeavours, was intolerable. His choices were limited: he could sign and swallow bile or resign. The latter was the path of conscience, but no easy matter for an old man, in uncertain health and with spinster daughters to support. In the end he was only obeying orders but he alone amongst the actors knew those orders to be wrong, to be cruel and unnatural and, in the end, he signed and cast such a millstone around his neck as would weigh him down for the rest of his days. Others would subsequently hasten to save their reputations, but Hill knew his signature was sufficient to compromise his honour irrevocably; for this I feel he deserves not censure but pity. That he came to be a tool in the scheme was regrettable, but it was not his work, and he condoned with a heavy heart. He deserves our understanding: he was a decent man in an indecent business, and one whose efforts deserved a better employer.

He had been ignored and slighted; Stair had dallied with grey John's defunct scheme for bribery, and his exposure of the Campbell's perfidious private clauses had been effectively brushed under the Government carpet. Now Hamilton, his second-in-command, was to all intents and purposes usurping his authority. In the circumstances, he rationalized his own dishonour as a justifiable attempt to re-assert his own authority. On 12th February he wrote in the following terms to Hamilton, and any hope of clemency for the people of Glencoe was thereby extinguished:

> You [Hamilton] are with four hundred of my regiment, and the four hundred of my Lord Argyll's regiment, under the command of Major Duncanson, to march straight to Glencoe, and there put in due execution the orders you have received from the Commander-in-Chief. Given under my hand at Fort William, the 12th February 1692 etc.[16]

With the final piece in the jigsaw of command decision-making at last in place, Hamilton dispatched a galloper to Duncanson with the order – this, as we have seen was couched in altogether less euphemistic language than that employed by Hill; 'the orders are that none be spared, nor the Government troubled with prisoners'. As soon as Duncanson had these orders, he in turn sent an urgent communication to Glenlyon; he could not have been aware that this would become notorious as one of the most infamous orders ever to be penned in the English language:

> You are hereby ordered to fall upon the rabelle [rebels], the MacDonalds of Glenco, and to putt all to the sword under seventy. You are to have a special care that the old fox and his sones doe not escape your hands. You are to putt in execution at five of the clock precisely. And by that time, or very shortly after it, I will strive to be at you with a stronger party. If I do not come to you at five, you are not to tarry for me but to fall on. This is by the King's special commands, for the good and safety of the countrie, that these miscreants be cutt off root and branch. See that this be put in execution, without fear or favour. Else you may expect to be dealt with as one not true to King nor countrie, nor a man fitt to carry a commission in the King's service. Expecting you will not faill in the fulfilling hereof; as you love yourselfe.[17]

This is totally unequivocal, and, moreover contains a strong threat as to the consequences should Glenlyon fail to carry out his orders. This reminder of the Campbell's officer's precarious position perhaps underlies a concern on the part of Hamilton and Duncanson that he might not be entirely fit for purpose. He had doubtless been selected, primarily because he understood the people and might, by right of his niece, be accepted, and that he, above all others, had sound reason for a deep, underlying hatred. That said, he was also known to be a drunkard and a braggart, a man who sought his commission in late middle age through desperation, and owed the same to patronage; intemperate in his cups, with the likely sentimentality of the toper, there would be a question against his logistical capacity to put his orders into significant effect. We have also to consider the disparity of timing: Hamilton plainly mentions seven as the relevant hour. Possibly Duncanson interprets this as meaning he should have completed the march (four miles) from Ballachulish by seven and mopped up accordingly so that by the time Hamilton appeared the glen, or at least the townships, would be secure. This would make sense of the command to Glenlyon to unleash the furies at five.

Another, more cynical view might be that Duncanson wanted no actual part in the killing, let that be done by Glenlyon. The tone of his order places a very strong emphasis upon the need to strike and strike resolutely. Perhaps, even at this stage, Duncanson was considering what furor might arise. Neither he nor Hamilton was a fool: this day's work might advance their careers, a prime objective in both cases, but, equally, it might yet rebound and destroy them. They could claim they were only carrying out superior orders, but they would be aware how rapidly blame is transferred downwards rather than the reverse. Glenlyon made an excellent choice of scapegoat: he had neither career nor prospects, and could expect scant support from either Argyll or Breadalbane who would be as hungry to throw an offering to the wolves as the rest. What was, nonetheless, essential was that Glenlyon did precisely what was required of him and did not allow brandy fumes or sentiment to interrupt the work.

On that Friday the weather once again had begun to change; the skies darkened and the wind swung around into the north-easterly quadrant from a puckish and mild breeze toward the swelling ice-laden tempest. There would be little sport on the haughs that day; bitter cold and razor-sharp blasts kept folks indoors, sergeants 'shrill commands whipped down the glen as shivering ranks stood numbly to mute attention'; heavy muskets clumsy in frozen hands, touch of cold steel as frigid as the grave.

John Prebble asserts that Glenlyon was ignorant of what was afoot until that evening when Drummond brought Duncanson's order to his lodgings at Inveriggan. With this I must disagree: there would be no point in giving such orders cold, and at so late a stage in the game. I suggest that Glenlyon had been aware of the likelihood of such instructions from the outset, and had advised his immediate subordinates accordingly. Otherwise the thing simply could not be done. For the business to be undertaken with due thoroughness, given that the men were scattered throughout he glen, required an element of pre-planning, that trusted subordinates such as Barber should have a strong party where required, and that Glenlyon himself should stand midway. In order that the rank and file could make ready in the time available, it is axiomatic that the officers were prepared. All that Glenlyon would not know when he left Inverlochy, was full confirmation that the matter was to proceed and the exact timing.

In the evening, Alasdair Og sat at play with his wife's kinsman in the house of Inverrigan. In this respect Friday was perfectly normal, Glenlyon did not neglect the bottle, his bonhomie burning almost fever bright in the leaden dusk, grey pallor of afternoon thickening into blackness of night, rising wind howling around the gables, whipping down the lanes and wynds of the huddled settlement. He announced he was to dine with the chief next day, but cards were interrupted by the arrival of Thomas Drummond. The younger MacIains would be aware this was the officious officer of grenadiers who had so uncivilly abused their father on his dash to Inverary, and by his boorishness, had imperiled them all. The introductions might have been a trifle stiff. Drummond brought Duncanson's order, which he curtly handed to Glenlyon. On reading the death knell of his hosts the Campbell betrayed no emotion. I am firmly of the opinion that such an order was fully anticipated and brought no surprises. It will become clear that Glenlyon had no particular enthusiasm for the work, but had neither the means nor the will to oppose. He simply begged that the chief's sons would excuse him, and said that he must forgo the pleasure of supping with them. Fresh orders he blustered, vague rumblings Glengarry's way, a soldier's lot was not an easy one bit, at least his hosts would be spared the continued burden of free quarter. This much at least was true.

CHAPTER 7

The 13th February, 1692: 'Murder Under Trust'

'You are hereby ordered to fall upon the rebels, the McDonalds of Glencoe, and putt all to the sword under seventy ...'

Duncanson's Order

'Dear to me are the white bodies of those who were generous, manly delightful men. Alas, that one should see our nobles defenceless at the mercy of those who hate them ...'

Murdoch Matheson

' 'Genocide' – The mass extermination of human beings, esp. of a particular race or nation.'

Oxford English Dictionary

The scene was now set for the events that were to become notorious as the Massacre of Glencoe. William III, King of England and Scotland, had signed an order for the mass-murder of a defined group of his subjects, orders issued at the urging of his Secretary of State for Scotland. These instructions had been communicated to the Commander in Chief, to Colonel Hill, Lieutenant-Colonel Hamilton, Major Duncanson, Captains Drummond and Glenlyon. Very soon the NCOs and enlisted men of their companies would receive their detailed orders for cold-blooded slaughter of their hosts, MacDonalds of Glencoe. Britain has a long history of violence, but not since the days of Aethelred has the Government of the day given the order for a deliberate mass-murder of its own citizens. The Jewish communities had suffered vicious pogroms in the medieval period before their formal expulsion, Roman Catholics had been dis-enfranchised and harried under Elizabeth and James I. In the civil wars, MacColla had preached a virtual annihilation of Campbells. The covenanters and their conventicles had been murderously suppressed in the Killing Time of the 1670s. But never, until this point, had a duly elected Government with the King at its head sanctioned the complete destruction of an identified section of the community. That was, on the night of 12/13th February 1692, about to change.

Midnight

It was a wild night, full of Wagnerian fury. Heavy, gray-bellied clouds had rolled ominously in the last hours of daylight, crowding down the glen behind a stiff north easterly, laden with chill. Snow fell in ever increasing drifts, heavy and persistent, making movement difficult, choking the narrows and piling against stonewalls. The steady dirge of the wind, now whipping to blizzard fury, drowned out sound and persuaded most to stay within, hunched over their smoky fires. Robert Campbell of Glenlyon, orders in his pocket, faced a considerable difficulty merely in getting round the outposts. Billeting arrangements were such that the men were widely dispersed, many crowded into the westerly settlements facing Loch Leven, at Invercoe, Carnoch, Brecklet and Inveriggan. The more westerly hamlets, Leacantuim and Achnacon, lay a mile or so to the east, whilst the most easterly, Achtriachtan was a good five miles from the

187

Loch-side. There were scarcely any roads worthy of the name and no lights intervening. The desperate cold and keening gale would claim lives but would equally be the salvation of many.

A primeval scene, one enacted through hundreds of winters' nights since men first came to the glen; people huddling in their crofts as their Iron and Bronze Age ancestors before them. Almost nothing has changed, until this night, after which it would never again be the same. Was Robert Campbell of Glenlyon aware he was about to make history, and that the work upon which he was about to embark would damn his name for generations, haunting his descendants to the extinction of their line? It may be he had no enthusiasm for the business. Nothing in his character suggests he might: he had eaten the bread of his victims, shared drink and dice with them; they were kin by marriage. When all came to all, he had no choice. He could have broken his sword but he was a penniless rake, living on charity, almost in his seventh decade; younger men might rise again, but not he. Duncanson might have already played him false, lying as to the timing, though he was not to know that, at least not in the dead cold heart of the winter's night. The storm raged like a shrieking demon as he struggled from post to post.

From a purely logistical viewpoint the situation was far from ideal. The dreadful weather implied that pursuit, once surprise was lost, would be nigh on impossible; the killing must be as swift, as silent and as complete as flint and cold steel could accomplish. Which was it to be? Clearly the bayonet would be quieter, for even in nature's uproar the crack and muzzle flash of the guns would tell. These MacDonalds were unsuspecting, but they all recognised the sound of gunfire when they heard it and knew precisely what it imported: 'The object of bayonet training is to fit the soldier to take his place as one of a team, with confidence in his own and his comrades' skill with their weapons, and thereby imbued with a mutual determination to close with the enemy'.[1]

As a weapon, the plug bayonet had been seriously flawed, the new socket version with its seventeen-inch needle pointed triangular blade would prove infinitely more useful and enduring. Modern semi-automatic assault rifles bear little resemblance to their flintlock antecedents. They fire at a rate of several hundred rounds per minute, using smokeless cartridges and with a range and penetrating power, coupled with a level of accuracy, that Glenlyon's men would have seen as the work of the Devil. But the bayonet has scarcely changed at all, nor has the manner of its employment. Once fitted it converts the most sophisticated rifle into a spear, the most basic of killing implements, and it requires a deal of practice and élan to be used effectively. When it is, the bayonet charge, perhaps still the epitome of valour even in today's armies, will still be irresistible. It is one thing to charge one's foes, shoulder to shoulder with screaming comrades, blinded by red mist, but to murder an unarmed civilian in his or her bed using the bayonet is another matter altogether.

Had this operation been a regular raid against fixed enemy positions, such as Eugene of Savoy's famous assault on Belgrade[2] or the so-called Paoli Massacre,[3] then the bayonet would have been the ideal choice. This was not, however, a regular assault; the men were to be called upon to murder their hosts in cold blood and without provocation. In such circumstances a man might hesitate. Use of the bayonet requires strength, skill and aggression. It is not necessarily an easy way of dispatching a foe and numerous thrusts may be required. As late as the Falklands War of 1982, when British troops were engaged in hand to hand fighting in the Argentine positions above Port Stanley, some combatants recorded their needing to stab their opponents many times to kill them, a grim and exhausting business. Even the most accomplished butcher might draw back from using his bayonet on a defenceless woman or child, thrusting uncertainly in darkness, the screams of his wildly writhing victim and the great effusion of blood fountaining from severed arteries.

Shooting was altogether less demanding. Nonetheless, the guns were noisy and inefficient; smoothbore flintlocks were scarcely accurate above 50 yards, a deal less in high wind and snow; bad weather could spoil the priming powder in the pan or the gale scatter the fine grains so the piece would not give fire. Misfires allowed for escape, as the victim would not necessarily be so obliging as to attend upon his murderer's convenience. At best the flint musket could discharge two rounds a minute, and the filthy belch of black smoke could swiftly obscure targets; with their weight and long barrels, the guns were not best suited for use in confined spaces. Gunshot wounds are more apt to cause death either instantly or shortly after impact. Soft lead balls would tend to flatten out in the air and thus strike the victim with a greater surface area, shearing off limbs and causing massive trauma with tissue damage, shock and exsanguination. The round, if it passes through the victim's body unimpeded, will leave a gaping exit wound, or shatter and break through in different places.[4] Bones, in turn, may fracture, creating a shower of bone shards which function as secondary projectiles. An untreated victim will quickly succumb through shock and blood loss even if the tissue damage as insufficient: septicemia and gas – gangrene will account for many who survive the original trauma.

Inevitably, a carapace of myth swiftly came to surround the events of 13th February, the dolorous superstition of the Gaels. The Great Man (*An Duine Mor*) was glimpsed by Loch Leven on the Friday before – such a sighting presaged death amongst those gently born. *Bean Nighe*, a spectral washerwoman was observed washing a shroud, a kind of Lady Macbeth figure; cattle unexpectedly stamped from byres. In the winter darkness a keening dirge the Caoineag sent shivers as sleepers huddled for warmth. The auguries were consulted and foretold doom, as auguries are wont to do. These tales are very probably apocryphal and added to the re-telling for dramatic effect, yet their existence may suggest a general unease amongst the MacDonalds. These troops, though bound by the laws of hospitality and Highland men themselves, were nonetheless Campbells, their red coats a badge of service to an alien king against who Clan Iain Abrach had risen. Glenlyon, as they had be aware, had little to thank them for, his present penury a consequence of their own depredations. Hatred and suspicion of 'King Campbell' ran deep, and none who had ever encountered Grey John would be likely to feel reassured.

There is no evidence that any of the enlisted men were privy to the orders until the early hours of the 13th, and the subsequent testimony taken from some, such as James Campbell of Glenlyon's company, would confirm this. Perhaps, among the sharper intellects, there was an inkling; for local tradition asserts that several soldiers, sickened by the baseness of what they must do, but feeling themselves nonetheless bound by their oaths did attempt to warn their hosts in various oblique ways. On the Friday, as the clan and their guests played shinty, one of the soldiers, taking his ease and watching the game in the company of a MacDonald youth, leant against the large boulder known as MacHenry's Stone. Having ensured he had the lad's full attention, the Campbell exclaimed: 'Great stone of the glen! Great is your right to be here. But if you knew what will happen this night you would be up and away'.[5] Another, as he sat by the fire, rather pointedly addressed his host's dog named Grey dog: 'if I were you grey dog, my bed tonight would be the heather'. The message was not wasted. At Brecklet, one of the men commented on the fine plaid the householder, a Robertson, was wearing, suggesting if he was the proud owner of such fine attire he had put it on to inspect his cattle in the fields that night; again the warning was wisely heeded. Even Glenlyon's piper, Hugh Mackenzie, for whom such a grim business could never be the stuff of bardic lays, played a sad lament from atop MacHenry's stone. Several MacDonalds interpreted this as a hint of trouble to come and quietly departed their homes that night.[6]

A Jacobite pamphleteer who subsequently wrote an account of the Massacre informs us that Alasdair Og, the more swashbuckling younger brother, maintained a deep mistrust of these redcoats infesting his father's glen. He did not trust Glenlyon, and kept careful watch into the small hours. What it was in the Campbell's demeanor that sparked Alasdair's suspicions cannot be guessed at, but was in a general uneasiness and unwillingness to look his hosts in the eye. Had the young MacDonald caught some glance or look that had passed between Drummond and he? As he watched, his alarm grew; the soldiers were about and active, the guard apparently being doubled.

More figures approached, their detail lost in the murk, and Alasdair was certain he recognised the older of the two Lindsays. Now seriously worried, he went to wake his older brother. John appeared less concerned; surely, he argued, it made sense to change the guard regularly as no man could stand long in such filthy weather. Alasdair was not to be mollified, and insisted both young men should acquaint their father with the younger son's fears. Reluctantly John rose, threw on his attire, and they went to rouse MacIain. No doubt the old man was testy, dragged from slumber in the bitter darkness. He did, however, consent to their making further enquiry. With that he went back to sleep, his last mortal rest.

Both MacDonalds knew their glen intimately, and were further shielded by eddies of snow gusted by the fanged wind. Undetected, they approached one of the bothies taken over as a sentinel post. Here was not one lone and freezing sentry, but a milling squad, fully accoutered. Despite the banshee wind they were able to pick up snatches of the men's talk. Guttering torchlight spread an uneven glow through the snow-laden curtain of night; light picking on scarlet coat and the polished musket barrels. One of the men, plainly uneasy, was declaiming to his comrades that he had no stomach for the work upon which they were engaged. Had he known that this would be their duty he would not have volunteered. He was as ready as any to engage the MacDonalds in a clean fight, but this was to be mere murder. Obviously, the rank and file had just been given their orders, and one of the others responded that the responsibility was not theirs for any blame would rest solely upon the officers – their duty was but to obey. Thoroughly alarmed, both John and Alasdair made haste to warn their father, but, on approaching his house once more, perceived it to be surrounded by a ring of steel, the night air punctured with the crash of gunfire. They were too late; the Massacre had already begun.[7]

Whether these events occurred as the Jacobite account avers is questionable. In their subsequent testimony neither brother refers to the alleged incident. Both state that, after playing at cards with

Glenlyon, they returned, unsuspecting, to their homes. John testified that he was awakened at some point in the small hours by a knot of soldiers looming beneath torches outside his property. The men were fully prepared, the light again gilding burnished arms, but they obviously intended him no harm – perhaps this was even a warning. As the blanket of freezing dark swallowed them, he returned uneasy to his bed, calming his wife's fears. Next, he dressed and made his way to Inveriggan where he found more troops, bayonets fixed and ready, though they did not accost him. He entered the tacksman's house to discover Glenlyon, his late companion in gaming, now engaged in the altogether more purposeful business of loading his pistols.

Deeply uneasy, he demanded an explanation, and, covering any surprise, Glenlyon brusquely lamented the vicissitudes of a soldier's life; the company must be ready to move at once, he said. This did not account for loaded weapons, but Campbell, with a flash of inspiration offered the very comment guaranteed to reassure John MacDonald. He laughed at the clear suspicion that local harm was intended; would he, after all, do harm to the family of his niece? This was, by all the conventions, conclusive: no Highlander, not even a Campbell, would injure his own flesh. Reassured, John went home. Had Glenlyon's host been able to interject he would have been significantly less sanguine; but John did not see Inveriggan, indeed, it was intended he should not, for the tacksman with eight of his household were lying helpless, bound, gagged and out of sight. Their fate was certain, and if Glenlyon had not dirked John MacDonald, it was not from any feelings of humanity. His orders said five and at five the killing would begin.

5.00 A.M.

Punctual as an undertaker, Lieutenant Lindsay, with a file of enlisted men, arrived at MacIain's door. They did not force an entry but roused one of the servants to summon their master: the reason being they must depart urgently, and the officer would wish to pay his compliments to a generous and agreeable host. In this, of course, there appeared nothing sinister. The twelfth Chief of Glencoe, roused, if we believe the earlier account, for the second time, now attempted to dress, probably ordering his departing guests sent upon their way with a warming dram, as would be the custom. This civility did not proceed, however, for even as the old man was in the act of pulling on his trews, Lindsay's party burst into the chamber firing at least two shots. One passed through MacIain's body, the second, at virtually point blank range, into the back of the head. This would shatter the skull, driving into bone and grey matter, then burst out, probably through the forehead, punching a gaping hole and sending a spray of blood, bone and brain tissue spurting across the room. Their victim was killed instantly, sprawling over his blood-deluged covers. Thus the twelfth chief of MacDonald of Glencoe, he who had so impressed at the Dalcomera muster, famous for his fine stature, proven valour and martial appearance, was squalidly done to death in the most cowardly manner, in the very act of bestowing further hospitality upon his murderers.

MacIain's wife, now a widow, who would likely be in her sixties, had also put on clothes; she, splattered with her husband's brains, was stripped and abused, any jewellery was stolen and the rings torn from her fingers, the soldiers using their teeth. The traumatised woman was left naked and despoiled. The killing frenzy had begun; Lindsay made no effort to restrain the bestiality of his men. The crack of gunfire and the screaming of Clan Campbell's slogan brought men stumbling into the swirling, snow-filled dark. Two who approached were felled by a volley, and a third man, Duncan Don, not even local but a kind of postman bringing correspondence for MacIain, was also hit and wounded. Blood now spilled onto the snow; bright scarlet patches beneath the guttering torches; the killers in the stamping fury of slaughter, dragging the dead Chief to his threshold and chucking his limp corpse with the pile they were building.[8] Donald Don was not dead but wisely remained unmoving, despite the shock and pain of his wounds, the blood and urine running from the corpses whose company he now kept.

John MacDonald, who remained awake, despite Glenlyon's assurances, had not heard the sound of those first shots; he had perhaps dozed but, in the gloom, he was suddenly shaken by a servant; the man had seen soldiers approaching. Instantly alert, John ran to check, and sure enough he could make out what appeared as the best part of a platoon, bayonets fixed, struggling through the storm to his door. He needed no more proof; the household was roughly aroused, grabbing what clothing they could, they fled out into the blizzard, away from those long bayonets. John's son, no more than a toddler, was probably borne by his nurse;[9] his wife Eiblin, was Achtriachtan's daughter.[10] Shocked and stumbling, in fear of their lives, the small party made for the lee of Meall Mor, where a small corrie offered some form of shelter. Behind them they abandoned their home and possessions, wearing whatever they could fling on and carrying little or nothing. They were not long alone, for other fugitives drifted in. Each new arrival must have produced a thrill of nerves lest they prove to be redcoats. Murdoch Matheson, the poet, with one of MacIain's household, Archibald MacDonald, was amongst the newcomers; and from Archibald John learnt what had happened to his father.

Alasdair Og had not slept; his fears too urgent. If he wandered it was momentarily, but it was still a follower who warned him the redcoats were surrounding his brother's house. Alasdair had already considered this moment, and had his family and household ready mustered. He ushered these new fugitives out into the howl of the wind and piling snow. Frightful as this was, it offered the perfect cloak, and the group reached temporary refuge without loss or discovery. With his wife and servants safe, at least for the moment, Alasdair took off to find his older brother. In light or dark, sun or shadow, he knew this ground intimately, and shrouded by the downpour he threaded the paths like a mountain goat. At this point he saw the danger as confined to his own vicinity, Inverrigan and Achnacone. Staying to the lower slopes of the south elevation he stayed immune and, despite the whirling, snow-fogged darkness met with his brother. Below and to their right, more gunfire erupted.

Achnacone himself, John's father in law, was also awake, up and dressed with eight of his people gathered in his hall, the company included his brother John MacDonald, tacksman of Achtriachtan. Sergeant Barber commanded the troops quartered here, he had his orders and made no bones upon their being carried out. In the dark, before the appointed hour of five, he had mustered his men, ensured their muskets were loaded, flints working and bayonets fixed. Each section fully briefed, they were then to make sure of every dwelling and byre in the small township. It was probably this movement which had alerted Achnacone's tenants, and they had come to seek his reassurance. What they received was a volley blasted through the narrow casements by a platoon, just under a score strong, led by Barber himself.

These townships were untidy and crowded places, not at all like the image of the orderly country village; houses and bothies a warren; frozen mire between, animals and men mingled; ordure piled on steaming middens, only the intense cold to drive out or suppress the stink of man and beast. Quartering such a place, in the dark and obscured by snowfall, was no easy task, though the men had had nearly a fortnight to develop their orientation and besides, many came from places very similar. As the MacDonalds huddled in the tacksman's principal room, grand by local standards with perhaps a fitful glow from the peat fire and rush lights, just enough to aim by, the crashing volley sounded like the clap of doom, as indeed for several present it was. The noise of the blasting muskets would be deafening, ear splitting; some certainly would suffer burst eardrums; a cloying, sulphurous discharge would fill the smoky room with acrid residue. John MacDonald fell dead, despite the sacrificial efforts of his servant, named Kennedy, as did a trio of others, their blood in great arterial gouts, drenching the room, spraying over floor and walls, the stench of defecation competing with black powder. Dying men screamed and jerked convulsively as their bladders and bowels voided in terror. The work was going well.

Achnacone, stunned, no more than winged, was amongst those who still lived. Barber kicked his former host, finding him annoyingly alive; this he prepared to remedy, but the injured man pleaded he be permitted to die in the open. This wish the sergeant was disposed to grant: he had, as he advised, eaten the condemned man's bread, so he would bear the inconvenience of assassinating his host in his own yard rather than in his hall. Achnacone was dragged outside to be stood against a wall. He was barely injured, and with the quick-thinking and strength of desperation cast his plaid over the execution squad, breaking through and off as they struggled, like a hare, into the darkness.

He escaped, and the alarum provided cover for the other wounded men to gather and slip through the back door. Undeterred by these setbacks, Barber's squads set to work with a will, shooting, stabbing and hacking. People were killed in their homes or as they stumbled out into the horror of a darkness lit by the flash of blazing muzzles, bullets plucking them into oblivion or the agonizing thrust of reddened bayonets, grinding on bone, spilling intestines. It was said that over a dozen people were immolated in one of the cottages; one octogenarian and a child were heaped with the dead; later, only the severed hand of the child could be found. Within a short space, the township had been transformed into a charnel house, the dead piled on middens and covered. Killing with musket and bayonet is a tiring business. With each discharge the barrel becomes increasingly fouled with powder residue, many victims would be dispatched by a mix of shooting, stabbing with the bayonet and bludgeoning with the brass butt plate. Many would take a disobligingly long time to die, writhing, shrieking and screaming as their life blood poured out upon the frozen ground; the bayonet going in a dozen or a score of times; blunted by bone or the mass of tissue, lodging in muscle and sinew.

Robert Campbell of Glenlyon, quartered with the tacksman of Inverrigan, had raised no scruple against the orders he had been given. Perhaps these were not unexpected, but if he had to play the assassin it is evident he did so without relish, certainly without that degree of enthusiasm shown by Lindsay or Barber. At precisely five of the clock the tacksman and eight of his household were dragged, still bound, from the house and dumped on the midden. Glenlyon then shot his host dead, and all but one of the remaining men was killed, after not a wild volley but systematic execution. Inverrigan, like Achtriachtan, died with Hill's letter of protection on his person. The irony of this cannot have escaped Glenlyon. That he had no stomach for murder was evident, for he attempted to save the last of his victims, a young man of perhaps twenty. By now Duncanson's companies were coming up so this would suggest that he had arrived earlier than seven.

Glenlyon had his victims trussed and ready for slaughter before five so the killing would take but a few moments. Amongst the later arrivals was Captain Drummond; as a captain of grenadiers he outranked Glenlyon and mercy was not writ within his orders or inclination. Brusquely he reminded Campbell of their firm instructions and dispatched the lad with his pistol. The horror was not done; from the darkness a child, perhaps in its early teens ran and clutched at Glenlyon's booted leg, screaming for mercy, until Drummond used his dirk. More MacDonalds died at Inverrigan, another, much younger child and at least one female shot, stabbed or clubbed in the frenzy. As at Achnacone, the dead were flung sack-like onto their own middens or bundled into shallow graves hastily scraped in the frozen ground.

Achtriachtan himself had died beneath his kinsman's roof and Barber's murderous fusillade, but at his township there was more killing to be done, in this most easterly outpost of Clan Iain Abrach, the village of poets. One of the soldiers, maddened by bloodlust and filled with vengeance, is said to have screamed an imprecation with every maddened thrust. At least two noted bards of the clan, Iain MacRaonuill Og and Aonghus MacAlister Ruaidh escaped. If the venerable Ranald of the Shield was still living then he was slain, though his sons fled to safety. Had Hamilton succeeded in scaling the Devil's Staircase and sealing the eastern end of the Glen then the toll from Achtriachtan would have been very much greater, but he had not arrived, and the dazed survivors scattered from their burning homes without further molestation. In this they may be deemed fortunate.

Above the carnage, shrouded by the dark and the falling of the snow, John and Alasdair MacDonald, with a swelling band of fugitives, listened to the destruction of their kin; watched the stabbing tongues of flame as muskets banged and the bright blossom of flame from lighted thatch. Perhaps, too they heard the shrieks of dying men and women, the terrified sounds of frightened animals, the scent of blood and waste pungent in windswept air. By now, as dawn approached, the slopes of Meall Mor offered little sanctuary, and the MacDonalds hustled their women and children southwards by the frozen streams of Gleann an Fiodh or Gleann Leac na Muidhe. Here there was no shelter to be found from the bitter, knifing wind, though each step took the survivors further beyond the reach of the hunters. As they stumbled over broken ground, hardened by iron frost; streams frozen, barren snow covered slopes rising, the cold would begin to take its toll of the most vulnerable: the very old or the very young, the sick and any who were injured.

Death for them would be kinder; hypothermia proceeds through three stages. In the first, the victim notices numbness in their extremities, difficulty breathing; stage two brings a sensation of warmth, the sufferer stumbles, speech becomes slurred, pallid and blue in the extreme. In the third and final stage, speech and walking become impossible and the victim's major organs simply shut down; death ensues. Many of the fleeing MacDonalds must have watched helpless as their kin succumbed, escaping the bullet or the thrust of a bayonet only to sink upon a cold hillside, never to rise, to become part of a shrouded landscape, their bodies twisted in the posture of frozen death.

7.00 A.M.

Duncan Don, lay huddled with the dead around MacIain's wrecked and pillaged house, soon given to the flames. Though wounded, he was not dead, and he later recalled that he saw Duncanson's 400 soldiers come up. Alhough, given his wounds and the trauma he had undergone he may have been understandably confused, it seems that the major must have arrived before seven, given that Lindsay had struck just after five. It was now Glenlyon's piper that struck up a Campbell rant, though perhaps this is hearsay. No man present would be keen to shout what he had done in the darkness, and the creeping light of a winter dawn would reveal the extent of the horror. A clan might exult in the slaughter of foes killed in the glorious heat of battle, but the mantle of fame does not cling to base murder. Duncanson might have been cheered by the sight of MacIain's corpse, but his terse enquiries as to the fate of his two sons went unanswered. Riding on to Inverrigan to ask the same question of Glenlyon, he received no better reply. MacDonalds had been killed, but simply not enough.

Another question Duncanson would have been forming was simply this: where was Hamilton? Without the eastern approaches sealed and the trap left open, many could flee over the Black Mount and scatter. It was altogether unsatisfactory, and Duncanson would already have a sense that Livingstone and the Master of Stair were anticipating a far higher body count than this. Killing the old chief was of little value unless his successors could be cut off at the same time. Had he been aware of Hamilton's movements since leaving Inverlochy, he would not have felt reassured. Of the three formations detailed to take part in the operation, the seven companies under Hamilton had, in terms of hard marching, the most onerous task. In the deepening storm they struggled southwards from the fort, following a drove road to the flank of *Meall a Chaoruinn,* then pushing eastwards for seven long and fatiguing miles to come out on the shore of Loch Leven. This was not the toughest part of their twenty-mile yomp; that would be the ascent of the Devil's Staircase, which climbs from Kinlochleven to Glencoe.

It begins with a relatively gentle ascent from the township for perhaps a couple of miles, then crosses the *Alt a' Choire Ochair-mhoir* a little distance from the waterfall, traverses the shoulder of *Sron a'Choire Ochair-bhig*, before fording the larger burn and passing Beinn Bheag to the east. It then sweeps down a sharp, twisting descent to enter the glen at *Altnfeadh*. The weary infantry would then have to continue their march for at least another four miles westward down the glen to reach Achtriachtan. To accomplish the full manoeuvre in the teeth of a biting February gale with driving snow and over a distance of a score of miles and more, was asking a very great deal of the men. This writer has, on numerous occasions, retraced Hamilton's march, in fine weather and without heavy pack; it is exhausting. How much harder then for those four struggling companies, mainly in the dark, laden with kit, the snow driving relentlessly in their faces. It was too much; by the time the men straggled into Kinlochleven they were spent; to continue in the teeth of such devilish weather was beyond them. For John Forbes, seconding Hamilton, this was a relief: this was not the type of military service he had envisaged. It was possibly now the two junior officers of the regiment, probably Francis Farquhar and Gilbert Kennedy, refused point blank to carry out their orders; they broke their swords and would have nothing to do with the business. Of the men who were marching that night only they behaved with honour. For the moment, however, they were placed under arrest; the oath admitted no grounds for conscience.

As the cold and weary foot took what shelter they could find in the mean township, huddled and freezing, it was apparent the march could not be resumed until dawn. The creeping light brought little relief. The line of march was scarcely appealing, low cloud and mist scurried by drifts of snow meant the second phase of the approach would be arduous, and it was late morning before Hamilton's command entered the glen and swung westwards toward Achtriachtan. They saw no one and found the hamlet smoldering and deserted. Only the grim silence and acrid smoke of destruction greeted them,;those who could flee had fled, and they were too late. By way of something to contribute, Hamilton ordered his men to burn the few bothies still standing and, like beaters, they flushed out an old man lurking unseen, presumably too aged to flee with the rest. A platoon volley killed him – the murder of one greybeard a rather poor return for the effort expended.

NOON AND AFTER

The killing was over. Hamilton's men met with Duncanson's probing eastward and the Deputy-Governor's sour humor was not improved when he now learnt that John and Alasdair MacDonald had slipped the net. Glencoe was a scene from Hell. What had the day before, been a scattering of townships was now skeletal ruins, with the stench of the charnel house hanging like a pestilence in the cold air. Every cow, sheep, goat and pony had been lifted and was being driven westwards away from the glen; anything of use or value had been pilfered, and no living soul remained. In all, nearly a thousand beasts, two hundred mounts and a considerable quantity of sheep and goats were added profitably to the haul; any foodstuffs and utensils were taken; many items stolen by the Campbells might, of course, have been their own previously.

Those survivors sheltering in the bleak bowl of the *Coire Gabhail* must have looked on with renewed despair as their animals were driven off. Since the stumbling horror of the darkness when they had fled their homes, they had huddled in the wind-lashed amphitheatre, bare, scree-studded slopes of Gearr Aonach and Beinn Fhada rising stark around, many already showing signs of hypothermia; others with life-draining wounds. Many must have wondered if survival was a blessing or trial.

Robert Campbell of Glenlyon might have repossessed his own fine, copper kettle from the wrack of MacIain's house.[11] Glenlyon's report suggested three dozen MacDonalds had been killed besides their chief, and this figure probably referred to males only. To this we must add women and children known to have perished; a total of thirty-eight is that generally agreed upon. For the effort expended, it was an unimpressive total, the twentieth century would manage much better; but it was killing enough. Vile as the weather had been, it was this that had saved so many, preventing pursuit. At least three of Glenlyon's men, stumbling after fugitives, were ambushed by the vengeful blades of Clan Iain Abrach and cut down.

It may well be that, as John Prebble points out, that the Campbells, for all the reasons they had to hate Clan Donald, were more scrupulous than Lowlanders might have been. For them the laws of hospitality were inviolable, and the notion of murder under trust utterly abhorrent. Many MacDonalds must have survived because their putative assassins simply looked the other way; the snow may have abetted consciences. One tale concerns a desperate fugitive from Inverrigan, a young mother with infant child, crouched, numbed and terrified beneath the span of the small bridge that led across the stream of Allt na Muidhe. The baby cried out, and one of Glenlyon's men was sent to deal with mother and child. Seeing his victims in desperate straits, he could not bear to strike and simply bayoneted the woman's dog. It is said the officer in charge recognised canine from human blood and ordered him back to complete his orders. He next hit on the expedient of using his short sword or hanger to cut off the child's little finger and smear blood on the blade; by such desperate remedy were both mother and child saved.[12]

If the ferocity of the blizzard had saved lives during the onslaught, Hamilton might have had some grounds for hoping the cold might account for many of the survivors. In this he was undoubtedly correct: the death toll amongst those who were stumbling up snow shrouded high passes, through narrow, freezing glens must have suffered dreadfully. The young, the old, the sick, those bearing wounds from the attack would all be particularly vulnerable. At least as many would have perished as had fallen to powder and shot. In the coming months of privation, hunger and despair, yet more would succumb.

In all, the final toll must have been around one hundred, possibly as high as twenty-five per cent of the total population.

In the glen itself as the winter afternoon drew on, a long column of scarlet and plaid would be seen herding herds of frightened beasts, wild eyed in the smell of blood, flocks of sheep and goats, all the animals bony and weakened by winter hardship. Each of the settlements marked by eddies of smoke and drifting ash, blackened zones where, until yesterday, was habitation. As the soldiers withdrew, knapsacks and bellies full, loot jangling and driven on four legs before, we can speculate as to how they felt about the night's work, now the cold light of winter's day had driven back the red mist of frenzy. Were they indifferent to what they had done; did they exult or did they carry the worm of shame? How many would realise that the name Glencoe would follow them and their descendants like a curse? Were many of the officers already secretly rehearsing what they might tell a subsequent inquiry? It is hard to escape the conclusion, in the cases of Hamilton and Duncanson, that both had an eye to excuse, Duncanson may have deliberately confused timings, and Hamilton had to have known his night march was infeasible.

Dusk

As light thickened, some of the bolder spirits stole down from the lee of the hills to find what remained of relatives who had vanished in the suddenness of the onslaught. Many corpses would have been cremated within the shell of their tumbled dwellings, others heaped upon middens, some hastily interred and others left stripped and bundled where they had fallen. Archibald MacDonald found the corpse of the twelfth chief; Duncan Don was still breathing and had escaped the bayonets of the soldiers. Ronald MacDonald, stealing back to the stripped and ravaged carcass of his dwelling near Carnoch, from where he gathered his father's bones, reported seeing the corpses of Achtriachtan, and those who had been murdered with him, heaped ignominiously on a dung hill. It is said that the bard Murdoch Matheson ascended Signal Rock to compose his lament for the fallen.[13] Lady Glencoe might have been bundled away by fleeing servants and tenants, or she may have been left, unmolested other than the injury and abuse she had suffered when her husband was shot, his blood and brains splattered. Her sons did what they could though she did not long survive, the long, cold walk to Appin proved too much, shock and despair too great. They undoubtedly tended to the mangled remains of their father, and it may be his body was, in due course, interred on Eilean Munde.

There was nothing more to be done in the glen. They could not remain; all of their livestock was gone, their roofs destroyed their possessions taken. Besides, the Campbells might yet return to complete that which they had so earnestly begun. There was no alternative but to lead the shocked survivors to the safety of Appin. Their route lay along the passes of *Gleann Leac* or *Glen an Fiodh,* the snout of *Meall Mor* swelling between. Hungry, cold and despairing the fugitives, intruders now in their own landscape, set off. Those already suffering would fall by the way as the relentless wind howled through the bare upland valleys and yet more snow came down. Some went northwards to Keppoch country, others, who had hid in the *Coire Gabhail,* found shelter in shielings on the Black Mount; but the clan was effectively dispersed, a diaspora as swift as it was brutal. For four centuries they had occupied the glen and now, in a few, short hours of shocking violence, they were driven out. For the survivors, their trials were just beginning; the spring and summer would be a time of hardship and continued suffering.

By dusk, the soldiers with their booty would be back at Inverlochy, about to settle into billets and congratulate themselves on a job well done or uncomfortable introspection. Any who thought the business of Glencoe was now concluded would have been very wrong indeed.

CHAPTER 8

Aftermath: 'It is no Joy Without Clan Donald'

''Ethnic Cleansing' – The practice of mass expulsion or killing of people from opposing ethnic or religious groups within a certain area.'

Oxford English Dictionary

'I said it was a far cry to Lochawe.'

Sir John Campbell, Earl of Breadalbane

It is no joy without Clan Donald,
It is no strength to be without them,
The best race in the round world,
To them belongs every goodly man ...

A race the best for service and shelter,
A race the best for valour of hand,
Ill I deem the shortness of her skein
By whom their thread was spun

For sorrow and for sadness
I have forsaken wisdom and learning;

One their account I have forsaken all things.
It is no joy without Clan Donald.

> Ni H-eibhneas gan Chlainn Domhnaill –
> It is No Joy Without Clan Donald

The Massacre of Glencoe, apart from the murderous savagery of the act, was a great propaganda coup for the Jacobite cause. This was the justice Highland clans could expect from a Williamite Government, one that rated them no better than savages, to be slaughtered with impunity and with at least the tacit connivance of the administration. It was a nasty, bad and bloody business; if it spread disaffection, then this could hardly be wondered at. By 12th April, the Jacobite press was beginning to make hay; the Paris Gazette broadcast:

> The laird of Glencoe was butchered several days ago in the most barbarous manner, although he was amenable to the present Government. The Laird of Glenlyon, a captain in Argyll's Regiment, following the explicit orders of Colonel Hill, Governor of Inverlochy, went at night to Glencoe with a body of soldiers; and the soldiers having entered the houses, killed the Laird of Glencoe, two of his sons, thirty-six men or children and four women. It had been resolved in this manner to wipe out the rest of the inhabitants, notwithstanding the amnesty that had been granted them, but about two hundred escaped. It has been rumored that the Laird was killed in an ambush with his weapons in his hands, in order to diminish the horror of so barbarous an action, which would have made all nations see what little trust can be placed on the words of those who rule.[1]

Murder Will Out

This account was remarkably factual. The number of casualties is slightly exaggerated and, of course, both MacIain's sons escaped – the Jacobites had clearly had sight of both Hamilton's and Duncanson's orders. The coffee houses of both Edinburgh and London were alive with talk of what had been done. Sir John Dalrymple was not abashed nor minded to proffer excuses, his tone remained both harsh and unrepentant – if he regretted anything it was that the job had been left unfinished:

> All I regret is that any of the sept got away, and there is necessity to pros-
> ecute them to the utmost. If they could go out of the country, I could wish
> they were let slip, but they can never do good there. Appin, who is the
> heritor, should have encouragement to plant the place with other people
> than Macdonalds.[2]

Others were to take a less sanguine view. By 5th March rumours that the Glencoe people had been killed in their beds were circulating. Those in Edinburgh could hear it from Glenlyon's lips, for Argyll's Regiment was ordered for Flanders and the captain was active and babbling in the coffee houses and taverns. He was voluble in his own defence, but so burdened with guilt his face told a different story. Boldly he blustered: 'I would do it again … I would dirk any man in Scotland or England, if my master the King ordered me, and never speir [enquire] the cause'.[3]

Hill had sat down to write up his report of the 14th February, directing his correspondence to Tweeddale as Lord Chancellor. He reported, blandly enough, that Glengarry had at long last hauled down his colours and handed over his castle, that punitive action in the Western Isles had been satisfactorily attended to and that, almost as a postscript: 'I have also ruined Glencoe.' He confirms the death of MacIain and his tacksman, with the killing of three dozen more, and ends with a prayer, no doubt heartfelt, that: 'I hope this example of justice and severity upon Glencoe will be enough.' There was little more the old man could say, he knew too well what had been done and that the dagger of complicity hung over him. One man who was greatly more implicated but now hastened with considerable, not to say indecent, alacrity to distance himself, was

Breadalbane. Grey John had spent the winter in London, entrusting matters in Scotland to the capable hands of his agent Colin Campbell of Carwhin. The earl expressed alarm and horror at the news; most of his concern, as ever, related to his own position and whether he might be implicated.

He claimed he had protested at the violence of the action (implying this was beyond any measure he had intended) and he makes a point that it was Argyll's men who had been responsible. He feared innocent persons might now suffer – by this he did not mean the surviving MacDonalds but himself. He explained he had discussed the matter with the Duke, who was blandly confident of royal support, but that, in Grey John's Campbell slang, 'I said it was a far cry to Lochawe'.[4] Breadalbane's well-tuned antennae were picking up the rumblings of outrage that would soon reach a full chorus. News from Carwhin that his name was being freely associated with tales of the atrocity only sharpened his venom toward Glenlyon, onto whom he was clearly hoping to shift the blame: 'It's villainy to accuse me for Glenlyon's madness ... ane ill and miraculous fate follows unfortunate Glenlyon the whole tract of his life. He is not to be mended. I hope he will go to Flanders.' This last was doubtless sincere, for posting to the Low Countries would take Glenlyon beyond the reach of those who would use him as a scaffold upon which to hang Grey John's reputation.

In modern parlance, it was time for 'damage limitation'. Argyll himself, not unduly concerned, was with Stair, departing for Flanders in the King's train. Grey John, markedly, was not, and could hear the daggers rattling on his Ides of March. The Duke had intimated that the Glenorchy men were buying Clan Iain Abrach's lifted stock at discount rates, thus adding profiteering to slaughter. In response, Grey John instructed his steward, Campbell of Barcaldine, to seek out the survivors skulking in Appin and offer them a deal. If they would absolve Breadalbane of guilt in the Massacre, he would intercede on their behalf to obtain good terms for their restoration. This gerrymandering went nowhere, and Grey John was soon issuing denials that rose swiftly toward virtual hysteria.

Livingstone, on the other hand, saw no reason to express regret. At the end of February he replied to correspondence from Hamilton who had brought in some prisoners, reminding his subordinate that the Government was not to be discommoded by captives: 'Let no prisoners be brought in, but let them be dispatched in the place where they are found, for such robbers and thieves are not to be treated as regular enemies …'. No officer would be left in doubt as to the nature of his orders. Stair's letter to Hill, quoted above, does, however, contain the bare skeleton of a disclaimer from the Secretary of State. He prefaces his quoted remarks with an almost throwaway reference to gossip that the MacDonalds had been murdered in their beds, a politician's line: 'for the last I know nothing of it'. As yet there was nothing official to deny, but Stair, practiced as he was, clearly had future denials in mind. The Master's antennae were easily as keenly tuned as Breadalbane's, and he could obviously discern the shape of thunderclouds ahead.

One of the more remarkable Jacobite sympathizers was Charles Leslie, an Irish lawyer, well born and who had also trained as a minister, deprived of his position when he would not swear the oath to William and Mary. In England he became a noted propagandist and, inspired by the early reports, made a full and due enquiry into the circumstances of the killings. Such was the sensitivity and so acute the censorship he was obliged to tack 'A letter from a gentleman in Scotland to his friend at London, who desir'd a particular Account of the Business of Glencoe' onto the wholly less controversial screen of a diatribe on the Protestant Church in Ireland. Both Hamilton's and Duncanson's orders were copied verbatim within the text. As Argyll's regiment was encamped in the south-east awaiting transport, he journeyed to Essex to seek first-hand testimony. He did not speak to any of the officers but found plenty men willing to talk. Of Glenlyon they opined: 'you may see Glencoe in his face'. Though Leslie's account was intended to be both partisan and sensationalist, it is remarkably accurate and consistent with testimony provided to the official inquiry. The tone is pregnant with outrage, but does not essentially depart from the facts:

And how dismal may you imagine the Case of the poor Women and Children was then! It was lamentable, past expression; their Husbands and fathers, and near relations were forced to flee for their Lives; they themselves almost stript, and nothing left them, and their houses being burnt, and not one house nearer than six Miles; and to get thither they were to pass over Mountains, and Wreaths of Snow, in a vehement Storm, wherein the greater part of them perished through Hunger and Cold. It fills me with horror to think of poor stript Children and Women, some with Child, and some giving Suck, wrestling against a storm in Mountains, and heaps of Snow, and at length to be overcome, and give over, and fall down and die miserably.[5]

The pamphlet, some 4,000 words in length, was cleverly written. Leslie himself was both the 'gentleman in Scotland' and his 'friend' and he neatly avoids any overt hint of sedition in the manner in which he points the finger of guilt, accusing none directly but clearly placing the full blame at the Government's door:

You desire some proofs of the truth of the Story; for you say there are many in England who cannot believe such a thing could be done, and publick justice not executed upon the ruffians: For they take it for granted, that no such order could be given by the Government; and you say they will never believe it without a downright demonstration. Sir, As to the Government, I will not meddle with it; or whether these Officers who murdered Glenco, had such Orders as they pretended from the Government; the Government knows that best, and how to vindicate their own honor ...[6]

While Breadalbane hid on his estates with the King and Secretary busily engaged in Flanders, (where, to William, lay the important business of the day) Glencoe was an unimportant footnote that should not distract anyone unduly. The ash smouldered in the Glen, amongst the charred timbers and broken walls, the scattered debris of sudden death and panicked flight. And there was silence, the sounds of spring did not come or fell upon a shrouded landscape. There would be no Beltainn fires in Glencoe that year. But Clan Iain Abrach were hardened and hardy, the weight of their suffering was great, but such horrors were not unknown in the Highlands and they themselves had meted out similar treatment in Glen Orchy and Glenlyon. As the days lengthened, braver souls began to drift back to the wreckage of their homes, salvaging what little they could and contemplating the task of reconstruction, no more than landless beggars on their own soil. The Appin men and others contributed a few cows, and John MacDonald, now thirteenth Chief, felt sufficiently confident in the Governor's goodwill to approach Hill at Inverlochy for protection, ironic perhaps but sound. Hill proved amenable, this at least was some salve to his conscience and, as ever, he sought to do the right thing.

On 3rd May the Scottish Privy Council, which could justly claim to have had no hand in the business, issued favourable instructions. Hill was thus able to offer provisional security to these persons:

> Either in general or particularly, of all security to their persons, lands and goods, and a cessation of all acts of hostility, trouble or molestation to them, upon the account of their having been in arms and rebellion against their Majesties, and to take what security he shall think meet for their living peaceably until his Majesty signifies his pleasure therein.[7]

This was pretty thin given the desperate straits the survivors now found themselves in, but it was a shield of sorts. Throughout that summer Hill lobbied ceaselessly for clemency, and moderates such as Tweeddale were perhaps disposed to listen. Not so for Sir John Dalrymple, whose attitude, and that of the King, did not countenance mercy. True, the Glencoe men were no longer to be hunted down, transportation was now felt to be the fitter course: ' … he [the King] is willing to pardon them, they going abroad to the plantations, Ireland, or any other place.' There was, at this juncture, no question of them returning to their ravaged glen.

Despite this, the old soldier continued to lobby; the blood of those killed weighed heavy; he pointed out that the other chiefs were coming in and that further reprisal could only be damaging. In August his patience and good sense was finally vindicated when the King relented and Hill was, at last, able to write to John MacDonald advising him to undertake his own journey to Inverary and there to swear the oath before Ardkinglas. The thirteenth chief replied in humble and grateful tone. this must have cost him dear, to dig deep of servility whilst the bones of his name lay amongst their shattered steadings, but he was keenly aware that Hill's efforts were sincere and thatIan Iain Abrach had very few friends. It was not until the autumn, October 3rd, that the King signified his final acquiescence and Hill was able to write, almost joyfully, to Forbes:

> The Glencoe men are abundantly civil. I have put them under my lord Argyle, and have Arkenloss' [Ardkinglas] surety for them till my lord comes; for they are now my Lord Argyle's men; for 'twas very necessary they should be under some person of power, and of honesty to the Government.[8]

If anyone saw the bitter irony in the remnant of Clan Iain Abrach now being under Argyll's protection given what had passed before, they doubtless kept it to themselves. Battered and impoverished, the people were not entirely without friends; both Appin Stewarts and Camerons did what they could whilst Archibald MacDonald from North Uist sailed from the Isles bringing a cargo load of meal which he landed safely on the shore of Loch Leven. His people had connections with Iain Abrach stretching back several centuries and, in the hour of desperate need, he provided desperately needed and life-saving supplies. For William III, 1692 was not a very good year; the Massacre was but the least of his concerns if he considered the business at all. His campaign in Flanders was going badly, very badly in fact. Hugh Mackay and a legion of others perished in the cauldron of Steenkirk, a bitter defeat. The King was not the only person of note beset by enemies. James Johnston of Warriston was now Joint Secretary with Stair and could discern in the Massacre the weapon he might use to unseat Dalrymple.

WHERE WILL THIS LODGE THE MURTHER?

Johnston was the son of Archibald, Lord Warriston (1611 – 1663), a noted champion of the Covenant and active during the first Bishops' War. Unswerving is his opposition to abuses of the royal prerogative, he remained an influential figure in the Scottish polity, taking a senior role in the negotiations with the dying Pym that brought the Scots into the war in England. Although he enjoyed cordial relations with Cromwell, he supported Charles II and, as Lord Clerk Register, condemned Montrose. With the Restoration, however, his star swiftly declined and he was obliged to flee to Holland; crossing unwisely into France he was taken and extradited to face execution. James had followed his father into exile and had waited for a quarter of a century for his chance to come. With the Glorious Revolution, he was clear to take the stage, respected by some, vilified by others including Swift, he was a force to be reckoned with, one of the few who could match Stair's intelligence and élan. He heartily despised Dalrymple, partly on account of his religious zeal, but mainly as the Master stood in his way, as Melville had done before with Stair himself. Glencoe was the perfect vehicle; from the start Johnston was not interested in Breadalbane, Livingstone, Hill, Hamilton or any down the chain of command, his sights were firmly fixed on Dalrymple. None could ever accuse him of impartiality, nor could it be suggested he was motivated by the need to provide justice for the survivors; as a good Presbyterian the clansmen were still just savages, but now they were, for the moment, opportune savages:

> And all the Reception it met with among many here in England, was, That it was a Jacobite story, on purpose to Reflect upon the Government, and that there was no such thing: But this is now confuted by the Proceedings in Scotland, this Summer Session, 1695. Wherein they have voted the killing of the Glenco-men to be a Murther; and yet have acquitted Sir Thomas Livingston, and Colonel Hill, who gave the Orders for Killing of them. Why? Because their Orders were but pursuant to the Instructions

they had from Court. Where will this Lodge the Murther? The Design, it is well-enough known, is to put it upon Sir John Dalrymple ... because he is not so Fiery a Presbyterian as the other Secretary, James Johnston.[9]

From the outset Johnston was assiduous in asserting that the true purpose of any inquiry would be to absolve the Crown of responsibility, thus avoiding a whiff of sedition. Furthermore, if the entire burden of guilt could be removed from the King's shoulders then who else was to blame? There could be only one culprit: the Master of Stair. William had no interest in such proceedings; Glencoe was but a historical footnote in the greater events unfolding in Flanders and the tide of those events was not flowing in a favourable direction. Losses on the scale of those incurred at Steenkirk made the taking off of a few Gaels even more immaterial. The Queen was far less sanguine. As a Stuart she continued to feel some measure of responsibility for the MacDonalds – lost sheep rather than irreconcilable savages – and she now added to the clamour. Barely a year after the blood of Glencoe had cooled upon the snow, William at last gave way and appointed the Lord High Commissioner the Duke of Hamilton to conduct a formal inquiry.

Survival instincts were already alerted. Livingstone could sense a mood of censure and thus wrote to Lieutenant Colonel Hamilton in April: '... some in Parliament mak[e] a talking about the business of Glencoe, and give out they design to have it examined.' This rather nonchalant tone had sharpened considerably within a month, however, when he wrote again to Hamilton:

> ... It is not that anybody thinks that thieving tribe did not deserve to be destroyed, but that it should have been done by those as were quartered amongst them, makes a great noise. I suppose I may have pressed it somewhat upon your Colonel [Hill] knowing how slow he was in the execution of such things.[10]

Thus Livingstone as Commander in Chief was already seeking to distance himself, if not from the order itself – which was patently impossible – then from the means of its being carried out. He is proposing to shift the blame onto Hill, in fact the least guilty of the senior officers implicated.

Matters did not proceed swiftly. The Duke of Hamilton, with admirable timing, now expired, and the King saw no immediate need to appoint a successor. But the clamour did not die down. Warriston and Stair's legion of opponents could sense blood in the water and were desperate to begin circling for the kill. A further two years passed and nothing was done, but the Scottish Parliament, so long ignored, now had the bit firmly between its collective teeth, egged on by such able riders as Johnston. Finally, anticipating the inevitable, William ordered another inquiry be undertaken, this time led by Tweeddale, as the new High Commissioner and the Earl of Annandale, established 'under the Broad Seal'. The commission was an affair of lawyers in the main, though quite balanced in its composition. Tweeddale himself was a staunch Williamite, Privy Councillor from 1689 and elevated to the Lord Chancellorship in the year of the Massacre.[11]

This time matters proceeded apace. It is possible to surmise the commissioners set about their task with some relish; their quarry was already in sight and it was rare for the Scots' Parliament to have the opportunity to flex any real muscle. Besides, the matter was something of a cause for celebration, the Jacobites stirring the pot for all their worth. Livingstone, Hill, Hamilton, Ardkinglas, Campbell of Dressalch, Lord Aberuchil, Sir Gilbert Elliot (Clerk to the Privy Council) the two junior officers, Francis Farquhar and George Kennedy (whom we may presume to be those who refused the order), together with an enlisted man, James Campbell, from Glenlyon's company, were all summonsed to appear. Of considerable significance are the names of those who were not able to be called as they were serving their country in Flanders: Duncanson, Glenlyon, Drummond, Lieutenant Lindsay, Ensign Lundie and Sergeant Barber with any other private men. Lieutenant Colonel Hamilton was by now in Ireland, and though his appearance was demanded, he failed to comply. The thirteenth chief of Clan Iain Abrach, his younger sibling Alasdair, Achtriachtan's heir Alexander and another seven MacDonalds gave evidence.[12]

When these Highlanders, in saffron and plaid, strode into the Great Hall of Holyroodhouse, they were as great a sensation as a deputation of Pathans or Zulus might have been 150 years later. Colonel Hill, supported by Glengarry, referred openly to the Private Articles arising from Breadalbane's Achallader summit and, whilst the existence of these might have been hinted at and even tacitly acknowledged, Grey John's perfidy was now out in the open and in full view of his enemies. Like Stair, he had few friends, and if his head was a lesser trophy it was not one to be scorned when offered on a plate. The Earl of Breadalbane presently, and in fear and trembling, found himself incarcerated in lodgings a good deal less commodious than he would wish. Rumblings of treason filled the air to add to his disquiet. Tweeddale, to his credit, was no witch-hunter, and petitioned the King for clemency. This request received no early reply, William would need time to consider his options and decide who, if any, was to be thrown to the wolves.

By 20th June, the commissioners had signed off their report and dispatched a copy to the King, in Flanders, who presently sat before the walls of Namur. The findings would make for uncomfortable reading.

What had been done was wrong and a considerable injustice had been inflicted on the MacDonalds of Glencoe. Their chief's submission should properly have been passed to the Privy Council. MacIain's submission had been known of, particularly by Stair, and, if there was a technical breach of the terms for taking the oath, worse culprits, such as Glengarry, had not been penalized. It was found that Stair's correspondence clearly indicated he had chosen to interpret the term 'extirpate' in a wholly more murderous sense than the King had intended, and that this resulted in barbarous murder.

Parliament was subsequently disposed to exonerate fully both Hill and Livingstone. Hamilton was censured and a warrant issued, though never executed – the Lieutenant Colonel was presently beyond the jurisdiction and clearly intended to remain so. The return for trial of Duncanson, Glenlyon, Drummond, Lindsay, Lundie and Barber was demanded but, unsurprisingly, nothing further transpired. By crepuscular argument the commissioners were careful to exonerate the King from any censure. They were pleased to interpret his order as being instructions to deal with the MacDonalds by due process of law. When he had referred, in his signed authority, to the separation of the Glencoe men, he intended such separation only if they had not submitted – which they now plainly had, and by 'extirpate' William, unlike his minister, was referring to punitive action within the law. Doubtless these findings were a great comfort to the King.

Their interpretation of Dalrymple's actions was a deal less circuitous. In his correspondence to subordinates he clearly exceeded, by tone and content, the instructions given by the King. Instead of authorizing a judicial reprisal, he had orchestrated an atrocity. The words used, and the earnestness with which the course of action was pressed, left no room for doubt, quite plainly establishing where the blame lay: it was all Stair's doing; he was wholly to blame. It was on 26th June that the Scots' Parliament sat and debated the report; that a witch-hunt was now in progress was gleefully obvious; for all of the Master's enemies this was payback time. For Johnston it was the prime and golden opportunity to be free of the fetters of joint office. Dalrymple had no friends, no powerful affinity that could rally and conduct a defence; only Argyll ventured to speak on his behalf and was swiftly brushed aside. It was left to Stair to submit his own defence, thrown in the teeth of the jackals now baying for blood, and penned by his brother, Hew. As might be anticipated, this was robust, spirited and unrepentant. He believed the commission was prejudiced, that his letters had been quoted wholly out of context and that he had been denied a voice. The victims were deserving of their fate, and it was only the manner of their taking off, a responsibility of the officers concerned, which was regrettable. The Master was, as ever, both erudite and thorough in his rebuttal. An equally lengthy response was drafted by Sir James Stuart, the Lord Advocate.[13]

Needless to say, it did him little good. The motion of censure, when it came, was passed with the anticipated, sizeable majority. On 10th July an 'Address by Parliament to the King, Touching the Murder of the Glencoe Men' was drafted and submitted to William. The document was swift to exonerate the throne and laid the blame entirely at the feet of the Secretary of State: 'we beg your Majesty will give such orders about him, for vindication of your Government, as you in your Royal wisdom shall think fit'.[14] Neither Argyll nor Breadalbane were mentioned; Grey John had ceased to be of interest, and it was requested that the King might extend some charity or compensation to the survivors, a body which had featured only anecdotally to date, for the real business of Parliament was the hounding of Stair, not restitution. Two key figures had now died: Queen Mary and Viscount Stair. The King thus had no nagging voices in his ear and the Master was now heir, thus providing a pretext for him to quietly slip beneath the radar of public life and retire, unrepentant, to his properties.

For the Jacobites, the savaging of Dalrymple was a rare gift. The indefatigable Leslie re-issued his earlier tract, embellished by a commentary upon the inquiry's report, under the bellicose title of 'Gallienus Redivivus' or 'MURDER WILL OUT, ETC Being a True Account of the DE-WITTING of Glencoe'. In this blast he likens the King to the Roman tyrant Gallienus, guilty of sanctioning the murder of his political opponents, and referring to the murder of the De Witt brothers, nearly quarter of a century earlier. Leslie does not hesitate in cutting through the commissioners' screen: 'the reader must likewise know that none of the 'Foresaid Instructions' were communicated to the Privy Council of Scotland, to whom by the Constitution of that Kingdom, and Continual Custom, all the Kings orders are directed.' They knew nothing of this matter: 'it was contriv'd to be Carry'd in such a Manner, as not to be prevented. And when Gallienus his Thirst of Blood is once Satisfy'd, then let Slaves Grumble, and make Inquiry!'[15] The pamphleteer scorned Johnston's whitewash and went so far as to accuse him of procuring Hamilton's escape.

Breadalbane too was now freed; his son had lobbied the King extensively, and William was irked not for the first time with his Scot's Parliament, which had taken upon itself the power to gaol one of his magnates who had been acting in pursuance of instructions, however liberally these may have been interpreted. Grey John also deemed it wise to return quietly to his own glens and say no more on the matter. It was in blustery October that the King returned from another fruitless season in Flanders and the year was drawing to a close, before he could direct his attention to the pernicious matter of Glencoe. It was not until 2nd December in the damp smog of a London winter that William summoned those Scots councillors then in the capital to attend.

He told them the Massacre had gravely afflicted him, but that he had not been aware of the brutal events until some eighteen months after. If either of these two statements caused surprise it may be certain the listeners maintained an absolute calm. Dalrymple was present, as was his nemesis Johnston, and the Master took the King's utterances (clearly shifting any censure entirely onto him as Secretary) as his cue to deliver a spirited and considered rebuttal of the commission's findings. Warriston seems to have replied in kind and, with these recriminations, the matter, to all intents and purposes, was concluded. Stair had surrendered his office, and whilst it was tacitly acknowledged that there was no position now for him in Government, the King fully and unequivocally exonerated him from blame. William found that Stair, so far distant from the actual events, was absolved from any guilt in the manner in which the instructions were carried out. Now the blame was shifted onto those actually responsible but who were, handily, removed from the clutches of Parliament by dint of their continued service in Flanders, where their more murderous inclinations were doubtless well employed. There was no question of any of the officers or NCOs being brought back for trial: the Queen was dead; her exhortation that those responsible should suffer hanging died with her. There was really nothing more to be said.

AFTERMATH: THE ROAD TO UNION

Throughout his reign, William's relationship with the Scottish Parliament was seldom altogether cordial. The overall position was complicated by the fact that a single monarch had two legislatures. The practical solution was simple: the two realms must be somehow made wholly separate, or the Parliaments must be combined into one. In the circumstances it would inevitably be the Scots' that would cease to exist. The spectre of Glencoe, even if thrust firmly beneath the Government carpet, could be said to have haunted William, and, after the Darien fiasco, the Scots had a second grievance to add. William's survival, initially was by no means guaranteed, but defeating the Jacobites in both Ireland and Scotland, coupled, in 1697, with the terms of the Treaty of Rijswijk, whereby Louis recognised William's legitimacy as King of England, severely dented the Jacobite cause. The Dutchman was by temperament an autocrat; he had little sympathy for popular Government. Scotland did not interest him. His life's work, as we have seen, was his crusade against French expansionism.

Nonetheless, such a stance, coupled with his aversion to popery, did win him some friends in Scotland. Opposition came most obviously from the Jacobites, but also from the Episcopalians, who resented William's acceptance of the Kirk. At the other end of the religious divide, the Cameronians, who had hoped for recognition of the Covenant of 1638, were also angered. Until the peace with France, there was some unease in Scotland over the continuance of the war, based on a lingering sentiment for the Auld Alliance. although this had been defunct since the Reformation.[16] The Scots regiments had taken heavy losses in the seemingly endless round of bloody and inconclusive battles.[17] These grievances, however, collectively paled into insignificance compared to the impact of Darien.

The Scots had not been idle in the swelling race for dominions. Despite legislative restrictions[18] they traded with the English colonies in North America and even planted some small colonies of their own. It was fashionable, and profitable, at this time to set up joint stock companies to exploit overseas business opportunities. In 1695 Scottish investors established a trading venture that, with the active backing of certain English interests, aimed to challenge the potent monopoly of the Honorable East India Company. In terms of capital for the new concern, some £300,000, a very substantial sum, was committed by both English and Scottish shareholders. William Paterson, a noted Scottish economist and founder of the Bank of England, suggested the members should turn their attention to the isthmus of Darien, where a trading colony would be able to straddle both east and west.

This appeared a sound notion. It was certainly threatening enough to cause ripples of alarm through the shareholders in the Honourable Company. Their considerable influence was brought to bear to frustrate the initiative. The English backers were scared off and sabres were rattled in the English Parliament. By this time the venture had caught the imagination of an entire generation of Scottish investors, who subscribed the whole cost of the project in the amount of some £400,000.[19] King William, anxious not to antagonize the Spanish, with whom he was in negotiations and who claimed Darien as theirs, became obstructive, demonstrably so. Despite these difficulties, the colony of New Edinburgh was established in October 1698. The founding was an unmitigated disaster; a markedly adverse climate and English intransigence ruined the settlement, which was swiftly abandoned. Next year, undaunted by their losses, the shareholders tried again and re-occupied the township. The Spaniards came to the aid of the climate and, though they were initially seen off in a fight at Toubacanti, returned with greater force, and the settlement finally capitulated on terms in March 1700.

Loss of life at around 2,000 souls had been great, the financial penalties a hundred times worse. William wrote to the Scottish Parliament in October, explaining why he had felt obliged to oppose the venture and providing vague assurances. As an attempt at appeasement this merely increased the ire of Scots. As a measure of this wrath, an unfortunate English skipper, Captain Green, with two of his seamen, was hanged five years later on a rather thin charge of piracy against one of the Scottish Company's few surviving vessels. To compound these injuries, the English Parliament, in 1701, passed an Act of Succession foreseeing that Queen Anne, who had succeeded her brother in law, might die childless.[20] The statute settled the succession upon the Empress Sophie of Hanover, a Protestant – it was also provided that the successor must be a communicant of the Church of England. The Scottish interest was simply overlooked.

James VII had died in 1701 and the torch of Jacobitism had passed to his son, to be known to Whigs as 'The Old Pretender'. In their outrage against the English, it was possible the Scots' Parliament would refuse to be bound by the Act and offer to the Crown their own nominee. If the Jacobite faction could seize the moment, it might even be James. When King William, early in his reign, had first mooted the notion of uniting the two Parliaments, the Scots had responded with some interest and it had been the English who demurred. A bill proposed in the Lords was rejected by the Commons. William never lost sight of the concept, and, immediately before his death he was urging Parliament to reconsider. He survived his father-in-law by barely a year, sustaining a fall from his horse which resulted in a fractured collarbone. Not in itself serious, but pneumonia set in and the King, his chest already weak, succumbed. It was said the mount had stumbled on a molehill; true or not, the Jacobites toasted the humble mole, 'the little gentleman in the black velvet waistcoat'.

Louis IV had already recognised James 'III' – Britain and France were again at odds in the War of the Spanish Succession, a conflict during which the Duke of Marlborough would win a series of dazzling victories that would shatter France's hegemony. Initially the war brought little hope for the Jacobites. The situation had changed since the days of the Nine Years War in the last decade of the preceding century. At sea the English were stronger than ever, the Jacobites no longer had armies in Ireland and Scotland, and their residual support in England had been exposed as minimal. In 1704 Marlborough utterly defeated the French at Blenheim and, within two years, Louis' armies had been chased both from Italy and the Old Spanish Netherlands. With the war proving disastrous for French arms, the appeal of an invasion to restore the Stuarts began to recover its lustre.

Queen Anne had the benefit of being free of the tarnish of Glencoe and Darien; moreover she was a Tory, immured in a sea of Whigs. This did not, however, imply she could afford to dispense with the idea of union. England and France were presently at war; Louis had recognised James, which necessitated continued antagonism to the Jacobite cause. In November 1702, the first serious set of negotiations took place. Whilst some accord was possible, important differences, particularly concerning economic matters, could not be resolved. In Scotland, the following year, the Whigs clung to power. The Tories comprised the conservative 'Country' faction and the more radical Jacobites; diehards like Fletcher of Saltoun ranted against the concept of Union. These opposition groups were widely disparate in their aims, united only by their dislike of England and the possibility of Union.

Jacobite sympathizers were cheered by two statutes, which the opposition did manage to steer through. The first provided that no monarch after Anne could declare a war in which Scots would be expected to serve without the concurrence of the Scots Parliament. The second allowed Parliament, within twenty days of the Queen's death, should she die without issue, as was likely, to nominate a successor – this should be one who was both a Protestant and of the Stuart line. With the war in the balance, the English were obliged to tread warily; victory at Blenheim implied they could be more bullish. The 'Alien' Act of 1705 was anything but conciliatory – if the Scots did not, within a deadline, accept the Hanoverian succession, then dire economic consequences would ensue. This blustering facilitated the appointment of the second Duke of Argyll as commissioner; his father had died in September 1703, possibly in the arms of his long-term mistress, Peggy Allison.

This Campbell was not a seasoned politician. A dour man by temperament, he was a constant and skilled soldier. His Whig pedigree was unimpeachable, the integrity of the Kirk, must go unchallenged but otherwise the negotiations could proceed on a constructive basis. The Commissioners would hold their appointment directly from the Crown, and all that was asked of the Queen was that she ensured the more confrontational provisions of the Alien Act were removed.[21] When the commissioners, thirty-one from each realm, were empowered, Argyll stood back, and, though convinced Jacobites were not excluded, both sides fielded a majority of Whigs. By July 1706 the bones of an accord had been hammered out. Pragmatism was the order of the day, the English wished, at all costs, not to have a hostile kingdom ruled by a Jacobite in their rear whilst at war with France.

The Scots would barter political independence for free trade. Though they had first held out for some form of federalism rather than a complete merger, the Scots themselves feared the Jacobite influence and a recurrence of civil strife. It would be a full and complete Act of Union. This Act would bring into being the Kingdom of Great Britain, a common flag – The Union Jack, a common currency and a guarantee of the Hanoverian succession; this last was a major blow to Jacobite hopes. As part of the complex financial settlement, some element of compensation, by no means inconsiderable, was to be paid to the Scottish investors in the Darien Company. The Scottish Parliament first debated the draft treaty in October 1706 and, once its terms were known, great howls of protest went up. In part this was orchestrated by the Jacobites and their Tory allies, but there was undoubtedly a revulsion against the notion that the Scots Commissioners had sold their independence to the English. Rioters took to the streets in Edinburgh, Glasgow and Dumfries. There was protest too from the shires and even from some in the Kirk, but the die was effectively cast on 16th January 1707, when the Treaty was passed by a respectable majority in both divisions, and the Scottish Parliament voted itself out of existence. Both bodies passed back-to-back legislation guaranteeing the

Kirk and Church of England respectively. As the Scots Chancellor handed the final version bearing the Royal Seal to the clerk, he is said to have remarked 'Now there's an end to ane old song'.[22] The sufferings of clan Iain Abrach played a poor second fiddle to the economic and social catastrophe of Darien and the great events preceding the Union. This latter looked forward to the Scottish Enlightenment not back to a dim Celtic past. Glencoe was already history.

GLENCOE ON HIS FACE

Robert Campbell of Glenlyon never returned to Scotland, serving the remainder of his days firmly wedded to Brown Bess, and rising to the rank of Colonel. He died at Bruges in August 1696, and his military career, begun so late in life and clouded by the horror of Glencoe, had done nothing to improve the wretched state of his finances. He died leaving an accumulated weight of unsatisfied debt. Even his funeral had to be subsidised by fellow officers such as Archibald Campbell of Fonab.[23] The 'curse' of Glencoe is said to have haunted the Campbells of Glenlyon. One of the lairds, 'The Black Colonel', served as a redcoat for most of his career. Dour and unmarried, he felt the cold hand of history ever on his shoulder. At the end of his service he was placed in command of a firing party tasked to execute deserters. In fact the wretched men were not to be killed but advised, at the last moment, of their reprieve. Unfortunately, as Campbell, who, as the officer in charge was the only one aware of the changed orders, drew the reprieve from his pocket he let fall his handkerchief, the signal to fire, and the men died ignorant of their release![24]

Grey John outlived his impecunious cousin, though he never took centre stage again, and his schemes to supplant Argyll as the senior branch never prospered; his career ultimately was not crowned with any lasting success; he earned the excoriation of many and plaudits of few. Still, as he grew old, he remained monarch in his own glens

and flirted actively with the Jacobites, driven as ever more by opportunism than conscience. When 'Bobbing John', the Earl of Mar, a
noted trimmer in his own right, unfurled the Pretender's banner at
Braemar to begin the 'Fifteen', Breadalbane sent his apologies; to be
fair he was now in his eightieth year. Some of his name did fight, and
fight well, at Sheriffmuir. When it was all over and the rebels were
either skulking or had fled, redcoats came seeking Grey John. But his
age, infirmity and the shield of his people was sufficient sanctuary,
and he was left in peace, dying the following year. It was one of the
MacDonald bards, inspired by the courage of the Breadalbane men
in the fight, who composed a eulogy; the irony of this must certainly
have amused him.

Sir Thomas Livingstone was elevated to the Viscountcy of Teviot,
and died, his reputation untarnished, in 1711. Lieutenant Colonel
James Hamilton disappears from history, but was certainly never
called to account for his part in the atrocity. Captain Thomas
Drummond, who served with distinction in Flanders, likewise escaped
any penalty, and later became embroiled in the Darien fiasco. Major
Robert Duncanson also fought for his King in the French wars. Now
a Lieutenant Colonel, he was ruined by the forced surrender of his
regiment at Dixemude, shortly after he had incurred considerable
outlay on its uniform and accoutrement. He stayed with the colours
and finally fell at the siege of Valencia de Alcantara in 1705.

With King William dead and talk of Union filling the air, it was
time for John Dalrymple to step back from the shadows. In 1703
Queen Anne granted him an earldom, and the first Earl of Stair
appeared, as he had always been, a champion of the Union with
England. Nobody, even his most determined enemies – who were
many – could deny the brilliance of his mind or the eloquence of
his counsel. Stair, his brother Hew, now Lord President, and their
kinsman Sir David Dalrymple, who was serving as Solicitor General,
were all members of the commission sent to hammer out details of
the treaty with Parliament in London. The earl was a tireless and
passionate advocate for a united kingdom and he strove mightily to

achieve this, his true life's work. However, exhausted by his endeavours, he died in January 1707 at the age of fifty-eight and never saw his dream realised. Had it not been for the shadow of Glencoe, history might have judged him a great man.

Inside the fort at distant Inverlochy, Colonel John Hill, slipping further and further into the grip of old age and infirmity, doggedly guarded his ramparts, a fort that nobody really wanted or cared about, yet the place where he had invested so much of his life and given so much of his heart. Hill may have faltered and acquiesced to the slaughter, but he was neither its author nor an actual perpetrator; he was simply a man who tried to do his duty and sought to do so in a decent and honourable manner and in this he did not fail entirely. His integrity was spurned and abused by an indifferent administration, and even the eventual knighthood probably conferred scant solace. For Hill, burdened by the weight of his own conscience, the shadow of Glencoe would never lift for so long as he lived.

Beneath the long ridge of *Aoanach Eagach* and in the lee of *Meall Mor*, below the fingers of The Three Sisters of Glencoe, the survivors of Clan Iain Abrach, the sentence of death and latterly transportation lifted, began the business of re-stocking their glen. Horrific as the events of 13th February 1692 had been, and furious the storm that sought to consume them, such brutal despoliation was scarcely an unknown commodity, and one which that they had themselves dealt in quite freely. That Campbell vengeance should catch up with them, whilst unfortunate, was not entirely to be wondered at. The thirteenth Chief rebuilt his father's shattered house, rising grander and more imposing than before. The people were hardy and resilient; this was their land, where they and their forbears had lived for generations: it would not easily be surrendered.

John MacDonald certainly learnt to be circumspect, no baying for revenge or the savage rant of the pipes. He appears genuinely grateful for Hill's continued intercession. Occasionally there were alarums, an echo of the old ways that Alasdair Og, always the more volatile of the two brothers, led a company beneath the Pretender's standard in 1715.

Thirty years on and MacIain's grandson, once the child carried to safety in the night of killing, John's boy, raised another company, 120 strong and with more to follow Prince Charles. The Glencoe men stood on the Jacobite left on the grim, sleet-lashed field of Culloden, where some, like so many of their MacDonald kin, would have fallen in the defeat. Afterwards, and in reprisal, fire and sword returned with the redcoats to Glencoe, and yet the clan survived.

It was 'the Great Sheep' that finally undid the work of so many centuries, when the Clearances of the late eighteenth and early nineteenth century destroyed the old ways forever. MacDonald of Glencoe ended not with a bang, not in a final, bloody *Götterdämmerung* but with barely even a whimper. The people simply left; only the names on the map recalling where they had once lived. MacDonalds had been in the glen since the fourteenth century but their long tenure was the continuance of a pattern laid down long before, beginning with those first Neolithic settlers, at least three millennia earlier. It was indeed an end to a very old song.

A ROMANTIC REVIVAL

As the ancient steadings were abandoned and the song of the people was heard no more; Glencoe and its history was largely forgotten. The Enlightenment was not enamoured of a Gaelic past with its dark warriors, Finn MacCool and Alasdair MacColla. The romantic image of the noble savage had yet to be invented. It was James MacPherson who created the influential romantic cult of 'Ossian' – the alleged discovery and translation of a corpus of ancient Celtic verse that offered the clans their very own Homer:

> Now I beheld the chiefs in the pride of their former deeds. Their souls are kindled at the battles of old ... Their eyes are flames of fire. They roll in search of the foes of the land. Their mighty hands are on their swords. Lightning pours from their sides of steel. They come like streams from the

mountains; each rushes roaring from his hill. Bright are the chiefs of battle
in the amour of their fathers, gloomy and dark their heroes follow, like the
gathering of the rainy clouds behind the red meteors of heaven.[25]

This turgid melodrama chimes with the contemporary vision of the
Noble Savage, the Highlander, follower of the White Cockade, his
reality safely defeated and consigned to memory, was rehabilitated
in fiction as the romantic hero. Even Napoleon Bonaparte, the arch
pragmatist, was said to be an admirer of Ossian. Dr Johnson, it
has to be said, was not, and it was his savage cynicism that largely
brought about MacPherson's eclipse, that and the author's inability
to validate any of his alleged texts!

By the third decade of the century the Highlands had become an
established tourist destination. Mendelssohn and Klingemann were
just two more distinguished visitors. If a further boost was needed
then Sir Walter Scott was the provider. With Sir Walter the Romantic
Movement came of age; his poems such as 'The Lord of the Isles'
and novels such as *Rob Roy* inspired a generation of travelers. Even
today his image of the swashbuckling Highlander, fierce but loyal
and enduring, persists. Johnson, initially discreetly, was the first to
lay the foundations of the cult of Prince Charles Edward Stuart. The
pair made their celebrated journey in 1773 when memories of the '45
were still fresh, too fresh for any overt admiration of the lost cause.
Boswell did not write his own account until some ten years later when
he told of the meeting between Johnson and Flora MacDonald.

His working of the tale of the Pretender's escape sparked the genesis of the cult, this at a time when Charles Stuart, an embittered
dipsomaniac, was still clinging to life in Rome. Once the aged relic
was safely buried in 1788, his heroic status soared. Old Jacobite airs
were revived; any gaps were swiftly filled by a swelling chorus of
nostalgic repertoire. From being a covert and dangerous expression
of extremism, the Jacobite movement re-emerged as a romantic phenomenon, a relatively safe symbol of sentimental nationalism. James
Hogg, the 'Ettrick Shepherd' and Scott's collaborator, was quick to
leap on the fast moving bandwagon:

Cam ye by Athol, lad wi' the philabeg
Down by the Tummel, or banks o' the Garry;
Saw ye our lads, wi' their bonnets and white cockades
Leaving their mountains to follow Prince Charlie?

Follow thee! Follow thee! Wha wadna follow thee?
Lang hast thou loved and trusted us fairly:
Charlie, Charlie, wha wadna follow thee,
King o' the Highland hearts, bonnie Prince Charlie.'[26]

It is doubtful that any of Clan Iain Abrach, in the wildest excess of alcohol fuelled optimism, would have recognised themselves in this turgid stream. Scott featured the '45 in 'Waverley' (1814). Though he initially disdained fiction as inferior to verse, his iconic status meant that by the 1820's he was the recognised authority of all matters appertaining to Scottish history. His great moment came in 1822 when he was appointed to organise the pomp and pageantry celebrating the state visit of George IV to Edinburgh. The King was to be treated to a spectacle of Jacobite fantasy; kilted Highlanders would once again conquer the capital.

This was a bold move, since some lingering resentment of the Act of Union still festered, and Highland dress had, until 1782, remained proscribed. George IV, as easily in love with dressing up as Scott, entered fully into the spirit and donned a florid version of Highland kit for a reception at Holyrood on 17th April 1822. Though some dissenters muttered, the Romantic Jacobite Revival had fully come of age; Scott was the hero of the hour; the fact that the tartan had been repressed for so long merely fuelled the passion with which it was now embraced. By a supreme irony, the revival was generally limited to the upper tiers of society and mainly concentrated in the Lowlands. The combination of Ossian, Bonnie Prince Charlie and Scott had otherwise proved unstoppable.

The fashion for Highland garb went on to spawn a whole industry devoted to the study and manufacture of tartan, an enduring fad that would totally have bemused any of those who stood on the field at Culloden. By the time Queen Victoria first toured the Highlands twenty years after George IV first dandified a plaid, the cult had become embedded and embellished with a historic pedigree of highly questionable provenance. Together with her beloved consort, the Queen fell for the Highland myth in its entirety. Their house at Balmoral created a whole style of 'Scottish Baronial' and inspired a rash of imitators from the wealthy strata of Victorian industrialists and tycoons seeking to invent pedigrees of their own. Tartan abounded, the ageing Queen Empress, desolate at the loss of her beloved Albert, sought solace in her Stewart roots and the cult of Charles Edward – notwithstanding he was her family's foe and, had he succeeded, she would never have reached the throne. Her journal entry for 12th September 1873 records:

> I feel a sort of reverence in going over these scenes of [the Pretender's trekking across the western Highlands] in this most beautiful country, which I am proud to call my own, where there was such devoted loyalty to the family of my ancestors – for Stuart blood is in my veins, and I am now their representative.[27]

Complete tosh of course. Whether any of those who shivered in the February blizzard on cold hillsides, so many years before, whilst the smoke from burning thatch eddied in the gale and the blood of their kin stained the snow, would have appreciated the irony has to be questionable. During the '45, the fourteenth chief led his 120 broadswords to fight for the Pretender, and was created a member of the Prince's council. When the army swept southwards, having outmanoeuvred Cope and occupied Linlithgow, they passed the Dalrymple property at Newliston. Doubtless fearful Clan Iain Abrach would be keen to take their revenge upon the stones and contents, the Jacobite officers sought billets elsewhere for the Glencoe men. MacIain would have none of it. He insisted his followers should be assigned as guards for the property so they might show they fought for honour and not for vengeance. And that, surely, must be the final word on Glencoe.

FINIS

Notes

INTRODUCTION

1. Loyd, A., 'My War Gone By, I Miss It So' (London: 1999), p.p.152 – 153
2. Bell-Fialkoff, A., 'A Brief History of Ethnic Cleansing' (http://www.foreignaffairs.org/19930601faessay5199/andrew-bell-fialkoff/a-brief-history-of-ethnic-cleansing.hmtl), 'Foreign Affairs' 72 (3): 110, summer 1993
3. Bingham, C., 'Beyond the Highland Line' (London: 1991)
4. ECHR Jorgic v Germany
5. http://www.balkansnet.org/ethnicl.html

CHAPTER 1: THE GLEN OF DOGS

1. Brander, M., 'The Making of the Scottish Highlands' (London: 1980), p.9
2. The Forts of the Great Glen were Inverlochy, Fort Augustus and Fort George at Inverness
3. Rannoch Moor is now preserved as a wildlife sanctuary and designated as a National Heritage site

4. A Munro is any peak over 3,000 feet in height
5. Stob Coire nan Lochan – in this writer's not unbiased view the finest in the Highlands
6. Now part of the Lochaber Committee Area of Highland Council
7. http://www.wikipedia.org/wiki/Glen_coe
8. Fionn mac Cumhaill – anglicized as Finn MacCool
9. Prebble, J., 'Glencoe' (London: 1966), p.21
10. Ibid p.p.21 – 22
11. From 'Clan Donald's Call to Battle at Harlaw'
12. Dunadd, the chief strength of Dalriada is still an impressive and haunting location
13. Magnus Bareleg – so called as he preferred the Hebridean style of dress
14. He was thought to have been behind the murder of Ranald Macruari, he was certainly the prime beneficiary, see Sadler, D.J. Clan 'Donald's Greatest Defeat – the Battle of Harlaw 1411, (Gloucs: 2005), p.p.65 – 66
15. Bingham, op. cit., p.97
16. Major J. 'A History of Greater Britain' (1521), p.p.48 – 49
17. Stevenson, D., 'Alasdair MaColla and the Highland problem in the Seventeenth Century' (Edinburgh: 1980), p. 17
18. The original Gaelic may have been cam beul (wry or twisted mouth), see Bingham, op. cit., p.100
19. Prebble, op. cit., p.43
20. The famous or infamous Rob Roy MacGregor doubtless savoured the irony of his sheltering beneath the name of Campbell!
21. Bannatyne, G., (1568), 'The Bannatyne Manuscript' (ed.) W. Tod Ritchie, Scottish Text Society, New Series, no 23, 1928
22. The much-photographed modern Highland cattle, predominantly russet in colour, are descended from these but are much stouter and larger in build
23. Bingham, op. cit.,
24. Prebble, op. cit., p.35

25. As observed by William Sacheverell
26. Brander, op. cit., p.101
27. Ibid p.101
28. Ibid p.101
29. Ibid p.102
30. Ibid p.102
31. It was during the sixteenth century that the Highland pipes developed fully, supplanting the earlier clairschach
32. Stevenson, op. cit., p.p.6 – 7
33. Ibid p.p.7 – 10
34. These minority kingships were those of James II, III, IV, V, Mary and James VI
35. Stevenson, op. cit., p.9
36. Ibid p.10
37. Ibid p.14
38. 'Blackmail' or 'Blackrent' was the custom of collecting what would now be termed 'protection money'
39. Prebble, J., 'Culloden' (London, 1961), p.47
40. The blood feud was endemic – perhaps the most notorious incident occurred in 1396, which may be likened to a gladiatorial combat, when thirty fighters from each of Clan Chattan and Clan Kay fought in a specially constructed arena before Robert III!
41. Forbes' property of Culloden House would feature in the battle
42. Prebble, op. cit., p.35
43. Ibid p.36
44. Ibid p.45
45. Some clothing from the period has survived in peat burials, sufficient to suggest that breeches were commonly worn
46. The kilt is a hybrid form of attire, which may have been the creation of an Englishman in the 1720s
47. Caldwell, D.H., 'The Scottish Armoury' (Edinburgh: 1979), p.p.19 – 20
48. Ibid. p.p.24 – 26

49. Ibid p.p.37 – 41
50. Curved blades in the Turkish ('Turcheach') style did exist
51. Caldwell, op. cit., p.p.56 – 58
52. Peterson, H.L., 'The Book of the Gun' (London, 1963), p.p.78 – 79
53. Caldwell, op. cit., p.p.64 – 70
54. 'Brosnachadh catha' – incitement to battle
55. An eyewitness account of the burying of English dead after the battle of Falkirk in 1746 recorded numerous fatalities caused by downward cuts to head and neck
56. Reid, S., 'Highland Clansman' (England: 1997), p.16
57. In 1745 it is said that the fiery cross travelled some thirty-two miles around Loch Tay in three hours!
58. Stevenson, op. cit., p.p.82 – 84
59. Reid, op. cit., p.16

Chapter 2: The Day of Clan Donald

1. Montrose was regarded as one of the greatest captains of his age, yet he was frequently and finally fatally let down by failures of intelligence and scouting, see generally Reid, S., 'The Campaigns of Montrose' (Edinburgh: 1990)
2. The Scots' army under Leven failed to distinguish itself in the battle, Leven at one point prepared to flee, believing the day lost
3. The name can be spelt in a number of ways – MacColla means 'son of Coll', his father being Alasdair MacColla Chiotaich
4. The principal strength was the dark tower of Mingary Castle, dramatically positioned on the coast of Ardnamurchan
5. In English this reads simply as 'Great Chief'
6. The courtyard or 'barnekin' wall, bearing bullet marks, still stands
7. Ardvreck, or its remains, still stands on a spur jutting out

into the still waters of Loch Assynt – Montrose's only memorial

8. Tam Dalyell, an eccentric cavalier who had served the Czar of Russia and as the builder of the family seat at the Binns

9. Sir George Mackenzie, the Lord Advocate

10. Stevenson, op. cit., p.267

11. Ibid p.p.270 – 271

12. Sir Ewan Cameron of Lochiel; in the course of a long and colourful career he listed amongst his accomplishments the killing of the last wolf in Scotland

13. Stevenson, op. cit., p.283

14. A bond or indemnity for good behavior

15. For a good and well-researched image of the chief with his tail of followers, refer to plate 'A' in Reid, S., 'Highland Clansman 1689 – 1746' Osprey Military Series, 1997

16. Stevenson, op. cit., p.p.280 – 281

17. Caterans appear in the fourteenth century and were effectively a professional warrior caste, likened to the Irish 'kernes' of the period; they varied immensely in quality from being an elite force to mere gangsters

18. Stevenson, op. cit., p.283

19. Ibid p.286

20. Ibid p.288

21. The matter was finely balanced: Argyll should have his wings clipped but without damaging the royal prerogative

22. Stevenson, op. cit., p.290

23. As these companies were expected to subsist from the land, they were as likely to form part of the problem as the remedy

24. Lochiel orchestrated a sham disturbance to present a notional and wholly fictional threat to the commissioners' safety, allowing him to usher them out of Lochaber on security grounds; see Stevenson, op. cit., p.291

25. Ibid p.294

26. Ibid p.295

27. Ibid p.293
28. From the Latin 'Jacobus' = James
29. The barracks that occupy the site date from the eighteenth century. In 1689, the medieval tower still stood
30. The spot named 'Soldier's Leap' is said to mark a terrific jump where a fleeing soldier leapt the River Garry to escape pursuit.
31. The pike now being obsolete, musketeers carried a bayonet though, at this early date, this was of the plug variety, which was thrust like a dagger into the mouth of the musket with the obvious effect that the weapon could not be discharged whilst it remained fixed
32. Hayes-McCoy, G.A., 'Irish Battles' (Belfast: 1969) p.214
33. Ibid p.235
34. English naval power was rising and continued to do during the eighteenth century and the Royal Navy proved a major obstacle to proposed French interventions
35. Black, J., 'Culloden and the '45' (New York: 1990) p.15

CHAPTER 3: THE GREAT FEUD: 'THE GREED OF THE CAMPBELLS'

1. 'Toom Tabard' was the unfortunate sobriquet heaped on King John Balliol
2. Thomson, O., 'The Great Feud' (Gloucs: 2000) p.p.3 – 8
3. Battle of the Western Isles (1586) took place on Jura Donald; Gorm MacDonald fought Sir Lachlan Maclean, and escaped the defeat.
4. Battle of Siol Tormoit, on the Isle of Uist; the MacLeods lost perhaps a score of men
5. Battle of the Shirts – only five Frasers and eight MacDonalds are said to have survived this bitter fight!
6. This particular atrocity occurred in 1581; the tune is still known as 'Kilchrist'

7. The chief who perished, besides Keppoch, was Dugal Stewart of Appin

8. Alexander MacDonald of Keppoch, twelfth Chief and his brother were murdered in 1663 in the Tobair nan Ceann, or Well of Heads, by Invergarry, marking the spot where the severed heads of seven assassins were washed

9. In 1694 Sir John MacDonald had seized Dunaverty from the crown, but he also was captured by MacIain of Ardnamurchan and subsequently executed

10. The name derives from that of the Lochaber area

11. Linklater, M., 'Massacre: The Story of Glencoe' (London: 1982) p.27

12. The severed heads were sent, preserved in a barrel, for the approbation of the Privy Council

13. The Maiden was an early form of guillotine invented by the Douglas, Earl of Morton in the sixteenth century; fittingly, he was one of the first to try its efficacy. It may be seen in the National Museum of Scotland in Edinburgh

14. This description was contributed by John Macky, a contemporary political observer and Government agent – see Macky, J., 'Memoirs of Secret Services' p.119

15. Prebble, op. cit., p.187

16. Linklater, op. cit., p.150

17. This is not a contemporary description but derives from recent atrocities in the Balkans, it is included to underline the savagery involved

18. Linklater, op. cit., p.48

19. Ibid p.48

20. Prebble, op. cit. p.p.50 – 51

21. Ibid p.51

22. A blunderbuss was a short barreled flint carbine with flared muzzle, equivalent of a sawn off shotgun; lethal at close range

23. Philip of Americlose (translated from the Latin by Rev. Alexander D. Murdoch; Scottish History Society, 1888)

24. Linklater, op. cit., p.61
25. This equates to £670 sterling, see Linklater, op. cit., p. 61
26. Prebble, op. cit., p.56
27. This was enacted by James VI in 1587 on the basis that a feudal superior was vicariously liable for the misdeeds of his tenants. The landlord was obliged to hand over the accused from his people, to make reparations and, where required, to provide surety
28. Prebble, op. cit., p.59

Chapter 4: The Gathering Storm 1690–1691

1. Chandler, D., 'Oxford History of the British Army' (Oxford University Press: 1996) p.47
2. Ibid p.47
3. Ibid p.47
4. Ibid p.99
5. Ibid p.101
6. See Appendix 2
7. Prebble, op. cit., p.59
8. Tabraham, C. and Grove, D., 'Fortress Scotland and the Jacobites' (London, 1995) p.39
9. Alasdair Og, younger son of MacIain of Glencoe, had been 'out' with Colonel Cannon
10. Tabraham and Groves, op. cit., p.39
11. Prebble, op. cit., p.81
12. Secretary of State for Scotland was the senior appointment in the Government of the kingdom, prior to the Union of 1707
13. The Rye House Plot was a Whig attempt to assassinate both Charles II and his brother James [then] Duke of York
14. The medieval castle, which was to feature in the battle of 1645, dates from the thirteenth century, originally a Comyn hold

15. Tabraham and Groves, op. cit., p.40
16. A 'covered way', essentially a passage by which troops could move without being exposed to enemy fire
17. Tabraham and Groves, op. cit., p.40
18. See the plans shown in Tabraham and Groves, op. cit., p. 17 and colour plate 3
19. Tabraham and Groves, op. cit., p.40
20. Prebble, op. cit., p.97
21. Mackay, 'Memoirs' p. 341 & p. 354; 'Life of Mackay' p.183; Leven and Methven Papers p.471
22. This may be the earliest purpose-built barrack accommodation in mainland UK – see Tabraham and Groves, op. cit., p.43
23. 'He was the merriest grave man I ever saw, and no sooner was anybody's name than he had some pleasant thing to say of him, mocked the while, and had a way of laughing inwardly ...' See Master of Sinclair, 'Memoirs' p.185
24. 'Highland Papers', p.p.53 – 56
25. This appointment was as the head of the Scottish judiciary
26. Chief legal officer for the Scottish Government and chief public prosecutor
27. Certain black legends clung to the Dalrymple name, episodes his legion of foes would be only too happy to believe: John's wife had been a victim of rape before her marriage. His mother was considered a witch and a gothic horror clung to the legend of his sister Janet's wedding night when she was said to have been murdered on her wedding night by the demented groom; this was certainly apochrypal as the young woman died of natural causes shortly after her marriage; see Prebble, op. cit., p.p.110 – 111
28. Ibid p.117
29. Ibid p.121
30. Buchan, op. cit., p.42

Chapter 5: Prelude: 'To Maul Them in the Long Cold Nights'

1. 'Highland Papers', p.10
2. Stevenson, op. cit., p.p.276 – 277
3. These letters, though given in good faith, would fail to protect either man on 16th February
4. Buchan, op. cit., p.35
5. Prebble, op. cit., p.156
6. Ibid p.163
7. 'Highland Papers', p.p.45 – 65
8. Ibid p.p.45 – 46
9. Dalrymple, p.215
10. 'Highland Papers', p.49
11. Ibid p.p.51 – 52
12. Ibid p.53
13. Ibid p.p.57 – 58
14. Prebble, op. cit., p.170
15. Ibid p.171
16. The Writers to the Signet are the oldest legal fraternity in the world; officially founded in 1594, but their role began earlier as advisers to the Scottish kings

Chapter 6: Preparations: 'A Great Work of Charity'

1. 'Highland Papers', p.p.58 – 59
2. Ibid p.p.60 – 62
3. Ibid p.65
4. Ibid p.65
5. Ibid p.67
6. Ibid p.67
7. Ibid p.70
8. 'Oxford English Dictionary'

9. Type 'A' ethnic cleansing involves the systematic clearance of the chosen ground with the slaughter of all males capable of resistance. Type 'B' is more insidious, where the subject and domestic populations are too closely entwined to permit a leisurely slaughter. Here the target group is relentlessly harassed and harried till they accept the option of mass-expulsion, see UN reports from Bosnia available at: http://www.un.org/ict

10. Buchan, op. cit., p.91

11. 'Gallienus Redivivus', p.32

12. Ibid p.44

13. Ibid p.p.15 – 16; this gives the appointed time as five, though in Highland Papers this appears as seven – see Buchan, op. cit., p.170, n.

14. Prebble op. cit., p.219 & n.

15. The evidence for Matheson's sojourn is to a degree anecdotal; the bard may have been the author of the celebrated Gaelic lament for the Massacre – see Prebble, op. cit. p.222 n

16. 'Highland Papers', p.73

17. Ibid p.p.72 – 73

CHAPTER 7: THE 13TH FEBRUARY 1692: 'MURDER UNDER TRUST'

1. 'A La Bayonet or hot blood and cold steel' Canadian Army Infantry Journal; http://www.members.tripod.com/~RegimentalRogue/papers/bayonet.html

2. Eugene's assault on Belgrade took place on 22nd August 1717, the incident at Paoli's Tavern during the American War of Independence on 21st September 1777

3. In the American War of Independence

4. As an example, though from a later war, an officer in the 1st Battalion Durham Light Infantry, Hubert Coddrington, was struck by a Mauser rifle bullet during the Boer War in 1901 and

the round exited through nine different wounds – DLI Museum & Art Gallery, Durham

5. Prebble, op. cit., p.p.231 – 232
6. Ibid p.232
7. 'Gallienus Redivivus', p.p.23 – 24
8. Details of the killings are those provided by survivors giving evidence before the Parliamentary Inquiry
9. The child survived to manhood and later led the clan contingent during the 'Forty-Five'
10. Prebble, op. cit., p.237 (n)
11. Ibid p.244
12. Ibid p.245 (n)
13. Ibid p.246

CHAPTER 8: AFTERMATH: 'IT IS NO JOY WITHOUT CLAN DONALD'

1. Prebble, op. cit., p.229
2. 'Highland Papers', p.75
3. 'Gallienus Redivivus', p.49
4. This expression is interpreted as Campbell slang – what occurs in the Highlands bears little relation to that which might happen in London
5. 'Gallienus Redivivus' p.p.20 – 21
6. Ibid p.p.4 – 25
7. 'Highland Papers', p.83
8. Ibid p. 87; 'Culloden Papers' p.22
9. 'Gallienus Redivivus', p.p.28 – 29
10. 'Highland Papers', p.90
11. The other members were Lord Murray, Sir James Stuart, Adam Cockburn of Ormiston, Sir Archibald Hope of Rankeillor, Sir William Hamilton of Whitelaw, Sir James Ogilvie and Adam Drummond of Megginch

12. The remaining Glencoe men comprised Alexander MacDonald, tacksman of Dalness, Ronald MacDonald of Leacantium, Ronald MacDonald and Duncan MacEanruig, (both of Inverrigan), Donald MacStarken of Laroch, Alexander MacDonald from Brecklet with Angus MacDonald in Strone; see Prebble, op. cit., p.271

13. 'Highland Papers', p.p.120 – 124

14. Acts of Parl. Of Scotland, ix, p.p.424 – 425

15. 'Gallienus Redivivus', p.p48 – 49

16. Cultural ties with France still lingered after the demise of the 'Auld Alliance'

17. Argyll's foot suffered heavy loss at the battle of Dottignes in July 1693

18. Scots' seafarers were trading with English colonies despite the restrictions

19. This was equal to something like one half of the nation's total available investment capital!

20. Anne had borne eighteen children, none of which had survived infancy

21. The offending clauses were deleted in the final draft

22. Mackie, J.D., 'History of Scotland' (England: 1964) p.262

23. Prebble, op. cit., p.289

24. Ibid p.291

25. Laing, M., 'The Poems of Ossian etc Containing the poetical works of James MacPherson with notes and illustrations in 2 vols'. (Edinburgh: 1805) 'Fingal' Book One, Vol. 1 p.p. 13 – 14

26. Bingham, op. cit., p.179

27. Ibid p.183

Appendices

A Note on Sources

'Gallienus Redivius or Murder Will Out etc Being a True Account of the De Witting* of Gencoe' first appeared in print in 1695 and is available in the facsimile edition published in 1885. It is remarkably in tune with the Report of the Commission of Inquiry. This is now lodged with the National Archives.** Other relevant and useful primary sources are the Maitland Club's 'Highland Papers'; Mackay's 'Memoirs'; Memoirs of Lochiel; Leven and Melville Papers; Culloden Papers; Lockhart Papers; Browne's 'History of the Highland Clans'; 'New Statistical Account of Scotland'; Clanranald MSS; Acts of the Parliament of Scotland; Argyll Papers; Balhaddie MSS; Barcaldine Papers; Brighouse Papers; Breadalbane Papers; Cromartie MM; Inverawe Papers; 'Regimental Rolls 1689 – 1691'; 'Registers of Scottish Privy Council; Tweedale Papers'.

Additional primary and secondary sources are as listed in the Bibliography.

* The brothers De Witt had been political opponents of William in the Netherlands and had been done to death by a partisan mob – the Stadtholder was believed to be heavily implicated.

** SP8/15 no.84

The Oath of Allegiance
and Articles of War

I do sincerely promise and swear that I will be faithful to their Majesties King William and Queen Mary and be obedient in all things to their Majesties, or to the Commander-in-Chief appointed by their Majesties for the time being; and will behave myself obediently to my superior officers **in all that they shall command** me for their Majesties service. And I do further swear that I will be a true, faithful and obedient soldier, in every way performing my best endeavours for their Majesties' service, obeying all orders and submitting to all such rules and articles of war as are, or shall be established by their Majesties. So help me God.

On the face of it the oath is absolutely binding: the common soldier is simply obliged to obey the orders given to him by his superior office. It says nothing concerning any moral choice or other equivocation – none exists. The private man carries out orders given to him by his officers, the supreme commander and through him the King and Queen. He need not trouble himself as to the consequences. It would not be until the Nuremburg trials after the end of the Second World War that the defence to an alleged war-crime raised by a subordinate 'I was only obeying orders' would be found wanting. The principle that the individual soldier has no responsibility to carry out an inhumane or immoral order, one that is repugnant to established standards of decency, was not necessarily recognised in the seventeenth century. Besides, the taking of oaths was considered a very solemn business and, in the case of Argyll's regiment, there were already strong bonds of clan loyalty in play.

Should anyone, officer or enlisted man, be given to entertaining doubts about the code which bound him, and as set down in the Sixty-nine Laws and Ordinances Touching Military Discipline, these were read aloud to each company at monthly parade:

Article 9: Giving any warning or intelligence to an enemy was a capital offence

Article 16: Refusal to obey any order was a capital offence

Article 19: Unlawful killing was punishable by death

Article 20: Looting and theft, punishable by death

Article 37: Where any man abuses the family with whom he is quartered, he shall be punished and an offence of rape should be punishable by death.

There are, as John Prebble points out, certain bitter ironies in the content and tenor of the articles; Argyll's men were to be tasked to obey Article 16 to the letter and, in so doing, place themselves in contradiction to Articles 19 and 37. In the circumstances the need to obey their orders without question was undoubtedly the article uppermost in the minds of their officers. Two officers, as we have seen, refused to carry out the order, which they regarded as inhuman and unlawful; their courage and fortitude is to be commended and admired; thus it was recognised that a moral dimension existed. Nonetheless, it cannot be said that the order was illegal. Hamilton and Duncanson were putting into effect an order issued or ratified by Colonel Hill, in compliance with prior instruction from the C- in-C who was himself acting on orders from the Secretary of State, approved and sanctioned by the King. We may be inclined to find, with the inestimable benefit of hind-sight, that the men would have been justified in disobeying the order, but to do so would in the circumstances be unfair; the rank and file cannot fairly be blamed. If we are seeking to apportion blame then it must rest far higher up the chain of command.

Muster Roll of Glenlyon's Company and Deummond's Grenadier Company Quartered in Glencoe, February 1692

Captain; one lieutenant, ensign, two sergeants, three corporals, two drummers and fifty-seven enlisted men (sentinels):

Officers: Captain Robert Campbell of Glenlyon; Lieutenant John Millan; Ensign John Campbell; Sergeant Robert Barber; Sergeant James Hendrie; Drummer Mungo Dalyell; Drummer Cuthbert Hunter; Corporal Archibald Campbell; Corporal James Macphail; Corporal Duncan Kennedy.

Sentinels: Alexander, John; Blair, Archibald; Bruntfield, Thomas; Campbell, Archibald (the elder); Campbell, Archibald (the younger); Donald Campbell (the elder); Donald Campbell (the younger); Campbell, Duncan; Campbell, George; Dumbar, John; Dyatt, Hugh; Fergusson, John; George, John; Gray, Archibald; MacAllom, John; MacCalloume, Donald (the elder); MacCalloume, John (the younger); MacCalloume, Duncan (the elder); MacCalloume, Duncan (the younger); MacCallum, Malcolm; MacChessag, Archibald; MacClewan, Donald; MacClewan, John; MacClewan, Malcolm; MacDiarmid, John; MacDugald, John; MacEacher, (?); MacHinbin (?), Martin; MacIntyre, Patrick; MacIvackeder, (?); MacIvor, David; MacKechirn, Patrick; MacKenthor, John; Mackinlay, John; Mackinlayroy, Duncan (the elder); Mackinlayroy, Duncan (the younger); Maclean, Archibald; Machnachton, Duncan; MacNicolas, John; MacPholl, Duncan (the elder); MacPholl, Duncan (the younger); Macray, Adam; Milne, Alexander; Morrison, Archibald; Nicoll, Gillies; O'Breyan, Terence; Patrick, Robert; Robertson, Donald; Robertson, Duncan; Robertson, Ludovick; Scott, Thomas; Sinclair, Archibald; Sinclair, Malcolm; Stewart, John; Tillery, Walter; Turner, John.

DRUMMOND'S:

Captain; two lieutenants; three sergeants; three corporals; two drummers and fifty-seven sentinels.

Officers and NCOs: Captain Thomas Drummond; Lieutenant John Kilpatrick; Lieutenant Robert Campbell; Sergeant Walter Purdie; Sergeant Walter Buchanan; Sergeant Walter Bruss; Drummer John Mitchell; Drummer George Lyon; Corporal Lauchlan Sinclair; Corporal William Ross; Corporal James Mackinlay.

Sentinels: Alam, William; Alexander, Adam; Black, Duncan; Blair, Donald; Brown, William; Buchanan, Patrick; Campbell, Archibald; Campbell, John; Campbell, Malcolm; Carmichael, Walter; Dawson, George; Duncan, William; Duncanson, Duncan; Erroll, John; Fergusson; Donald; Fergusson; John; Fisher, Donald; Forester, Alexander; Fraser, James; Graham, Richard; Grey, Patrick; Grey, Rorie; Hossack, William; Howatt, John; Jameson, Hugh; Johnston, William; Kerr, James; Lamont, Walter; Loudon, Abraham; MacArter, Donald; MacCallum, Gilbert; MacEadam, John; MacElbrid, Hugh; MacEwan, John; MacFarland, Walter; MacFinn, Donald; MacIntailer, Donald; MacKellar, Duncan; Mackellar, Patrick; MacKellar, William; Maclean, Hugh; MacNeill, Thomas; MacHickol, Archibald; MacNish, Duncan; NacRie, John; MacSimon, Donald; MacVurish, Neil; Monss, John; Morrison, Duncan; Muirhead, James; Mulliken, John; Scott, John; Sim, David; Smith, Neil; Taylor, John; Taylor, Thomas.

The Order to Sir Thomas Livingstone from William III, dated 16ᵗʰ January 1692

The copy of that paper given in by Mckdonald of Auchterau to Colonel Hill hath been showen to us. Wee did formerly grant passes to Buchan and Canon, and Wee do authorize and allow you to grant passes to them, and for ten servants for each of them, to come freely and safely to Leith, from that to be transported to the Netherlands before the [] day of March next, to goe from thence where they please, without any stop or trouble.

Wee allow you to receive the submissions of Glengary and these with him, upon their taking the oath of allegiance and delivering up the house of Invergarry, to be safe as to their lives, but as to their estates they must depend upon our mercy.

In case you find that the house of Invergarry cannot probably be taken in this season of the year with the artillery and other provisions that you can bring there, in that case Wee leave it to your discretion to give Glengary the assurance of intire indemnity for life and fortune, upon the delivering of his house and armes, and taking the oath of allegeance. In this you are allowed to act as you find the circumstance of the affair doth require; but it were much better that these who have not taken the benefits of our indemnity in the tearmes, and within the dyet prefixed by our proclamation, they should be obliged to render upon mercy. And the taking of the oath of allegiance is indispensible, others having already taken it.

If Mkean of Glencoe, and that tribe, can be well separated from the rest, it will be a proper vindication of the publick justice to extirpate that sect of thieves.

The double of these instructiones are only communicated to Colonell Hill.

January 16th, 1692.

The Glen Today and the 'Massacre Trail'

'Mile after mile, the only sound that indicates life is the faint cry of a bird of prey from some storm, beaten pinnacle of rock. The progress of civilization, which has turned so many wastes into fields yellow with harvests or gay with apple-blossom, has only made Glencoe more desolate ... and in truth that pass is the most dreary and melancholy of al the Scottish passes, the very Valley of the Shadow of Death.'

Thomas Babington Macaulay

As with most of Scotland's tragedies, the Massacre has provided a solid boost to tourism. Like Culloden, yesterday's horror is easy to market and, of course, the place does not disappoint. As late as 1769 the old ways still continued, but significant economic and social changes at the end of the eighteenth century, which are lumped collectively and emotively as the Highland Clearances, expunged the ancient life more surely than any redcoat's bayonet. Sheep completed the work Glenlyon's men had attempted and, in the longer term, proved more damaging. By the time writers like Dickens or Macaulay journeyed through the pass, what had happened there and the life of the people for centuries was already history.

The Scottish Enlightenment witnessed a period of commercial and cultural expansion unparalleled in the history of the northern kingdom. Scotland, in the latter half of the eighteenth century, would be the power house of the Enlightenment. The building of the New Town in Edinburgh would herald the arrival of the nation's capital as one of the great cities of Europe, a position that has never been relinquished. The Union, so much despised, would generate unimagined opportunities as Scots participated fully in the building of a great British Empire, as much a Scottish as an English phenomenon. The Seven years War (1756 – 1763) would witness Scottish soldiers fighting as redcoats around the globe, particularly in North America and Canada.

In the Highlands, the clan system died after Culloden. It was undoubtedly moribund beforehand and the brutal transition ushered in by the failure of the 'Forty-Five', completed a process that would have occurred in time. In its way savage repression was successful, for old loyalties did die out. In the space of a generation chiefs, no longer educated in Paris, became facsimiles of English gentlemen. Within a few decades the Highland Clearances would change the face of the landscape and add considerably to a diaspora spurred by the events of 1746. By the time of the romantic revival in the 1820s, engineered by Sir Walter Scott, Jacobitism was a historical anomaly, an ancient grudge, as dead as the clansmen who had charged on Drummossie Moor. Like all lost causes, it improved in the telling and acquired that romantic veneer which fuels a significant slice of the Scottish tourism industry.

Writing in the early nineteenth century, one observer noted of Glencoe: 'The sheep farming system has done the work of extirpation more effectively than … the Massacre'. Many from the glen joined the diaspora to the New World but there was new local industry; burgeoning slate quarries by Ballachulish; by the mid-nineteenth century the labour-force was nearly 600 strong producing 26,000,000 slates (source National Trust for Scotland).

When the seventeenth chief, who had spent his career in medicine, died in 1837 without male issue, his heiress sold the estates to Lord Strathcona. In 1935 the Lord Strathcona of the day sold off the whole, and the National Trust purchased some parts for Scotland ("NTS"). A later gift added the Dalness Estate to NTS holdings.

Today the glen is largely managed by NTS, though, and apart from the landscape, virtually no trace of the settlements which existed in 1692 remains; most are simple single steadings and even Glencoe village, though picturesque, is a much later construction. No trace of MacIain's fine house or that rebuilt by his eldest son survives; the foundations of the chief's summer house which may be viewed are, at best, suspect. To this writer the traces are distinctly nineteenth century in character. NTS maintains an excellent visitor centre and there is a monument to the victims of the Massacre in the village, together with a modest folk museum. The Trust produces a well-illustrated guide to the glen, which covers history, geology, wildlife, walks and mountaineering.

Little trace survives of Hill's Fort William, one stretch of curtain wall and bastion and the gateway which was latterly preserved and now welcomes entrants to the cemetery. Panelling and effects from the Governor's office are preserved in the West Highland Museum in Fort William, the former Maryburgh. The old medieval castle of Inverlochy largely stands, immured in a drab and decaying industrial estate. These are really the only tangible monuments to the events of 1692; at the time of writing Kilchurn castle remains closed for repairs, though most of the construction is intact.

The Glen, despite the inroads of mass tourism, is still a wild and lovely place. This writer has seen both eagles and wildcats, soaring above and offering a tantalizing glimpse on a scree-covered slope. Perhaps we should leave the final word to a dedicated local historian, the late Arthur Smith, who recorded a poignant and tempting postscript to the Massacre, taught him by his grandmother:

One of the stories told to me by my granny was of a local witch, Corrag. At the time of the Massacre Corrag had warned everybody that the Redcoats were up to no good; but nobody listened. The evening before the Massacre, Corrag fled up into the hills, wrapped herself in a plaid and stayed out all night. She came back the next day and the village was empty, the houses were burned, the cattle had been driven off and there was just the haze of smoke lying over the Glen. The myth is that she went to where MacIain, the chief, had been shot by the Redcoats and she took his broad-sword down the Glen to the Narrows, where she threw the sword into the water: Corrag made a prophecy that the men of the Glen had suffered enough, and as long as that sword lay undisturbed by the hand of man, no man from this Glen would ever die by the sword again.

Timeline

1354 – John of the Isles assumes the title 'Lord of the Isles'.

1411 – Battle of Harlaw.

1449 – John MacDonald becomes fourth 'Lord of the Isles'.

1476 – Forfeiture of the earldom of Ross.

1493 – Fall of the Lordship.

1603 – James VI of Scotland becomes also James I of England.

1638 – Signing of the Solemn League and Covenant.

1644 – Beginning of Montrose's and MacColla's campaign,
the first raid on Argyll.

1645 – 'Year of Miracles': in December the MacDonald's
raid Breadalbane; second ravaging of Argyll.

1646 – MacDonald's raid Glenlyon, battle with the Campbell's at Sron a'Chlachain.

1649 – Execution of Charles I.

1654 – Cromwell in Scotland, first fort at Inverlochy.

1655 – 'The Raid of Colin's Cows'.

1674 – MacIain of Glencoe, briefly incarcerated in Inverary, somehow escapes.

1688 – November: the Glorious Revolution.

1689 – Spring: William is offered the crown of Scotland by Argyll and Stair.
 – July 27th: Battle of Killiecrankie.
 – August 18th: Jacobites defeated at Dunkeld.
 – 24th: Argyll's regiment's first muster.
 – Late summer: the MacDonald's raid Glenlyon.

1690 – March: Colonel Hill arrives in Edinburgh, Breadalbane is given a commission to treat with the Jacobite chiefs.
 – May: Livingstone defeats Buchan's Jacobites at Cromdale William III orders the construction of a new fort at Inverlochy.
 – June: Mackay marches north to Loch Leven to establish the garrison.
 – July 1st: Battle of the Boyne.
 – July 3rd: Hill at Inverlochy.
 – December 6th: First muster of Hill's regiment.

1691 – January: Stair is appointed jointly with Melville as
Secretary of State for Scotland.
– April: Duncanson, Glenlyon and Drummond all granted
their commissions in Argyll's regiment.
– June: the Achallader conference organised by
Breadalbane.
– July: Alasdair Og of Glencoe with Appin Stewarts attacks
supply vessels in Loch Linnhe; King William empowers
Queen Mary to confirm Breadalbane's treaty negotiations.
– August: the Jacobite officers leave Scotland for France to
secure James' release of his adherents from their prior
obligations. On 17th August William III offers indemnity
to all provided the oath is taken by 1st January 1692
On the 28th Forbes confirms to Hill the true content of
Breadalbane's agreement with the chiefs.
– September: Stair writes reassuringly to Breadalbane.
– December: Melville is removed from office leaving
Stair as sole Secretary of State.
– December: Stair writes to Hill intimating the possible need
to make an example of those clans that do not submit;
by the 15th troops are being ordered into the Highlands
and Breadalbane arrives in London. On 21st Menzies
of Fornooth reaches Edinburgh with James to release
the chiefs. This does not reach Lochiel until over a week
later. On the 30th Lochiel attends Inverary to swear
the oath.
On 30/31st MacIain attends Hill at Inverlochy, but Hill
is not empowered to administer the oath.

1692 – Jan 2nd: After a difficult journey MacIain arrives at Inverary
but cannot swear the oath till 5th/6th; on 7th January,
Stair writes to Livingstone.
On the 9th Stair retorts he is sorry to hear MacIain has
sworn within the time. On 11th Stair confirms his orders

to Livingstone to proceed against those who have not come
in. He now knows MacIain did not take the oath in time.
On the 16th Stair sends again to Livingstone with the King's
additional instructions to 'extirpate' MacDonald are
of Glencoe; writes also to Colonel Hill.

– 29/30th January: Duncanson's troops have arrived at Fort
William. He and Hamilton plan the attack.

– Despite the fact that Stair is aware MacIain did take the
oath, though not within the stipulated period, he does
not vary his earlier instructions.

– 1st February: two companies of Argyll's under Glenlyon
are quartered in Glencoe.

– 12th February: Hill orders Hamilton to proceed – Hamilton
then writes to Duncanson to arrange for the massacre to
begin the following morning at 7.00 a.m.

– 13th February: the Massacre of Glencoe.

– By 12th April, the 'Paris Gazette' is reporting the fact of
the atrocity and in May Charles Leslie publishes 'A Letter
from a Gentleman in Scotland'.

1693 – Hamilton is ordered to begin the inquiry into the massacre
but dies in the following year.

1695 – April: Tweedale advises the Scots Parliament that the
Commission of Enquiry is to proceed.

– June 20th: The Commission of Enquiry sends its report to
the King; no action follows.

1702 – March: William III dies.

1707 – Death of Stair; Act of Union passed, Scottish Parliament
ceases to exist.

Dramatis Personae

Barclay, Sir George (1636 – 1710)
A noted Jacobite and James' agent in the Highlands, it was he who, in August 1691, journeyed to the exiled Stewart court to seek consent to the chiefs swearing the oath of allegiance to William and Mary; the former King's vacillation materially contributed to the murderous outcome in Glencoe.

Cameron, Sir Ewan of Lochiel (1629 – 1719)
Arguably the most influential of the clan chiefs, known as the 'Gentle Lochiel' he had, nonetheless, torn the throat from a Cromwellian opponent in his youth, his guardian, after his father died young, was the Marquess of Argyll; fought at Killiecrankie and his son led the clan at Sheriffmuir.

Campbell, Archibald first Duke and tenth Earl of Argyll
(1658 – 1703)
Eldest son of the ninth Earl who was executed for treason in 1685; he married Elizabeth Tollemache, daughter of Lionel third Baronet of Helmingham, though he preferred the company of numerous mistresses. He raised his foot regiment in 1689 that carried out the Massacre of 1692 and, though he may have had a hand in conceiving

the affair, he escaped censure to die in the arms of his favourite courtesan. On his death, his son, John, who became 2nd Duke of Argyll, succeeded him.

Campbell, John, first Earl of Breadalbane and Holland (1636 – 1717)

'Grey John', one of the principal actors in the drama of Glencoe; married (1) Mary Rich, daughter of the first Earl of Holland and (2) Mary, widow of the Earl of Caithness, he had many enemies and few friends. Alternately a staunch Williamite and sometimes supporter of the exiled Stuarts; 400 of his clan fought at Sheriffmuir in 1715 for the Old Pretender, though the earl survived to die peacefully in his bed.

Campbell, Robert of Glenlyon (1630 – 1696)

Fifth Laird of Glenlyon, he inherited an estate mauled by Clan Donald and ruined by his own degeneracy. At the age of fifty-nine he had to take a commission in Argyll's regiment to try and clear some of his debts, the truncated estate which he held by right of his wife having again been taken up by the Glencoe men. Haunted by his role in the killings, he served afterwards in Flanders, and died at Diksmuide in 1696.

Dalrymple, John, first Earl of Stair (1648 – 1707)

Had he not been the principal recipient of blame for the Massacre, Stair might have been better remembered for his work in connection with the Union of 1707, which he did not live to see. A gifted advocate and zealous Secretary of State, he abhorred both Covenanters and Jacobites and was cordially detested by both; with Breadalbane he is regarded as the architect of Glencoe.

Drummond, Captain Thomas

It was Drummond who captained the elite grenadier company of Argyll's Regiment and took part in the latter stages of the killing on 13th February. Hard and brutally efficient, he had previously incarcerated MacIain as the chief attempted to reach Inverary to swear the oath. Though condemned by the Parliamentary Commission in 1695 he suffered no consequences.

Duncanson, Major Robert of Fassokie (died 1705)
He was from an established Stirlingshire family with a connection to Argyll; a tough professional soldier, he proved a malleable tool in planning the Massacre with Hamilton. He it was that issued the infamous order to Glenlyon, and though Parliament wished to prosecute him, he was never brought to account. He served loyally until his death at the siege of Valencia de Alcantara. John Buchan asserts that the Major may also have held the office of Procurator Fiscal to the Duke of Argyll, (this is not mere speculation and the suggestion is evidenced by a comparison of handwriting).

Graham, John, first Viscount Dundee – 'Bonny Dundee'
(c1648 – 1689)
Bonny Dundee or 'Bluidy Clavers', depending on the speaker's partisanship; a loyal adherent of James II & VII, he led the clan forces in the first Jacobite rising winning posthumous glory at Killiecrankie and epic if phyrric victory. To Clan Donald he was 'Dark John of the Battles'.

Hamilton, Lieutenant Colonel James
Second in command of Hill's regiment of Foot and Deputy-Governor at Inverlochy. Possibly of Irish origins and with an unspecified cloud hanging over him, he was anxious to impress – a perfect agent for Stair. He resisted the request and summons to explain his conduct before the inquiry, and slips out of history.

Hay, John, first Marquess of Tweeddale (1625 – 1697)
A noted trimmer, Tweeddale was remarkable for the shift in his allegiances during the civil wars; this did not hamper his appointment as Lord President of the Scottish Council, following the Restoration. Toward the Covenanters he pursued a policy of moderation which

brought about his dismissal in 1674. He came back into his own under William III, becoming Lord Chancellor of Scotland, and it was he who ordered the enquiry into the Massacre; his support for the Darien fiasco engendered his final fall.

Johnstone, James of Warriston (1655 – 1737)
Son of an adjudged traitor hanged after the Restoration, a noted advocate and Williamite; appointed Joint Secretary with Stair, against whom he was happy to conspire, and he used the Inquiry as a means to secure the sole position for himself.

Johnstone, William first Marquess of Annandale (1664 – 1721)
Descended from the border name, he supported both Monmouth and later the Jacobites, being goaled for his perceived role in the Montgomery plot, and heavily involved in the Glencoe enquiry.

Livingstone, Sir Thomas first Viscount of Teviot (1652 – 1711)
Livingstone came to England with William III and led the Crown forces that routed the rump of Dundee's forces still under arms in the Rout of Cromdale. He became Commander-in-Chief of HM Forces in Scotland, and transmitted Stair's orders for the Massacre to Hamilton, a course of action of which he appears to have heartily approved.

MacDonald of Glencoe, Alasdair twelfth Chief of Clan Iain Abrach (c.1630 – 1692)
MacIain was a larger-than-life character, hugely tall and imposing; He served under Dundee at Killiecrankie and attempted, at the last minute, to swear the oath. Technically, he was late in doing so, an omission that proved fatal to him and over three-dozen of his tiny clan.

MacDonald of Glencoe, Alasdair Og, younger son of MacIain
Alasdair Og, more of a firebrand than his brother, mistrustful of Glenlyon and his company's presence in the glen. He, with his family, escaped the slaughter and later, like the other survivors, returned to rebuild.

MacDonald, John, elder son thirteenth Chief (died c.1714)
John, on his father's murder, became thirteenth Chief. He behaved subsequently with great circumspection and led his people in their attempts to rebuild. Despite the severity of their lesson, *Clan Iain Abrach* sent men to the '15 and to the '45.

Mackay, Hugh of Scourie (c.1640 – 1692)
A Highlander from Sutherland, Mackay was a career soldier. He fought for a spell for the Venetians and later commanded the Williamite forces at Killiecrankie. It was due to his experience and cool nerve that the withdrawal did not degenerate into a complete stampede. He served with distinction in Ireland and finally fell at Steenkirk.

Maitland, John first Duke of Lauderdale, third Lord Thirlestane (1616 – 1682)
Maitland, scion of an ancient border-line began his career as an ardent Presbyterian and became a member of both Privy Councils. After the Restoration, he adjusted his sensibilities toward serving Charles II and his own advancement. He abandoned Argyll and overcame any scruples concerning episcopacy. He survived numerous attempts by his many enemies to out him, but was finally dismissed in 1680.

MacKenzie, George first Viscount Tarbat, first Earl of Cromarty (1630 – 1714)
An ardent Royalist, he remained in exile between 1654 and 1660; appointed Lord of Session in 1662 and a sworn enemy of Lauderdale. He served as Chief Minister in the Scottish Parliament from 1682 – 1688. Created Viscount Tarbat in 1685, he survived the Glorious Revolution and subsequently held several important offices.

Melville, George, fourth Baron, first Earl of Melville
(c.1634 – 1707)
A staunch champion of the Kirk, Melville was obliged to go into exile after the Restoration but came back with William and Mary, at which time he was appointed as Secretary of State for Scotland. He was concerned with the pacification of the Highlands; Stair was made Joint Secretary and soon undermined Melville, who was reduced to the role of cypher.

Stuart, James, VII of Scotland, II of England (1633 – 1701)
James was a committed Roman Catholic and, in his short reign, sought to reverse the Protestant establishment. He easily defeated Charles II's bastard Monmouth, but was unseated by this daughter Mary and son-in-law William of Orange in the largely bloodless Glorious Revolution of 1688. He was obliged to flee in disguise and his exiled court at St. Germain became the hub of the Jacobite movement (In Latin Jacobus = James).

William III of England (1650 – 1702)
Having been appointed as Stadtholder in the United Provinces, William became the chief opponent of Louis XIV and stoutly resisted French expansionism. This policy did not change when he became William III. His attention and considerable abilities were firmly focused on affairs in Flanders; matters in Scotland, in which he had scant interest, would never amount to anything beyond a mere sideshow.

Bibliography

'An Account of the Depredations committed on the Clan Campbell and their followers during the years 1685 and 1686'; A report drawn up by Ewing of Bernice, 1690, ed. Alex. Kincaid (Edinburgh: 1816)

'An Account of the Proceedings of the Estates in Scotland, 1689 – 1690'; ed. E.W.M. Balfour-Melville, Scottish History Society (Edinburgh: 1954 – 1955)

'Annals and Correspondence of the Viscount and the first and second Earls of Stair'; ed. J. M. Graham, 1875

Anderson, M.S. 'War and Society in Europe of the Old regime 1618 – 1789' (London: 1988)

Argyll Papers 1640 – 1723, (ed.) James Maidmont (Edinburgh: 1834)

Bain, R., 'The Clans and Tartans of Scotland' (London: 1983)

Balfour, P.J. 'The Scots Peerage' (Edinburgh: 1904 – 1914)

Bingham, C., 'Beyond the Highland Line' (London: 1991)

'Black Book of Taymouth' (Edinburgh: 1855)

Black, J., 'Culloden and the 45' (New York: 1990)

Black, J., (ed.) 'Britain in the Age of Walpole' (London: 1984)

Blackmore, H.L. 'British Military Firearms 1650 – 1850' (London: 1961)

Bland, H., 'Treatise on Military Discipline' (London: 1727)

Brander, M., 'The Making of the Scottish Highlands' (London: 1980)

Buchan, J., 'Montrose' (London: 1928)

Buchan, J., 'The Massacre of Glencoe' (London: 1933)

Caldwell, D.H. 'The Scottish Armoury' (Edinburgh: 1979)

'Calendar of State Papers' 1689 – 1696

Campbell, A., 'History of the Clan Campbell', Vols. 1 – 3 (Edinburgh: 2000 – 2004)

Campbell, D., 'The Clan Campbell' (Edinburgh: 1913 – 1922)

Chandler, D.A. 'Guide to the Battlefields of Europe' (London: 1989)

Coventry, M., 'The Castles of Scotland' (Musselburgh: 2001)

Chandler, D.A. 'The Art of Warfare in the Age of Marlborough' (London: 1976)

Cruickshanks E., (ed.) 'By Force or Default? The Revolution of 1688 – 1689' (Edinburgh: 1989)

Cruickshanks, E., (ed.) 'Ideology and Conspiracy: Aspects of Jacobitism 1689 – 1759' (Edinburgh: 1982)

'Culloden Papers 1625 – 1748'; 1815

Cruicksanks, E. and J. Black, (ed.) 'The Jacobite Challenge' (Edinburgh: 1988)

Duncan, A.A.M., 'Scotland; The Making of the Kingdom'(Edinburgh: 1975)

Forbes, D., 'Culloden Papers' 1815

'Dewar Manuscripts' the, vol. 1; ed. Revd. J. MacKechnie (Glasgow: 1964)

'Gallienus Redivivus; or Murder Will Out etc., Being a True Account of the DE-WITTING of Glencoe' (Edinburgh: 1695)

Gillies, W.A., 'In Famed Breadalbane' (1938)

'Glencoe' National Trust for Scotland

Grant, I.F., 'The Lordship of the Isles' (Edinburgh: 1935)

Grant, N., 'The Campbells of Argyll' (Edinburgh: 1959)

Gregory, D., 'History of the Western Highlands' (London: 1881)

Hayes-McCoy, G.A., 'Irish Battles' (Belfast: 1969)

Henderson, A., ''The Life of John, Second Earl of Stair' (1759)

Herman, A., 'The Scottish Enlightenment' (London: 2001)

Hill, J.M., 'Celtic Warfare' (Edinburgh: 1986)

Historical Manuscripts Commission Reports, 15, Appendix Part IX

Hopkins P., 'Glencoe and the End of the Highland War' (Edinburgh: 1986)

Howell's State Trials, Vol. XIII; T.B. Howell 1809 – 1815

Hughes, B.P., 'Firepower 'Weapons Effectiveness on the Battlefield' 1630 – 1850' (London: 1974)

Jarvis, R.C., 'Collected Papers on the Jacobite Risings' (England: 1972)

Jones, G.H., 'The Main Stream of Jacobitism' (Cambridge Mass.: 1954)

Judiciary RRRReports of Argyll and the Isles 1664 – 1705; The Stair Society 1949

Keegan, J., 'The Face of Battle' (London: 1976)

Lang, A., 'A History of Scotland', 4 vols. (1909)

Lenman, B., 'The Jacobite Risings in Britain 1689 – 1746' (London: 1980)

Lenman, B., 'The Jacobite Clans of the Great Glen 1650 – 1784' (London: 1984)

Leven and Melville 'Papers, letters etc. Bannatyne Club' (Edinburgh: 1843)

Linklater, M. and C. Hesketh, 'For King and Conscience' (London: 1989)

Linklater, M., 'Massacre: The Story of Glencoe' (London: 1982)

Loyd, A., 'My War Gone by I Miss It So' (London: 1999)

Lynch, M., 'Scotland: A New History' (London: 1991)

MacDonald, A.J., and A.A. MacDonald, 'The Clan Donald' 3 vols. (1896 – 1904)

MacDonald, C.M., 'History of Argyll' (Glasgow: 1950)

MacDonald, N.H., 'Clan Ranald of Lochaber' (Edinburgh: 1972)

- 'Clan Ranald of Knoydart and Glengarry (Edinburgh: 1995)

MacDonald, R.A., 'Kingdom of the Isles' (Edinburgh: 1997)

'Memoirs of Great Britain and Ireland, 1681 – 1692' Vols. 1 & 2, Sir John Dalrymple of Cranstoun, 1771

'Memoirs of Sir Hugh Mackay', Maitland Club, (Glasgow: 1833)

'Memoirs of Secret Services', J. Macky (London: 1733)

Mackerral, A., 'The Clan Campbell' (Edinburgh: 1979)

Mackie, J.D., 'A History of Scotland' (England: 1964)

MacDonnell, J. M., of Keppoch, 'The MacDonnells of Keppoch and Gargavach' (Glasgow: 1931)

Mackenzie, A., 'History of the MacDonalds of Clanranald, 1881

MacPherson, J. and M. Laing, 'The Poems of Ossian etc.' 2 vols. (Edinburgh: 1805)

Mactavish, D., 'Inverary Papers' (1939)

Martin, Martin, of Skye, 'A Description of the Western Islands of Scotland *c.* 1695, including a voyage to St. Kilda' (1703)

Memoirs of Hugh Mackay, Maitland Club (Glasgow: 1833)

Murray, W.H., 'Rob Roy' (Edinburgh: 1982)

Memoirs of Sir Ewan Cameron of Lochiel (ed.) John Drummond (Edinburgh: 1842)

Napier, M., 'Memorials and Letters illustrative of the Life and Times of John Graham of Claverhouse' (1859 – 1862)

Original Papers containing the Secret History of Great Britain from the Restoration to the Accession of George I, ed. J. Macpherson: 1775

Papers illustrative of the Political Conditions of the Highlands of Scotland from the year 1689 – to 1696, Maitland Club, Glasgow 1945 ('Highland Papers')

Parker, G., 'The Military Revolution' (Cambridge: 1988)

Peterson, H.L., 'The Book of the Gun' (London: 1963)

Philip, James of Almericlose, 'The Grameid, an Heroic Poem descriptive of the Campaign of Viscount Dundee in 1689' (Scottish History Society, 1887 – 1888)

Prebble, J., 'Glencoe' (London: 1966)

Register of the Privy Council of Scotland 1681 – 1691

Reid, S., 'The Campaigns of Montrose' (Edinburgh: 1990)

Reid, S., 'Highland Clansman 1689 – 1746' (England: 1997)

Report of the Commission of Enquiry (NA SP 8/14 no 84)

Rixson, D., 'West Highland Galley' (Edinburgh: 1998)

Roberts, M., 'The Military Revolution 1560 – 1660' (Belfast: 1956)

Rogers, Col. H.C.B., 'Artillery through The Ages' (London: 1971)

Sacheverell, W., 'An Account of the Isle of man, with a voyage to I-Columb-kill' (London: 1702)

Sadler, D.J., 'Scottish Battles' (Edinburgh: 1996)

Sadler, D.J., 'Clan Donald's Greatest Defeat – The Battle of Harlaw 1411' (Gloucs: 2005)

Scottish Art Review 'Ancient Scottish Weapons', vol. 10 no.2 (1965)

Sellar, W.D.H., 'The Earliest Campbells' in Scottish Studies, 17, 1973

Seymour, W., 'Battles in Britain', vol. 2 (London: 1969)

Skene, W., 'The Highlanders of Scotland' (1837)

Smout, T.C., 'A History of the Scottish People 1560 – 1830' (London: 1969)

Speck, W.A., 'Reluctant Revolutionaries, Englishmen and the Revolution of 1688' (Oxford: 1988)

Stevenson, D., 'Highland Warrior: Alasdair MacColla and the Civil Wars' (Edinburgh: 1980)

Tabraham, C. and D. Grove, 'Fortress Scotland and the Jacobites' (London: 1995)

Thompson, O., 'The Great Feud: Campbells and MacDonalds' (Gloucs: 2001)

Young, Brig. P., 'The British Army 1642 – 1970' (London: 1967)

List of Illustrations

1. The Coire Gabhail – It was up this steep defile that the MacDonalds' of Glencoe are alleged to have driven stolen cattle. The narrow path is steep and precipitous, even allowing for a smaller, hardier and more nimble breed of cattle, the likelihood seems remote (author's collection).

2. A view over the landscape of the upper glen; harsh upland terrain of bog and scree, ground out over millennia by the glaciers; a landscape of legend and myth (author's collection).

3. The main road now traverses the glen, otherwise little has changed; over this landscape in the teeth of the biting blizzard dazed survivors fled. That exhaustion and exposure should take their toll is hardly to be wondered at(author's collection).

4. This is the glen in spring, where but a few moments before a warming sun had been shining, until sleet laden showers chased between the lines of mountains, the land reverting to the chill and frozen winds of winter (author's collection).

5. The nineteenth-century shepherd's bothy is dwarfed by the steep slopes behind. Basic as such dwellings are, they represent a significant increase in levels of comfort and sanitation from the altogether cruder crofts that would form the townships in 1692. No trace of these now remains (author's collection).

6. The cairn – the ostensible cairn upon which each successive chief of MacDonald of Glencoe was installed (author's collection).

7. Glencoe – a further view of the approach to the Coire Gabhail amidst the grandeur of the 'Three Sisters', Stob Coire Nan Lochan stands behind. The author has, in the past, seen the elusive wildcat on these slopes (author's collection).

8. Glencoe – the defile leading to Coire Gabhail – the landscape has barely changed since the late seventeenth century (author's collection).

9. Glencoe – a view across the placid waters of Loch Achtriachtan; the township of that name has disappeared. On the night of the massacre it was a scene of horror (author's collection).

10. The Devil's Staircase – modern signpost at the Glencoe end (author's collection).

11. The Glencoe end of the Devil's Staircase – it was down this precipitous pathway that Hamilton's weary companies trudged through the fierce snow (author's collection).

12. Glencoe – the rampart of mountains on either flank provide the glen with its topographical identity and protected the MacDonalds as surely as fortress walls; but walls also contain as well as shelter and trap fugitives like driven game (author's collection).

13. Glencoe – light thickens in snow-laden air, such conditions would mirror those that obtained the day preceding the night of the Massacre (author's collection).

14. Eilean Munde – traditional resting ground of the chiefs of Clan Iain Abrach the chapel is long decayed, the atmosphere, however, survives intact (author's collection).

15. The Gateway to Fort William – this no longer stands where once stood the fort but has been moved to form an impressive entrance to the town cemetery (author's collection).

16. The inscription on the gate: 'This arch was erected in 1690 over the main entrance to the Fort and re-erected here in 1896 where Sir Allan Cameron of Erracht in 1793, raised the 79th or Cameron Highlanders, a Regiment which distinguished itself on

many a hard fought field for King and Country'. Thus, by donning a red coat the recalcitrant rebel becomes the cutting edge of Empire (author's collection).

17. Rannoch Moor – storm clouds gather; a view the Glen Orchy Campbells would doubtless have been familiar with, as attackers and cattle disappeared from sight (author's collection).

18. The approach looking over the Black Mount, home to the MacDonalds summer shielings. Now only the mournful cry of the curlew and the roar of traffic on the highway disturbs the calm (author's collection).

19. Glencoe – The lower ground looking eastwards up the glen; here were the townships, winter grazing and cultivation (author's collection).

20. Inverlochy Castle – originally a Comyn hold in the thirteenth century, the castle featured in the action at the battle of Inverlochy in 1645, the MacDonalds' most spectacular and bloody success against their rivals Clan Campbell. Argyll himself wisely if uninspiringly watched the action from his galley and sailed serenely clear of the wrack of his army; the bulk was less fortunate (author's collection).

21. The Meeting of the Waters Glencoe – spectacular and wildly romantic the tumbling waters collide, cold and clear (author's collection).

22. Memorial by the present Glencoe village: 'This cross is reverently erected in memory of McIain Chief of the MacDonalds of Glencoe who fell with his people in the Massacre of Glencoe of 13th February 1692, by his direct descendant Ellen Burns MacDonald of Glencoe August 1883 – Their Memory Liveth For Evermore' (author's collection).

23. The memorial with the glen behind. This is really the only feature to commemorate the massacre and a simple annual remembrance is held on the anniversary (author's collection).

24. Pap of Glencoe viewed looking northwards from the Monument. (author's collection).

25. Glencoe viewed looking from the area of the Monument (author's collection).

26. Lochleven – the castle, which occupies an island site in a strategic position on the Edinburgh-Stirling-Perth axis, is associated most popularly with Mary Queen of Scots. It was strengthened by Robert I and David II. Originally more strongly placed than its contemporary remains would suggest: the water levels in the loch dropped considerably after canalisation works in the nineteenth century (author's collection).

27. Dumbarton – this great hold atop its volcanic plug has an ancient lineage, being the capital of the Strathclyde Britons. It fell to the Norse and then came into the possession of the King of Scots, remaining a royal stronghold. Its importance declined after the close of the civil wars, but the defences were upgraded in the later period as a further deterrent to the Jacobites (author's collection).

28. The Old Tolbooth, Edinburgh – the original gaol was built in 1480 and re-built some eighty years later, adjacent to the Signet Library. Many Highland chiefs would find themselves familiar with its interior, and it housed many celebrated prisoners before finally being demolished in 1817 (author's collection).

29. The Marquis of Montrose – James Graham, Marquis of Montrose (1612 – 1650), is regarded as a great commander of the civil wars. Though tactically brilliant his failures of intelligence and reconnaissance led to near misses and eventual disaster. During his 'Year of Miracles', the clans moved to centre-stage in the greater struggle being waged throughout the Three Kingdoms (author's collection).

30. The Execution of Montrose – after his final defeat at Carbisdale on 27th April 1650, the Marquis fled the ground and, after some days' wandering, unwisely accepted shelter from Neil MacLeod of Assynt. Ardvreck castle proved a 'deadly refuge' when MacLeod, in defiance of the accepted laws of hospitality, betrayed his guest. The jubilant Covenanters degraded their

Index